MILITARY REMINISCENCES
FROM THE NORTH WEST

Military Reminiscences from the North West

Fifty accounts of military life from servicemen and women from or connected to the North West

Edited by Ashley Toms and Graham Kemp

First published in Great Britain in 2015

Scotforth Books
Carnegie House, Chatsworth Road
Lancaster
LA1 4SL

ISBN: 978-1-909817-24-1

Designed and typeset by Scotforth Books, Lancaster
www.scotforthbooks.com

Printed and bound in the UK by Jellyfish Solutions

We would like to thank the Morecambe branches of the Burma Star Association, the RAF Association and the Militaria Association as well as Lancaster Military Heritage for their support. In addition we would like to thank the Cumbrian branch of the Canal Zoners, with special thanks to their secretary Raymond Gill and finally to the Westmorland Gazette for their help.

We would also like to acknowledge with a special thanks to the patience of Mrs Jill Charnock for typing up many of the accounts and to David Macgiveron and Rod Webster for the proof reading.

Contents

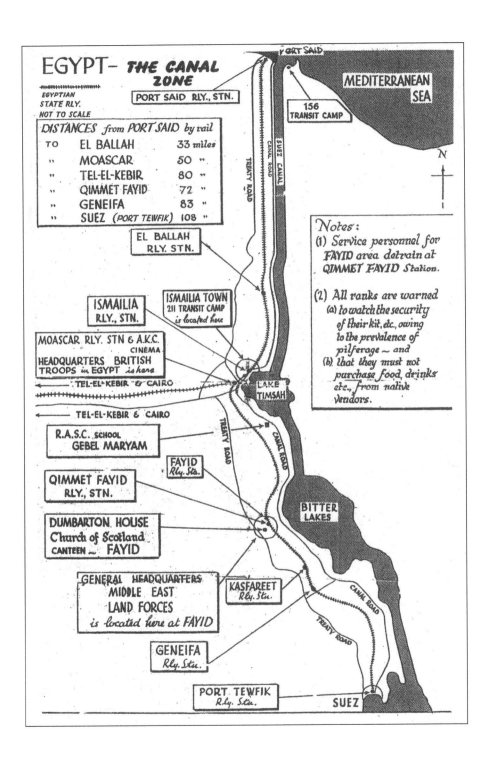

EGYPT– *THE CANAL ZONE*

EGYPTIAN
STATE RLY.
NOT TO SCALE

PORT SAID RLY., STN.

DISTANCES *from* PORT SAID *by rail*

TO	EL BALLAH	33 miles
,,	MOASCAR	50 ,,
,,	TEL-EL-KEBIR	80 ,,
,,	QIMMET FAYID	72 ,,
,,	GENEIFA	83 ,,
,,	SUEZ (PORT TEWFIK)	108 ,,

MEDITERRANEAN
SEA

PORT SAID

156
TRANSIT CAMP

SUEZ CANAL

TREATY ROAD

CANAL ROAD

N

EL BALLAH
RLY. STN.

ISMAILIA TOWN
211 TRANSIT CAMP
is located here

ISMAILIA
RLY., STN.

MOASCAR RLY. STN & A.K.C.
CINEMA
HEADQUARTERS BRITISH
TROOPS *in* EGYPT *is here*

TEL-EL-KEBIR & CAIRO

TEL-EL-KEBIR & CAIRO

LAKE
TIMSAH

R.A.S.C. SCHOOL
GEBEL MARYAM

TREATY ROAD

CANAL ROAD

FAYID
Rly. Stn.

QIMMET FAYID
RLY., STN.

DUMBARTON HOUSE
Church of Scotland
CANTEEN – FAYID

BITTER
LAKES

GENERAL HEADQUARTERS
MIDDLE EAST
LAND FORCES
is located here at FAYID

KASFAREET
Rly. Stn.

CANAL ROAD

TREATY ROAD

GENEIFA
Rly. Stn.

PORT TEWFIK
R.ly. Stn.

SUEZ

Notes:
(1) Service personnel for
FAYID area detrain at
QIMMET FAYID Station.

(2) All ranks are warned
 (a) to watch the security
 of their kit, etc., owing
 to the prevalence of
 pilferage – and
 (b) that they must not
 purchase food, drinks
 etc., from native
 vendors.

Introduction

What was it like?

To look for a baby under fire in Florence
To give Corporal Jones Turd, a military burial with full honours
To sun yourself on some exotic foreign beach, such as Waikiki
To be a bookie behind Japanese lines on D-Day
To not be able to wash in a submarine
To be tucked into a small nuclear bomb shelter
Waiting to see if nuclear war will come.

This book comprises fifty stories of the lives of men and women who served in the military, mainly from north Lancashire and Cumbria. Others had connections to the region. These fifty people volunteered to tell their stories in order to pass on their experiences to future generations. Their stories cover all aspects of military service from the First World War to the present day and of all three services. They include volunteers, conscripts and National servicemen, submariners, engineers, aircraft fitters, pilots, officers and soldiers. They reveal that military life is not just about action, it is about surviving basic training, the boredom and the irrational quirks of military life. The book covers a breadth of experience from jungle warfare, to biding one's time in remote bases, from drinking and relaxing with comrades and to being pinned down under enemy fire. To honour these men and women, we have kept each story separate, so it is their story. We gave them control of the final editing, to keep as close as we could to hearing their stories as they told them.

Some are short, some are long, but in all you will discover gems of military experience and accounts not often found in the standard military books.

Several themes stood out for us when we heard these stories, the first was the strong sense of comradeship that develops out of military life, camaraderie forged not only in the face of the enemy, but also in the face of the harshness of basic training, great lifelong friendships developed often not found in civilian life. As one contributor said, 'you had to rely on your mates to survive and that developed trust and comradeship, which runs deep ever afterwards.'

The horrors of war take their toll; and often the real victims of war are the ones who come home. Many here were not fully prepared to talk about the impact of combat and in the telling of their stories it was obvious that deep pain still lingered. One needs to acknowledge that service personnel do not just face the threat of death or serious physical injury, but also long lasting mental trauma and pain that combat can cause while serving for their country.

Humour was another consistent theme, it relieved boredom, stress and the bewildering pointlessness of military life, as one contributor commented, 'humour is at the heart of British military life, it is what keeps one going under stress.'

Several of the accounts cover events that are often forgotten in the passing of time. There are stories from the Forgotten 14th Army in Burma, the Forgotten East Indies Fleet, (1943–1946) and of 'Little British Expeditionary Force', which had to fight their way out of France after the Dunkirk evacuation. There are also accounts of the forgotten emergency of the Canal Zone (1951–55), overshadowed by the later Suez Crisis. Little has been written on the Canal Zone, yet, over 80,000 British National Service men were employed, with fifty-four killed in action against Egyptian insurgents and many more dying as a result of the appalling conditions they faced in what was called a large hot fly-ridden sandbox with a ditch (Suez Canal) running through. We are grateful to the members of the Cumbrian Canal Zoners for their rich contributions about life in the Canal Zone, only recently has their service being recognized by the issue of a campaign medal.

Some of the stories cover the same aspects of military life from different viewpoints. There are differences in opinion on the harshness of basic training. One contributor revealed that he was less fit after the training than he was at the outset! In contrast, accounts of parachute and Guards basic training reveal a very harsh regime.

There are several comments on our allies in arms. Bob Hayton's account of being with Australians on the 38th Parallel in the Korean War supports the stereotype of their laid-back attitude to army life. Rueben Boyd's experience of the Australians though was not such a happy affair. We were struck by the consensus of those who worked alongside the Americans, that it could be the hazardous experience.

We felt honoured and often touched in doing this project, most were interviewed between 2005–7; whilst others contributed written accounts to be included in this book. We hope this book does them justice.

Ashley Toms and Graham Kemp
2015

Section One

Army Life

National Service in Malaya with 'Pig' (courtesy of Reuben Boyd)

The Army Across the Century

We have grouped the following three accounts under the above title. They account for much of the experience of army life in the 20th century, covering the three of the main conflicts of the British army – The Great War 1914–18, The Second World War 1939–45 and the Northern Ireland Campaign – the Army's longest campaign of the century.

The first account is by William Coggins, who was interviewed in 1989, at the age of 92. He is the only First World War veteran in this volume. He was in the 1/4th of the Oxfordshire and Buckinghamshire Light Infantry; and was called up on 4th August 1914. As his unit was a territorial unit it was not sent out until 1915. His account covers the life and death of routine trench duties, first at Ploegsteert (pronounced by the British as Plugstreet) and later at the Hébuterne sectors on the Somme. William, at just eighteen was promoted to CSM (Company Sergeant Major) one of the youngest CSMs ever in the British Army.

The second account, 'Westmorland and Cumberland go to War', are two complimentary accounts by two comrades of the 4th Battalion of the Border Regiment, Adrian Grimes and Jack Laidler. Adrian's recall was exceptional; he sat for three hours without stopping or hesitating and gave a detailed account of 4th Battalion's actions in the Second World War from its time in France in 1940, through to the Middle East and the siege of Tobruk 1941, Burma 1943–4 and finally Norway 1945.

We also interviewed Adrian's comrade, Jack Laidler, who supplied a complementary account, which emphasized vividly, a recurring theme among those involved in action, how far luck plays a role in survival. Unlike Adrian's broad sweep of the 4th Battalion's actions during the war, Jack was able to give us a detailed account of just a single action that the men of the 4th Battalion were involved in, while in Burma.

The final account given here is that of John Woods in Northern Ireland; the Army's longest campaign of the twentieth century. John joined the Ulster Defence Regiment in 1972, at the outset of the 'troubles' and his account reveals some of the dangers of being a volunteer in UDF, as well as some of its humour. It is a short but poignant account and to compliment it we recommend John Spooner's account in Northern Ireland in the Grenadier Guards section of the book.

The Army's Youngest CSM

William John Coggins

Service Number 200100
Company Sergeant Major

Born:	18th January 1896 Wichford, Warwickshire
Service Dates:	1914–1934
Unit:	1/4th and 2nd Battalions The Oxfordshire and Buckinghamshire Light Infantry, The Royal Flying Corps and TAVR
Awards:	DCM, 1915 Star, 1914–18 Victory Medals
Main Theatres:	Western Front, Italy, Ireland and home front

This record is based on two interviews with William John Coggins, known as Jack by family and friends. These interviews took place in 1989 when Jack was 92. His memory was very clear, but we have referred to the 1/4th Battalion diary to help organise the anecdotes in chronological order. The 1/4th were mainly recruited from Banbury and district.

Jack joined the 1/4th OBLI as a boy and like his father before him became a bugler. As the 1/4th was a TA battalion, it was not mobilised for the BEF in 1914. Instead, they were sent to be trained at Whittle. near Chelmsford. Training consisted of route marches, patrols and live firing up to 500 yards.

In March 1915, King George V inspected them in Hylands Park along with the rest of the 48th (South Midland Division). On the 29th March, they entrained for France and soon after arrival, they were inspected by General Horace Lockwood Smith-Dorrien. [Smith-Dorrien was one of a handful of survivors of the battle of Isandlwana, 1879 and commanded the II Corps in 1914 and won the battle of Le Cateau on the retreat from Mons] The battalion then moved to Ploegsteert ('Plugstreet') Wood, in the Ypres Salient. On Jack's arrival, his CO asked Jack if he would give up his bugle badge so that he could be promoted. Jack agreed and became a Lance Corporal before he was 18 years old. He was immediately sent on a Lewis gun course at Etaples for three weeks so he could instruct other members of the battalion in its use. Jack commented that Ploegsteert was a quiet part of the line, but even so, they had not been there long before his friend Tommy Sharman was killed by a sniper as he looked over the firing step. His parents had lived next door to Jack on the Causeway in Banbury. Jack also recalled:

> We did a dammed silly thing in Ploegsteert Wood. Lieutenant Pickford, my platoon commander, came to me and said, 'It's a foggy morning, we will go as close as we can to the German lines and give them a tune' [on a gramophone]. We played this tune but before we got back the mist had lifted and they really gave it to us! German artillery opened fire on the trenches and two men were killed. The Lieutenant was given a real roasting by the CO who held him responsible.

In July of 1915 the battalion was moved south to the Hébuterne area on the Somme. [Sector G, Hébuterne to Serre and Sector K Hébuterne Gommecourt] Activity for the next year consisted of trench routine and raids. Jack particularly liked patrolling in no man's land, prompting his men to ask, 'Sergeant, have you got cat's eyes?' Jack, explained:

> Just look over the German trenches through a periscope for prominent objects on the skyline. Get them fixed in your brain box and you can always find your way back!

Jack went on listening patrols, where two or three men would get close to the enemy trenches and listen to the German conversations, leading him to conclude that the enemy were regularly entertaining young ladies. In addition to these small teams, there were also full fighting patrols consisting of ten to sixteen men. Jack recalled one such patrol:

> We had a young lieutenant straight out of England and Captain Edmonds, my CO, asked me to get a few men to take him into no man's land, because he wanted to see what it was like. That night an array of Very lights showed that the patrol had been detected. None came back so I went out the following night and found the lieutenant with his stomach hanging out and close to death. The others were presumed captured.

Jack did not like shellfire, 'It's not very nice. You cannot explain what it is like, shrapnel is the worst because it bursts in the air, gas shells just made a thud when they hit the ground.' He remembers a body in a tree after one barrage, with eyes staring straight down.

Promoted to Sergeant, Jack did night rounds with Captain Edmonds to inspect the sentries. One night they found a sentry asleep. The conversation regarding the sentry went as follows:

Edmonds:	*'What shall we do?'*
Jack:	*'It's up to you sir, but if you report him you know what will happen. He will be sent for a court martial and shot'*
Edmonds:	*'I'll tell you what I'll do. I'll give him a good bollocking in the morning!'*
Jack:	*'I think that would be best sir, It's a devil if you have to find a firing party to shoot someone.'*

A soldier was never shot by his own battalion. Jack remembers a kid from the Royal Berks who was convicted of cowardice in the face of the enemy. He detailed Corporal Tommy Lewis to take a squad to shoot the lad, but the Corporal did not want to do it. Jack formally ordered him and Tommy was so upset he nearly cried.

Jack described the winter of 1915 as, 'a devil in the trenches. We had to put whale oil on our legs to prevent frostbite. They called it trench-foot then and we were issued with a fur jerkin!' [The 1/4th were not deployed on the first day of the Somme in 1916 but were held in divisional reserve at Serre, ready to exploit breakthroughs. It was committed on 19th July, between Ovilliers and Pozieres, taking a lot of casualties in the subsequent weeks. Jack was involved in an attack on Sickle trench.] He carried a Lewis gun across no man's land with his friend and number two, Dennis Taylor, who carried the ammunition. Dennis was mortally wounded before they were half way across. On reaching the enemy trench Jack set up the gun. There were hardly any other soldiers with him and before long they were ordered to withdraw. There were bodies everywhere. Jack said they were rotten and rat eaten and the stench was awful. Blowflies were everywhere and interfered with him eating his food.

After the battle, the battalion was withdrawn from the line and given light duties. This consisted of being sent to a field dressing station where the wounded were triaged and those who would not survive were put into a tent and left to die. No one visited them. They received no water. The following morning, the dead were taken out, sewn into blankets, loaded on to a horse and cart and taken to a nearby cemetery, where French civilians were employed to dig graves. A Pastor was there for the internment, which was carried out with dispatch and the minimum of formality.

Eventually in March 1917, they were able to cross the Somme to Peronne, by this time Jack had been promoted to Sgt Major, although he was still only twenty years old. He believed he might have been the youngest man to hold that rank in the army. In the square at Peronne a couple of soldiers found a dummy tied to a lamppost dressed up as a French soldier, it was a booby trap which exploded and killed them as they tried to cut it down. Whilst at Peronne they encountered an Uhlan [German Cavalry] patrol. The officer wore a black leather helmet with a silver eagle badge. Jack killed him with a burst from the Lewis gun and the rest of the patrol ran away. He gave in the helmet to the Quartermaster but it subsequently disappeared.

On the 23rd November 1917 the 1/4th OBLI, with the rest of 48th Division, were sent to Italy to support the Italian army which was experiencing increasing pressure from the Austrians. The battalion arrived in Genoa where they were able to undertake more training. One exercise involved walking across the river Piave, which was thigh deep and running fast. Lt Barrett, who commanded the platoon, ordered his men to parade in the afternoon of the same day, as he had been dissatisfied with the condition of his men's rifles. His men refused and the platoon sergeant came to Jack for help. Jack attended the incident which he said constituted a mutiny:

> I went to every man and asked him if he refused to go on parade.
> The Lance Corporal came at me with a fixed bayonet but I

knocked it to one side and put him under close arrest. He was later sent to prison for two or two and a half years. That probably suited him, as he wanted to get back to England.

The remainder of the platoon escaped punishment but the CO gave Lt Barrett a dressing down for unnecessarily harassing them. [May 1918 found the division on the Asiago Plateau facing an Austrian army in the foothills of the Alps.] On the night of the 14th May 1918, Jack said that he swore at an officer for the only time in this career, He was accompanying Lt Miles and 11 Platoon on a patrol, sent out to take prisoners. It was 11.30pm and they had crawled to within fifty yards of the enemy position when they saw three Austrians or Magyars. The conversation went as follows:

Miles:	*'Look at the bastards. I'm going to take a pot at them.'*
Jack:	*'What with?'*
Miles:	*'My pistol'*
Jack:	*'Don't be a bloody fool! Your flash will give the game away'.*

The officer fired and what happened next was described in the London Gazette, in the citation for the DCM that Jack was subsequently awarded.

200100 CSM W.J. Coggins

On the night 14/5/18 he was with a fighting patrol of one officer and thirty other ranks which attacked an enemy post just outside the enemy wire south of Asiago. The officer became a casualty in the first rush but CSM Coggins immediately took charge and led the platoon after the retreating enemy, of whom one was taken prisoner and several killed. He set a splendid example of pluck and initiative in the attack and afterwards organized a rear guard that prevented the enemy, now reinforced from interfering with the carrying of the wounded officer.

Jack shot six men that night. Two weeks later the Brigadier came to the Company HQ. Jack said, 'He gave me a 'wigging as I was not supposed to go on small raids and then recommended me for the DCM.' A month later on the 15th June, the 1/4th found themselves at the sharp end of a big Austrian attack. A tremendous bombardment commenced at 3am that destroyed communications and a big supply dump. The main infantry assault came in at 7am with seven battalions heading for the 1/4th front. The outlying companies were heavily engaged. Jack said,

> I could not understand why my Lewis gun was not firing. I got onto the road, it was a silly thing to do but the trench continued on the other side. Of course, the first bullet got me before I was no more than two or three paces across the road. That was the one that went straight through. Of course, it knocked me down. I started choking with blood but managed to crawl to the far side. When I got there all the lads were dead as the gun was knocked to pieces by shellfire. As I lay there an Austrian stood over me. I thought he was going to pull out his pistol to finish me off. I had got the DCM ribbon on. He seemed to know what is was and simply cut it off. I don't remember much after that until my stretcher team picked me up.

Jack was evacuated to a hospital in Genoa where he was treated for a chest wound, the bullet having passed completely through his body without doing major damage. He also had a bullet wound to the elbow. He was recovering next to an Austrian officer who had been wounded in the foot and he kept making a lot of noise: 'I gave him such a whack but the doctor came along and said, 'Don't do that Sgt Major, I know he is not as badly wounded as you'. After a few weeks, Jack was sent back to England where he found that he had been recommended for a commission. He wanted one in the infantry but there were none available as the war was ending. He therefore became a pilot cadet in the RFC, flying patrols across the Channel.

With the end of the war, the chance of a commission in the RFC was also gone, so he decided to join the regular army as a CSM in the 52nd Oxfordshire and Buckinghamshire Light Infantry. 1921 found Jack with the battalion in married quarters in Cork. One night Jack had been out on a 'Sinn Fein raid' that involved arresting suspected members and handing them over to the local police. On his return to Victoria Barracks in the early hours, he found his wife in labour. Major Brett, his CO, offered to take them to the nursing home. As they approached the home they could see dead bodies. Continuing gunfire prevented them from entering safely. Eventually at dawn, they managed to gain access and Jack's first son was born quickly. Soon afterwards, the battalion came back to Wellington Barracks in Lichfield but because of increasing tension, they were promptly posted to Dublin. Here they took part in the siege of the Law Courts in Sackville Street where the rebels were holding out. Eighteen pounders from

Phoenix Park shelled the buildings until the garrison led by Rory O'Connor surrendered and they were handed over to the Irish Free State forces.

The British commander in the area, Major General Boyd felt concerned about the numbers of soldiers in hospital with V.D. Jack was sent to investigate with two sergeants. On interviewing the patients, the common factor of a public house called Deer's Head, off Sackville St, was identified. Jack and his colleagues went there to investigate. Young ladies who drank copious amounts of 'gin and it' quickly befriended them. At the end of the evening, Jack asked, 'Where are you going to take us then?' They went into the cellar of the pub, where on every step and all over the floor were couples in varying stages of coitus. Jack's report was passed via his CO to the Irish authorities and he believes this led to the girls being arrested and the pub burnt down.

His next task was considerably more dangerous, he was sent to Belfast to find out who was the area commandant of the IRA. Incredibly, he went into normally out of bound areas in Belfast in full uniform and was eventually introduced to the man himself. Jack reported that they got on very well. The man had been a corporal in the RAMC during WWI and he could not understand why the British army continued to remain in Ireland interfering in internal Irish affairs. Jack was neither harmed nor threatened.

Jack finally left the army in 1934, but Hitler ensured that his services were still required. In Banbury, in 1940, there was an important aluminium works protected by an anti-aircraft battery, persuaded to join the TAVR, Jack became battery Sergeant Major under Captain Ashby. Jack thought the gun crew were very sloppy and he used to visit them in the early hours to catch them out. On one occasion, he walked straight into the post without being challenged, so he took their Lewis gun and walked out with it, presenting it to Captain Ashby the following morning. As a result, the NCO in charge was arrested. Jack later turned out the guard and presented arms to King George V1 who was passing through Banbury on the way to Coventry. Towards the end of the war, Jack was sent on a course to learn about the new 20mm Hispano AA guns and was offered a job as a lecturer. On his return to the battery, he asked the captain what he thought, 'You're not bloody well going,' he said and that was that.

All three of Jack's sons fought in WW2, one in the navy, one in the RAF and his eldest was in the Queen's Own Oxfordshire Hussars and was wounded at Arnhem. At the time of the interview Jack had been a regular visitor to the battlefields of WW1 and was in particular demand to lay wreaths, being one of the few surviving soldiers with a DCM.

Westmorland and Cumberland go to War

The Experiences of James Adrian Grimes & Jack Laidler

4th Battalion, Border Regiment

Jack Laidler, Jack Huddleston and Adrian Grimes, Burma 1944

As they are 50 years later

A World War
France, North Africa, Burma, Norway

James Adrian Grimes

Service Number 3600146

Born:	1920, Ambleside
Service Dates:	May 1939 (TA) March 1947
Place of Enlistment:	Ambleside
Units:	6th Battalion Border Regiment, 4th Battalion Border Regiment
Awards:	1939–45 Star, Africa Star, Burma Star, Defence Medal, Victory Medal, Territorial Long Service Medal
Main Theatres:	France, North Africa, Syria, Burma, Norway. Germany

In May 1939, as war loomed, the call came: 'come and join the TA.' Adrian, with about 40–50 men, went along that night to the local drill hall in Ambleside to join up. The response was so great that they ran out of enrolment forms; in fact so many had enlisted into the Border Regiment; that they had to form a 6th Battalion. (East Cumberland.) It was the 6th that Adrian joined.

TA life consisted of a uniform; an evening's drill once a week and a fortnight's camp. At the end of August, they were due to camp at Abergavenny in South Wales, but as war was imminent, they were sent instead to Halton camp. Their first duty of the war was to form a guard for the RAF Maintenance Unit at Carlisle for two weeks. Adrian remembers one building contained only propellers and a second was just full of machine guns. After the two weeks, they were sent home, but they still drilled every morning. Then they were dispatched to the Kendal depot for a month.

At Kendal, volunteers were wanted for the 4th Battalion (Westmorland and Cumberland). There were not enough volunteers, so volunteers were 'suggested,' including Adrian. They entrained and were joined by conscripted men at

Oxenholme before all proceeded down to Aldershot to join the 4ᵗʰ Battalion. They expected to go to India, as the battalion had done in the First World War, but they were told that they were going to France instead. So on 17ᵗʰ November 1939 the 4ᵗʰ Battalion was in France, guarding the ammunition dumps in Brittany. These dumps, Adrian commented, stretched for miles, behind hedges and down small country lanes.

Nothing happened until May 1940, when the Germans attacked France. The fear was German parachutists would land on these ammunition dumps, so the 4ᵗʰ Battalion was dispatched to spend all day going round in trucks looking for them, but they never saw one.

On 15ᵗʰ May, they moved to Rouen, where they were met by refugees coming from Belgium and Holland. The battalion then got orders to move up to the Somme to join the remnants of the 51ˢᵗ Highland Division. On Empire day (24ᵗʰ May), they went into action for the first time. That morning they were on what they thought was a routine route march. They passed through a village just south of the Somme, where a lot of elderly French women came out and greeted them with kisses. Suddenly a machine gun opened fire. They had met the German army.

Their first orders were to cross a railway line and take the bridges the Germans were holding. They got the bridges but took heavy casualties, which included the platoon officers. Tanks were meant to arrive in support, but did not turn up. This was not unusual as they later heard, so without support they had to retreat.

Meanwhile in the North, Dunkirk was about finished and the 4ᵗʰ Battalion began its own retreat. It was part of what was called little BEF, made up of base depot troops – the 'odds and sods,' hoping to defend Calais and western France.

The next few days saw mainly skirmishes, but more serious were the constant air attacks. 'We were machine gunned and bombed, almost every time we moved,' Adrian pointed out. They lost much of their transport. They had no news of what was going on and streams of refugees blocked the roads. They then heard they had to get over a certain bridge by midnight, as it was to be blown, but the refugees delayed them. Fortunately, for the battalion, the blowing up of the bridge was delayed for half an hour, so they got across.

Moving toward Le Havre, they reached Fecamp. As they came down to the town in trucks, they came under fire from both sides at the crossroads. They got across the crossroads, but took casualties and were forced to take to the houses. In early evening, (and Adrian reminded us that days were long then), they decided to attempt a break out. They got the few trucks that were left and drove up a sunken road, but were stopped by Germans in front of them. They then realised they were totally surrounded and the Germans had tanks. Firing went on into the night, where upon the order came again to try a break out. This time they had to leave behind the trucks and the wounded. They gave the wounded morphine and then stole quietly away.

They discovered there were now no bridges across the Seine, thus no means to get into Western France, so they would have to head for Le Havre. They split into groups, one led by the CO and the other by his second in command. Adrian chose to go with his CO. It was a good choice, as the second group under Major Kidd were all eventually captured.

They formed single file behind the CO. They were very tired, but if anyone fell asleep, he was left behind and had to catch-up as best he could.

As they approached Goderville they were confronted by a large barricade of farm carts, (French farm carts are larger than English ones). Behind the barricade was a huge naval gun manned by French sailors, one of whom came forward to warn them of the position of land and antipersonnel mines.

At Goderville, they decided to split into smaller groups of two and three. It was now midday; Adrian's group met up with a retreating truck, which had room only on the canopy, so they climbed on top. It held for a while but then broke and they fell on the men below.

They finally arrived at Le Havre, which was illuminated by the fire of the oil fuel depot, the largest in France. They were informed there was a chance of a boat out of Le Havre that night, the ex Heysham-Belfast ferry *Duke of York*. So that night they left France. Coincidentally they had sailed on her sister ship the *Duke of Lancaster* into Cherbourg seven months before. They sailed all night and in the morning, land was sighted, but to their chagrin, it was not England, but France again! – Cherbourg. They had been re-landed to form a new line of defence. They were camped in the gardens of a Chateau and were joined by a Canadian battalion. The Canadians soon departed and were shipped back to England. After a few days it was realised a second line of defence was not a realistic option and they were all to be shipped back to England. This time it would be on a small coal boat, the *Alnwick* with its wheelhouse at the back. They had to use makeshift ladders to get all 200 of them down into the hold, where they brewed tea in a dustbin. They sailed all day and saw no other ship, not even an escort ship, eventually arriving safely at Poole. First, they were taken by bus to an empty school in Bournemouth and then sent on by train north to join up with the other remnants of battalion. The battalion was officially reformed in Sheffield and then sent to Kingston, Hertfordshire. Here they got re-enforcements but no trucks, so they had to commandeer vehicles from local civilians. This led to the battalion going round in butcher and baker vans, still advertising their wares. (They did get some National Express buses, which were more comfortable.) They now formed part of 25th Brigade, 2nd London Division TA, to defend South Wales and Birmingham's water supply at Rhayader.

In early 1941 at Great Malvern, they were issued with eastern tropical kit and sent to board the *SS Orontes* at Avonmouth. They were escorted up to the Clyde to join a convoy; all convoys for the east sailed from there. They had a strong escort, including the battleship *HMS Nelson* and an aircraft carrier. The convoy itself consisted of 12 liners. They stopped at Freetown, West Africa, for water. Water was used as ballast for the ships and the troops had used so much that the ships had become unstable. Water carriers had to come out to the liners, as the liners could not dock at Freetown. On reaching South Africa, half the convoy went to Durban, the other half to Cape Town. Adrian was in the Durban half and commented that they felt lucky, as Durban was more pro-British than Cape Town. They had a great reception and a 3-day leave; the Lady Mayoress invited them all to a concert hall where she sang. She proved an excellent singer. (Known to all as the Lady in White.) They then got a day with local families. Adrian commented that heavy drinkers had a great time as drink was free and many got severely intoxicated.

Joined by the rest of the convoy from Cape Town, they sailed for Port Tewfik and into the Suez Canal. They came to the Sweet Water Canal, which Adrian remembers was anything but sweet. This canal was built during the construction of the Suez Canal to supply freshwater. Now the British encampments stretched for miles along its banks, with filtration units supplying sweeter fresh water. The town of Ismailia formed the centre of these camps and as the main base for the British Army and RAF.

They then spent a fortnight getting use to the temperature, which was 127° F in the shade. (As stated in the English version of Egyptian Mail at the time – they were having a heat wave and Egyptians were dying in the streets.) As a result, they were not allowed out during the day and kept under double-layered tents. 'It was so hot,' Adrian said, 'it toasted bread in minutes and melted butter in seconds.' Getting out of the tent was like opening an oven door. It was very dry heat and caused mirages. You would look out and see a lake, but by evening, there would be no sign of it. 'Unbelievable' was Adrian's final word on the experience.

After acclimatising, they were sent up to the Libyan border (Sidi Barrani) for 2–3 weeks, as part of the 23rd Brigade, 6th Division. They were then sent to the Palestine-Syrian border, because of the rebellion in Iraq. Iraq was important to the RAF as a staging place. To help the rebellion, the Germans sent men through Turkey and Syria to Iraq. (Syria being Vichy.) The 4th Battalion was sent up through Palestine by train to Haifa and by truck up to the Golan Heights. Adrian remembered the Sunday bells ringing in Nazareth as they passed through.

They took positions on the Golan Heights, which is very rocky and mountainous and joined up with the 6th Australian division, (mainly consisting of Australians and South Africans.) They did not attack, as the mountains were so bad, so they – with other forces – advanced up the coast instead, where the French Foreign Legion opposed them. Following an arranged armistice with Vichy controlled Syria, they got to talk rather than fight these Legionnaires. They were mainly Poles and East Europeans, with German NCOs and French Officers. They had loads of money and were prepared to fight for anyone who paid them, but had no sympathy for any one or any cause.

After the armistice, they moved up to Aleppo in North Syria. Some of the battalion companies went to the Turkish border to stop trains, in order to search out and prevent any Germans or anyone of military age getting through to Iraq. Turks proved very friendly and Adrian heard many British forces personnel, in civilian clothes, (e.g. Royal Engineers,) helping the Turks with their defences, against any possible German attack. They had also no trouble with the Syrians, who were just so glad to see the French go.

Adrian then got three days leave in Beirut. After which the battalion was sent back to Egypt, to a transit camp near Alexandria. This was October 1941. They were told they were going somewhere and they were not to disclose any facts about that. A week later, they boarded destroyers in Alexandria, Adrian on the *HMS Jackal*. They sailed at midday and stayed on the decks, as there was not much room below. Towards evening, the sailors came up and lowered the railings, as if to prepare for action. It then started to get rough, with waves breaking over the decks dispatching kit overboard. Then as darkness fell they found themselves at the entrance of Tobruk harbour; about to become part of the longest siege in British History.

The harbour was full of sunken ships, so lighters came alongside to take them in. In the dark, they spied a big building, which was Tobruk hospital. They had come to replace the Australians. The Australian Prime Minster had in face of the increasing Japanese threat, recalled them for home defence. Australians boarded the lighters and were taken out to the destroyers – they had a rough time. It had taken months to replace the Aussies with the 70th Division, to which the fourth Battalion now belonged. Adrian commented, on landing, 'we were told to get mugs and get some tea – it was terrible, very salty; I think the Aussies were pulling a fast one on us.'

Trucks then took them to various parts of the fortress. Adrian was allocated as a private to the 4th ack-ack platoon, with four captured Italian 75mm field guns dating from the First World War. They did not have a great range. They had orders not to open up unless all guns of Tobruk opened up, for being so close to the front line their position would be easily spotted. There were twelve to fifteen men to operate and service all the guns; their position was just behind a low hill, just back from the front line in a salient. In front of them were four companies of infantry manning the trenches. These trenches had been the Italian defences – a series of massed concrete tunnels beneath the desert. As Ack Ack crew, Adrian added, it meant they were exempt from manning those trenches. On their right was a Polish Carpathian division.

From October to December there was little fighting, just patrols sent out each night to capture a few of the enemy for interrogation and intelligence. Adrian remembers picking up a shell fired by the enemy, which had landed nearby and found it to be the same as theirs. He added there was so much ammo under the sand; one could easily get more just by digging it up. Tobruk was defence-less from the air and the Italians and Germans bombed every day. In addition, German and Italian big guns on the perimeter of the defences (e.g. the Barda Bill) could reach any part of Tobruk. Conditions were bad and no fresh food was available. Supplies had to be brought in by sea every night, but if there was a full moon, no supplies came.

Sandstorms could be both dangerous and unpleasant, as they could cover an enemy tank attack. Unpleasant, as one could not take cover, as you had to keep watch in case of such an attack and sand got into your eyes and mouth.

In December, they moved out of the perimeter to El Duda, where big tank battles were taking place in what was called the 'The Cauldron.' The 4th Borders, the Durham Light infantry and Essex Regiment formed the 23rd Brigade; they were to attack Point 162, a point just outside Tobruk at El Adem.

The Essex began the attack then the Borderers and the DLI followed up. Then the DLI took up position to support the Borderers who made the final attack on Point 162, which overlooked the El Adem aerodrome – the final objective. There would be tanks to support them. It was dark and Adrian remembers seeing tracers from the Bofor guns bouncing off the tanks in the distance. They passed Italian and German positions as they advanced and could hear them talking. However they did not come out to investigate, which surprised Adrian as tank tracks make a lot of noise on rocks. They passed right through them without firing a shot. At dawn he went up with the adjutant to fire a vary pistol – the success signal – and it was then the enemy opened up with shells. They imme-diately took cover, digging in and making Duvres (hollows in the ground with lumps of stone as cover.) It was not the best of cover, as bullets could ricochet off the stones in any direction, but the best one could do quickly in the desert.

Suddenly an Italian appeared with a white flag and nervously advanced towards them. Then another appeared and then another and suddenly loads of them appeared. No shot had been fired. This, Adrian felt, was remarkable, as only 2 days before an attack on another point held by Italians had been repulsed with heavy losses. (Moreover, that been held by what was felt to be a weak unit, although they were usually told that before any attack…)

They were now faced with a few hundred Italians, plus a few German prisoners. Suddenly a German motorcycle came into view. The driver realised they were British, turned round and drove off as fast as he could. They fired at him, but he got away. With so many prisoners, they had to create POW camps, but the Germans and Italians would not mix and so had to be separated. They got to the hospital at El Adem aerodrome, which was full of New Zealander casualties, manned entirely by German doctors and nurses. Adrian added that Germans in the desert did act as gentlemen – Rommel not having SS troops.

After the attack Adrian now found himself lethargic, with no desire to do anything, even defend himself or dig in. On reporting to the MO, he was found to have jaundice, which was common among Tobruk defenders due to reliance on tinned food and lack of fresh food. He was put in an ambulance back to Tobruk and to the beach hospital; anyone sent to the beach hospital, as Adrian knew, was for evacuation. He noted some men used the opportunity for a swim, but Adrian did not fancy it, it was cold. He was taken out by lighter to the Hospital Ship (all white with a green band) and sent back to Alexandria. They had to wear hospital blues, as no uniforms are allowed on Hospital ships. Ships are also floodlighted at night so the enemy can see them clearly.

Back in Egypt, he was sent to the Number 6 Hospital, near Ismaili, in fact very near where the battalion had first been based when it came to Egypt. Here he spent Christmas 1941 and was visited by his cousin. He had met his cousin on his way up to Syria a few months before in a canteen, so he knew he was in the Middle East. He wrote a letter and his cousin came down from Port Said where he was currently stationed, to spend a day with Adrian.

Adrian was 2 months in hospital and had good food, including as much tinned fruit, as he wanted, but no fat. The battalion came back from Tobruk and was stationed close by, so Adrian and a number of others sneaked out of the hospital, putting overcoats over their hospital blues in order to go to the battalion canteen for a good egg and chips dinner.

Adrian knew that on discharge, if he did not know where his battalion was, like others in that position would he be sent to an Infantry base depot at Genafa called 'The Hill. It was a place to 'harden you up' and had a notorious reputation. Thus Adrian was so glad to discover his battalion had moved back to Egypt and was close by. On his discharge, he got a three-day pass, but he never used it, as it was cancelled. The 70th division, which included the 23rd Brigade (although the

DLI had now left the brigade for Malta,) was to leave Egypt immediately. In fact Adrian points out that in all the time he was in Egypt he saw none of the sites, such as the Pyramids – he saw only the 'hard parts.'

They were taken down to Tewfik to board the brand-new liner *Mauritania*. Adrian said that all her finery and luxury were covered in plywood for protection. She was fast, thus given no escort as she headed for Rangoon. What puzzled Adrian was that all their equipment, such as trucks, was coming separately on a slower boat. On route, they heard Rangoon had fallen and so they were diverted to Bombay. It was now May 1942. Adrian met another cousin in Bombay and spent his leave with her, rejoining his battalion at Kirkee. (A big arsenal near Puna, 80miles NE of Bombay.)

From there they went to the semi-hill station of Ranchi, (Semi as it is only 3000 feet up, not 6–800 feet, which would make it a proper hill station.) They were there as a reserve in case of an invasion of the east coast of India by the Japanese. They were also there for internal security. In August 1942, they went to Patna University, to throw out the students who were rioting.

Adrian was now in the intelligence section of the Borderers, working on coding and decoding and he recalls that the summer of 1942 was a very bad time – all bad news. He remembers a secret message from Divisional HQ (70th) to 23rd Brigade, saying that morale of the division was at its lowest point. The fall of Tobruk, Adrian added, hit the 70th hard, but general morale lifted with the news of the victories at El Alamein and Stalingrad.

They then moved to the semi-hill station of Bangalore to begin jungle training. It was a good station, a lovely place where they had a good time. In April 1944, they heard they were to form part of Wingate's special force, known as the Chindits. In November they were sent up to Jhansi, to practice river crossings with mules. This was also a lovely spot, green grassy banks, with the jungle 100 yards away from the river. In their training, they learnt how to lay out a ground sheet, put their kit into it and wrap it across the seam into a sausage; this would then form a float for two men to cross the river. They also learnt that no man should be ever left on his own. Adrian was part of the reconnaissance unit, which crossed first. Horses came next and then the mules; men would hang on to the mules, which were great swimmers and could swim 3 times faster than a man.

The battalion was then split in two columns, the 55th and the 34th, Adrian being in the latter. (8 Columns made a brigade, with the artillery forming an infantry column of its own.) The battalion was to be called 34th Division to fool enemy intelligence. They were to fly into Burma in gliders, as part of Wingate's command. The gliders, Adrian added, were able to carry even bulldozers in order to create airstrips. This would then allow the troops to be supplied by air. They were the last brigade scheduled to go into Burma. The battalion was now sent by train to Mariana airbase, where their gliders were waiting for them. There was a fear that the Japanese may break out as they were only 20 miles away, so the battalion travelled with the officers in the Engine and the men in the coaches, their rifles sticking out of the windows. By the time they got to Mariana General Wingate had been killed in an air crash and General Slim saw his chance to take over the 23rd Brigade for his own purposes. He would use them to act behind the Japanese right flank at Kohima where the Japanese were besieging the British at the key position of Imphal.

Thus they were redirected to Mokokchung and into the Naga Hills and during the monsoon season. For the next four months (April to June 1944), they operated in the Japanese rear. Their objective was to cut and disrupt the supply lines of the Japanese army. They continued to move southwards from Kohima, cutting supply lines so effectively that the Japanese often mistook them for a division rather than a brigade. When the Japanese army were pushed back from Imphal, the 23rd Brigade became like a guerrilla force, helping to turn the Japanese retreat from Imphal into their greatest military disaster.

British and USA Dakotas supplied them every four days and in those four months, they were in jungle the RAF only failed once not to deliver, due to a low mist. Each column had a RAF officer, who kept in contact with the airbase. They helped bring in fighters as air cover when and if the column needed them.

Each drop came in chutes of different colours to show which supplies were in them. Due to the steepness of the Naga Hills, if a drop missed by a 100 yards, it could end up miles away as it plunged down the steep sides of the hill. The local Naga Indians were very trustworthy and headed down the slopes to retrieve the supplies, particularly as supplies would often contain salt, a commodity the Naga highly prized. The supplies contained US K-rations and were in Adrian's words 'a wonder to behold' compared to normal British rations. It was the first time Adrian was to come across Nescafe. In fact, all equipment they were supplied with was exemplary; Wingate had ensured his forces got the best. They had Kashmir wool blankets, (dyed green,) US Carbines and Garrand rifles – far superior to standard British weapons.

Airdrops had their dangers as well. Adrian recalled a bale of hay killing one man, while with another drop the chute did not open and an ammo box landed on a tent, just as two men vacated it. Having said that, in four months no other brigade had such light casualties: 13 killed, 30 wounded. Wounded were always evacuated, as not to do so would have had a bad effect on morale. To do this they used the Auster light aircraft, strapping a man on each wing. The Austers could land and take off on a very short strip. Adrian added that communication with the outside world was so good you could send a letter from behind Japanese lines and it would be in Ambleside in three days. To transfer mail they set up two poles with a rope tied across; the mail and documents were attached to this rope and aircraft would fly low, with a hook on the front, grab the rope and thus take away the mail. If they took any prisoners they would send them back via the indigenous Nagas, who were paid with silver rupees. Each man carried 20 silver rupees to help engage Naga help if needed.

Adrian also mentioned that with the Jungle so thick, ambushes were easy. So being so close to Japanese lines, as added precaution, on waking they always moved to another mountain before starting breakfast.

In the final days of the Japanese retreat from Imphal the battalion witnessed the total destruction of the Japanese army. Along the sides of jungle tracks many hundreds of the enemy lay dead, many burned black. Finally, they reached Ukhrul, their job in destroying the Japanese Army finished. They marched part of the way to Imphal, past the 2nd Borderers, who had taken up position in case of any Japanese counter attack. Then they boarded trucks for Manipur. On arrival they were greeted with cut down oil drums of heated water. They were told to take off all their clothes, which were then taken away and burnt and after a good soak in the oil drums, they were issued with a completely new set of clothes and kit.

Their action in Burma was now over. They moved to Bangalore, a lovely spot, for a well-earned leave over the summer of 1944. In September, they heard about Arnhem, which would have a direct effect on the battalion in the future. In September, Adrian took his final leave in Bombay. He discovered on his return that those troops with three years, nine months continuous service were to be repatriated. It was a bolt from the blue, but as that applied to Adrian, he was therefore off back to England. The Suez and Mediterranean were now open, so the replacements now took two not eight weeks to get to India,. Thus allowing them to bring the war weary troops in India, home quicker. In preparation for the departure, they were moved to Deolali, before finally boarding the SS Orion, another Barrow built liner, at Bombay. On arrival at Gibraltar they were told not to worry about the explosions going on around the liner. There were depth charges being dropped to prevent 2-man enemy submarines operating in the harbour. Finally, they reached Britain, Glasgow in a snowstorm and promptly set off for three weeks leave.

On his return from leave, Adrian was to join the 1st Battalion of the 1st Airborne Division, which needed replacements after its heavy losses at Arnhem. He was again in the Intelligence section. However every time an airdrop was

planned it was soon cancelled as the ground forces had already captured the intended target. This remained the case right through 1945, so Adrian and the 1st Battalion never did get into a glider.

Two days after VE day, they were told they were being sent to Norway, flying in Halifax bombers from Cambridgeshire. They would be the first allied troops into Norway. As they flew into Norway, the sky became black with clouds and they were ordered to return. However, six planes went on, dipping down every now and then to see under the clouds. Adrian was in one of these six.

They came in over the aerodrome just north of Oslo at 200 feet, with little fuel left and as they landed two of the six planes crashed into nearby mountains with a total loss of life.

On landing, they got into German trucks, (having none of their own) and set off to Oslo. They were greeted by what seemed the entire German Army of Norway coming the other way; not even in France or Africa had Adrian seen so many Germans or German units, including horse troops, bicycle battalions, infantry and artillery units. They had been, on their surrender, ordered to a designated area just outside Oslo.

Adrian found himself billeted in a school opposite the Gestapo building, which had been bombed and destroyed by British aircraft. The battalion formed the guard of honour for the arrival of King Haakon VII, on his return to Norway from London. Afterwards they were sent to Bergen to return on another Barrow built liner, *SS Stratheden* to Liverpool.

After a week's leave Adrian got married (he had got engaged when he came home from Burma,) and was dispatched to Germany, near Haan Munden, south of Hanover. In March 1947, he was finally demobbed. After the war he went back to work at the Windermere and District Electricity Supply Co. The firm eventually became part of Norweb and finding this too regimented, ("too much like the army", he said) he left to set up his own business as an electrical contractor. He had four employees, although later this was reduced to one man, whom he gave the business to in 1985 when he retired. At time the interview he was residing in Ambleside next door to the house where he was born. As he said, 'I have almost come full circle.'

Bullet Proof Jack, Battalion Bookie

Jack Laidler

Platoon Sergeant
Service No 3600602

Born:	5th January 1919 Windermere
Service Dates:	15th September 1939–late 1946
Place of Enlistment:	Carlisle
Units	4th Battalion, 1st Battalion Border Regiment
Awards:	Mentioned in Dispatches (Burma) 1939–45 Medal, Burma Star, North Africa Star
Main Theatres:	France 1940, North Africa, Burma, Norway and Germany

Jack joined up ten days after the war had started and always saw himself as a lucky man. He was in France in 1940 as part of the Little BEF retreating before the German advance. They were supposed to be evacuated from Dieppe but instead were marched to Cherbourg and then onto St Nazaire. There were no trucks, so they marched day and night. Thousands were waiting on the quayside when they reached St Nazaire and two liners the *SS Lancastria* and *Georgic* were in the harbour to take them out of France. They boarded tugs to go out to the liners but as Jack's tug set off, the harbour came under air attack. As they approached the *SS Lancastria* bombs that had just missed the liner, sent a wall of water before them and the tug veered off towards *SS Georgic* instead. Thus Jack was not on the *Lancastria,* when a few hours later, at 15.48, she was hit by three bombs and went down in 20 minutes with a loss of over 4000 lives. This represented a third of the British losses in France and was kept secret from the public.

In Tobruk (1941) Jack was injured out. Shortly afterwards, the 13th Platoon, of which he was a Sergeant, was wiped out. At the end of war he was meant to fly into Norway with the 1st Battalion, as part of the force to take the surrender of the German forces. However, just as he was to board the aircraft Jack was switched to a boat heading for Trondhiem in order to deliver a special package to the Russians. He was then to return by boat to Oslo, via Bergen, to rejoin his men. His platoon went on to Oslo by air, but perished when their aircraft crashed on the way in. (See Adrian Grimes' account).

Jack and Adrian were in the same battalion and Adrian gives a detailed account of the battalion through the war. Jack instead offers us a more in depth description of life and action in Burma.

Jack relates that when the battalion first got to India there were riots, as well as sabotage of bridges and telegraph lines. His first job in India was to be in charge of a boat on the Ganges, where it was difficult to know whom you were fighting as the 'enemy' were not in uniform.

The battalion was retrained as Chindits, but just before going with the rest of the Chindit battalions into Burma it was diverted by General Slim. The battalion instead advanced into the rear of the Japanese forces, attacking Imphal. Jack's real role in the battalion was that of bookmaker. This was not officially allowed, but the CO, Lt Col. Johnny Burges, sent for Jack and said;

> The Colour Sergeant tells me you are bookmaker. Know that this
> is not allowed, but I give you permission as you are doing a good
> job. Give the lads something to do.

Jack reckons he was probably the only official bookmaker in the British Army. He would take bets everyday on all sorts of things. For example: if a VIP was visiting, bets were made on whom it might be. He remembers that when they came out of Burma they had a visit from three VIPs. The CO had asked the battalion not to cheer until they were instructed to do so. The first VIP stepped out of the plane, then the second, General Wavell and then finally the third, General 'Bill' Slim. He was immediately greeted by spontaneous cheering from the men, much to annoyance of the CO. The cheers were from those who had guessed the VIP and won the bet.

Adrian says Jack was a good bookmaker because he always honoured the bets. He took bets for races such as the Derby even though it would take several days for the results to reach them. Jack tells of someone in the Signals who got to know the results beforehand and then craftily place a bet each way so as not to arouse suspicion. Jack discovered this only after the war when a mate from Ipswich visited him with the man from Signals, who informed Jack of the deceit.

On the Kei River, Jack arranged a 'Mule Derby,' with colours and jockey caps made by the local natives. Jack went down in the morning and rode all the mules to see which ones could not run, in order to set the odds. The whole battalion turned out for the races and big bets were made on one particular mule. Jack knew it was one that could not run, so he was not too worried. You can imagine therefore, his surprise when it won! A friend later revealed that all the other mules had been filled up with two gallons of water.

Adrian relates how Jack went missing on Derby Day 1944, while the battalion was deep behind Japanese lines at Imphal. There was confidence amongst the battalion that Jack would turn up in time for the Derby day results a few days later. Jack related in detail what happened in those three days he was missing and thus gives us a full account of a single action.

The night before Derby Day Jack and his men were ordered out to secure the road for the battalion to march down the following morning. The Japanese were known to be about. Jack made his foxhole, surveying and securing the road, whilst his lads slept. At first light, the battalion came past and went up the hill with the mules. Jack's instructions were to wait one hour and then rendezvous with the rearguard at the village on the hill. As they waited, the rations arrived – 14 days of K-rations, weighing about 100 cwt. He was faced with the choice of two routes, to re-join the battalion either the direct way, 300–400 yards up the steep incline, or the easier route which was ¾ of a mile. He opted for the latter, considering the loads that needed to be carried. The local natives were ordered to carry the rations but they refused, dropping the bags and running off. It was assumed it was because the baggage was too heavy.

Picking up the loads, Jack and his men went along the easier road. A new lad, Corporal Clifford, was leading and Jack pushed up to the front to talk to him. They had only covered 20–30 yards and as Jack addressed the Corporal with a, 'Hey up,' the Japanese opened fire from ambush. Jack pushed the lad off the road and down a steep scree slide. He would not see this lad again, though he did hear later that the lad had survived the war. (Jack assumed he had wandered off and found another unit and attached himself to it.)

Jack dropped to the ground initially pretending to be shot but then swivelled round and ran down the road to where the rest of his lads were. He thought his backpack had probably saved him, but he was surprised to find that it had not been hit at all. Yet another lucky escape. The Ghurkhas who were with him had fixed bayonets and grenade caps on their rifles and were ready to attack up the road. 'No,' ordered Jack, 'you'll get killed, Follow me.' Jack had little faith in the grenade caps. He remembered from training that there was no guarantee where they would fall and he expected they would harm his own men as much as the Japanese. The only other alternative was to go back and take the steep road. He also suspected that the real reason the natives did not want to carry the loads down the easier road was that they anticipated the ambush. Jack, with his Ghurkha scout, led the way back. Both had lost their bush hats and as Jack pointed out. The British identified their own soldiers by their hats, so there was a risk they might be mistaken for Japanese. Jack took the lead, as he felt he was more likely to be recognised as they approached the British position

He had walked 20 to 30 yards up the steep road when he came under fire. He assumed it was the Japanese again but it was in fact the battalion opening up on him as a suspected Japanese soldier. Jack dropped to the ground so they would think he was shot, took a grenade and pulled the pin. He then got up and rushed them, throwing the grenade (which luckily did not go off) then instead of heading back down the track as they would expect him to do, he dived off to the left. He had seen a row of bushes and into these he dived with bullets flying round him, only to discover that these were not bushes but the tops of 50–60 foot trees, poking up over a steep edge! Jack found himself falling off a sheer slope. When he came round, his legs were on each side of a tree. He tested himself by wiggling his limbs and found he was alright. The tree had stopped him a few yards above the road where the Japanese had ambushed him earlier. In case they were still there he followed a parallel path to the road below him, back to his original position. On his return his Ghurkha scout rushed up and hugged him with relief. His men felt that Japs were all around, but Jack was convinced that the last ambush had been British, as Jap rifles go 'yap yap' and British, 'thud thud'. His men were sceptical, but Jack was in command and he took them slowly back to the village where the column was meant to be. The Japanese had surrounded it, so it took three days to get in. When they entered it was dead silent, with no sign of anyone. Jack took a grenade off one of his men, advanced on a hut and kicked the door in. No one was there. Suddenly he heard 'Larry?' Turning, he saw Sergeant Chapman from Newcastle rushing towards him. As Jack realised that they had found the rest of the battalion fatigue overwhelmed him and he collapsed, Chapman caught him as he fell.

Jack woke up the next day in the MO's tent. On getting up to meet the rest of the lads, he discovered he had only one boot. The lads were sitting at the far end of the village.

'What has been happening in the past three days?' Jack asked.

The reply came, 'We were attacked by a Jap with a grenade – but we got him.'

'How do you know? Did you find the body?' Jack inquired.

'No he went over the hill in two halves' answered the men. (When Jack went over the hill some of his kit went one way and he the other.)

'Well,' exclaimed Jack, 'The Jap you shot at is talking to you now!'

They all laughed and thought Jack was 'doolali'. He realised he would need to prove it to them and demanded two volunteers to come with him to find his kit.

They set off to the spot where he had leapt over the hillside and Jack saw the skid marks he had made as he descended but there was no sign of his kit. He then realised that the local natives would have his kit by now. He set off back up the hill on his knees, as it was so steep. The sun was shining and as he looked up, there 60 feet up a tree, standing vertical on a branch against the trunk, was his rifle. With difficulty, as he was still weak, he climbed up to get it. It was an excellent rifle, American and deadly to 800 yards. It was the proof he needed and Jack was henceforth nicknamed, 'Bullet-proof Jack.' The official report stated that 47 rounds had been fired at a Jap and the officer did not look best pleased at having to rewrite the report; but at least Jack was no longer officially dead. He was back in time for the Derby Day results, which came in 14 days after

Later, the Japs were firing artillery at them from across the valley. They could not fire back as they only had grenades so Jack set out to attack them at close range. He went down to the river, where his Ghurkhas built a bamboo bridge. The river was in full flood and it took 2 hours to complete the bridge. When they arrived at the spot where the Japs were supposed to be, there was no sign of them because they only came at dusk and dawn to fire their weapons. The Japs were then spotted coming down a path, so Jack set up an ambush. It was not successful however because in the end the Japs took an alternative route and took up a commanding position just 40 yards away. Jack pulled his men out but came back the next day to try to ambush the Japs again, only to find that they had gone. The gun position was so well hidden that you could be within 15 yards of it and not notice it.

They then found a hut near Ochra, containing a Japanese printing press, set up to print Japanese pink notes with an equivalent value of £50. Jack had pressed about a dozen for himself, when he heard shouting outside. He was being ordered to take his platoon to a village 12 miles away that had been overrun. They set off immediately. [At the time of this interview Jack still had the notes}.

Arriving at the village they were greeted by another platoon, commanded by Dick O'Dowd. Since Jack's platoon had marched 12 miles, Dick decided he would attack first and give Jack's platoon time to rest. The attack did not go well and Dick's platoon came back carrying his dead body. Jack's platoon then attacked and killed 11 out of the 12 Japanese soldiers. Jack commented, 'Bloody warfare – war makes you do killing – it has to be done, no option.' They buried Dick at the village.

After the war, Jack was in the 1st Battalion and was demobbed late in 1946 in Germany. He had a grand time there, using his football skills to captain the battalion football team to win the Corps cup. Before the war he had been a professional footballer playing for Carlisle and he resumed his career after the war, moving on later from Carlisle to Hartlepool FC and then to Morecambe FC (The Shrimps). After he retired as a professional footballer, he established a very successful business of nine shops across Cumbria, including hairdressers and tobacconists.

King George VI in the London Gazette, July 19th 1945 for his service in Burma mentioned Jack Laidler in dispatches.

Ulster Volunteer

John Wood

Service No 24275529

Born: 5th June 1948 Newtownards NI
Service Dates: 1972–73
Unit: 7th Battalion Ulster Defence Regiment
Awards: GSM Northern Ireland
Main Theatres: Northern Ireland

In 1972, John returned to Northern Ireland after working for a while in England. He was disturbed by the extent to which paramilitary organisations were controlling important aspects of Ulster life, like the petrol supply. He thought that by joining the U.D.R. he might be able to influence events for the better.

He joined the 7th battalion as a part time soldier and received just one week's training at the Palace Barracks Hollywood. This training was entirely functional, concentrating on weapon handling, radios, getting in and out of vehicles, such as Land Rovers and helicopters and how to patrol. The soldiers were expected to work one night in four from 7pm to 7am, while continuing to do their normal work during the day. Their main job was to guard vital installations, for example, RUC stations and the dock cranes. In addition, they formed mobile patrols in the dock areas of Belfast and around residential districts. Although armed with SLRs they were supposed to avoid firefights if possible and call the army. John was acting as a spotter from a high crane in the dock area when he saw men firing at his patrol. Though he was a marksman and in a great position to shoot, he was told to wait for the regular soldiers.

John said his company and platoon consisted of Catholics and Protestants and from his point of view; their activities did not favour either side. In consequence, when patrolling in residential areas they were treated courteously and were rarely fired on. John feels that their largely non-combative role was meant to inspire public confidence and trust. One of their frequent tasks was setting up a vehicle control point. (VCP). On one occasion, the whole of Belfast centre was sealed off and all vehicles searched. Sometimes they did a swap with other companies in the countryside and they were often given the worst jobs such as guarding tracks on windswept hillsides. On one such VCP, they were there for several hours and the only vehicle that came through was a tractor driven by a drunken farmer. When eventually a car came through, it was 4am and they were all asleep.

If members of the force lived in dangerous areas, or had to pass through them they could apply for a pistol licence. One of John's corporals was refused a license. He was eager to possess a pistol in order to show off, so he got a friend to put a bullet through his front door and applied again. This time the license was granted. Playing with his new gun at home, he shot and destroyed his new stereo, then, on the way back from the pub one night, after he had been displaying it ostentatiously, a car followed him. He decided to fire at it, only to find it was a police car. No one was hurt, but his UDR career was quickly terminated.

John left the UDR after about eighteen months because of work commitments and thinks that the regiment was eventually disbanded because it was associated with the Protestant side, although he never experienced anything to indicate that they were anything but impartial.

The Army in World War Two
The Little BEF

The exploits of the BEF (British Expeditionary Force) in France in 1940 are well known with the retreat before the advancing German armies, through Belgium and France back to Dunkirk. What followed was one of the greatest legends of British military history; the evacuation of the BEF from the beaches of Dunkirk. What are less known are the actions of other British Units in France at the time. These forces were known as the Little BEF. This consisted partly of the troops guarding the ammunition depots all over northern France and Normandy, as outlined in Adrian Grimes' account. Their last minute advance from their reserve positions to support the BEF and then their fight to get out of France, is well represented in Adrian's account.

The Little BEF also included those forces sent to Calais and sacrificed in order to distract German forces from Dunkirk. These forces were the 3rd Battalion Royal Tank Regiment, the 229th Anti-Tank Battery of the RA and the Queen's Victoria Rifles (QVR), who arrived on 22nd May. These forces were so hastily sent that the tank crews had no time to test their armaments and were still without radios, while the QVR (a motorcycle unit) had most of their motorcycles left behind. On the 23rd May the main body of the 30th Motor Brigade arrived, consisting of the 1st Battalion of the Rifle Brigade and the 2nd Battalion of the King's Royal Rifle Corps (60th Rifles.) In total, 3000 British alongside some 800 French troops were to defend Calais. Against them was the 10th Panzer Division, (15,000 men and 300 tanks) who were ordered to take Calais. Rather than evacuate, Churchill ordered this force to, 'fight to the death' to delay the Germans. This lead to a heroic sacrificial battle which was fought between the 24th and the 26th May. Whether this sacrifice helped save those at Dunkirk has always been in dispute. What has not been doubted , is the tenacious battle that these forces put up in the defence of Calais. The following account by Frank Dowding of the QVR details this action, his capture and his later escape from a PoW camp. As we tend to concentrate in military history on the major battles, in terms of heroism, action and sacrifice, we should not forget that there were many less well known actions that deserve to be remembered.

The Little BEF
for Bravery in the Field, at Calais

Frank Dowding

Private
Service No 6896198

Born:	23rd November 1918, Lambeth London
Service Dates:	1938–1945
Place of Enlistment:	London
Units:	KRRC 1940, RASC 1944–5
Awards:	Military Medal 1939/45 Star, France and Germany Star, Defence Medal, 1939/45 Medal
Main Theatres:	Defence of Calais 1940, Normandy 1944.

In 1938, Frank joined the Queen's Victoria Rifles (TA), a battalion of the King's Royal Rifle Corps (KRRC). At the outbreak of war, he was taken into the regulars and shipped to Calais as part of the 30th Infantry Brigade commanded by Brigadier Nicholson. This brigade was selected as a mobile force to act as a rearguard to the retreating BEF. The 30th Brigade had been part of Eastern Command when it got sudden orders to embark for France. Leaving Southampton it moved to Dover and proceeded to Calais. Frank's unit was amongst the first to disembark on the 22nd May along with the 3rd Royal Tank Regiment. There they joined three companies of the French territorials and some French naval ratings. The Queen's Rifles were to secure Calais, while the rest of the Brigade was to join them the next day to act offensively towards Dunkirk. As a result, the Queen's Rifles did not have their transport sent with them, which proved to be a handicap later on. The battalion at the time had been trained as a motorcycle unit. Each company had ten Bren guns and five anti-tank weapons, but one third of the other ranks were armed with pistols instead of rifles. The battalion was ordered to guard six roads approaching Calais, as well as to guard the submarine terminal west of Calais and to watch the beaches in case of German parachute landings at low tide. The length of the front the battalion was guarding was about 15 miles. On the afternoon of 23rd May, the rest of the Brigade arrived: the 2nd KRRC, the 1st Rifle Brigade and the 229th Anti-Tank Battery RA.

On the night of 23/24th May these units attempted to advance, to try opening the road to Dunkirk to get rations through to the BEF. The Germans reacted quickly, sending two German Panzer Divisions to force a quick decision at Calais. Outnumbered and outgunned, the 30th Brigade refused to accept the surrender offered and fought for four days before finally being overwhelmed, but not before they had forced the Germans to send a third division from the Dunkirk front to support their attack. Frank remembers being engaged with the Germans and firing at motorcycle combinations across a canal, followed by street fights where he and his mates were cornered in a basement and had to surrender to avoid grenades being dropped onto them. Churchill paid this tribute in the House of Commons to the 30th Brigade's defence of Calais:

> The Rifle Brigade, the 60th Rifles and the Queen Victoria's Rifles with a battalion of British Tanks and 1,000 Frenchman, in all about 4,000 strong, defended Calais to the last. The British Brigadier was given an hour to surrender. He spurned the offer and four days of intense fighting passed, before silence reigned over Calais, which marked the end of a memorable resistance.

The Navy brought off only thirty survivors and we do not know the fate of their comrades. Their sacrifice however, was not in vain. At least two armoured divisions which otherwise would have been turned against the British Expeditionary Force had to be diverted to overcome them. The time gained enabled the Gravelines water lines to be flooded and to be held by French troops. Thus it was that the port of Dunkirk was kept open.

The rest of the 30th Brigade, including Frank, were now prisoners of war. Frank was sent to a French cavalry barracks in Marseilles which had been converted into a PoW camp. Frank managed to escape and he was hidden by a small French boy in an attic. He remembered cycling along the banks of a canal, in the company of two French women. As Germans cycled past in the opposite direction on the other bank, the women exclaimed, 'Look at the bastards over there.'

He then managed to obtain false papers that portrayed him as a US citizen. With these, he was able to pass through France and over the border into Spain. Finally, he was repatriated via Gibraltar

On his return to Britain, he rejoined the KRRC and was awarded a Military Medal. (MM). He later joined the RASC because of a recurring knee injury. He landed in Normandy a week after D-Day and followed the advance across France to Germany, working in stores, until the end of the war.

Home Front

Following the fall of France, the British Army prepared for the expected invasion of Britain in the summer of 1940. Following the RAF's victory in the Battle of Britain, which ended the threat of invasion, the British Army could now consider intervening overseas. The entry of Italy into the war in May 1940 threatened the British supply line through Egypt and the Mediterranean. To defend against this, Britain dispatched troops to Egypt to face the threat of invasion from Italian Libya. This did not mean there was an end to the war on the Home Front, as shown by the following two accounts. The first is from Maud Hools, (nee Armstrong), of the Auxiliary Territorial Service (ATS). The ATS was set up in September 1938 as a women's branch of the British Army. It was attached to the Territorial Army. In the evacuation from Dunkirk some of last to leave were the BEF's ATS telephonists, yet the womens' rate of pay was only two thirds of that of the men. Initially the role of the ATS was clerical support and women were barred from serving in battle, but due to the shortage of men, many ATS women took over more direct support roles. Maud was assigned to the anti-aircraft batteries defending Britain. By the end of the war, the ATS had expanded to 190,000 and had Princess Elizabeth as a member. Maud, undoubtedly one of the first of its members, gives an account which reveals much of the comradeship, as well hard work, of London's AA batteries.

The second account is by Dickie Toms of the Oxfordshire and Buckinghamshire Light Infantry. He reveals some of the hidden dangers of the home front, as in the case of the shooting of the vicar's daughter. He also indicates the problems of 'reserved occupations.' The First World War had clearly indicated the importance of not allowing all men to join up, but to keep back skilled labour in key jobs for the economic support of the war, such as miners, engineers, dockers and railwaymen. This caused anger in many young men who were thus prevented from being called up and some of them felt stigmatised. Dickie's fight to stay in the army clearly reveals this tension. For cross reference on accounts about life on the home front; see also Adrian Grimes and John (Jock) Wilson.

Battery in the Blitz

Maud Hool (nee Armstrong)

Auxiliary Territorial Service (ATS)

Born:	5th April 1921 Whitehaven, Cumberland
Service Dates:	December 1939–March 1945
Place of Enlistment:	Lancaster
Units:	613 AA Battery
Awards:	1939/45 Star, Defence Medal, 1939/45 Medal
Main Theatres:	London

In 1939, Maud was living in Lancaster, working at the Williamson's Linoleum factory. With the outbreak of war, she was called up and reported to the Bowerham barracks, now the University of Cumbria. She remembers that the drill involved a lot of marching and the drill sergeant shouting at her, *'Don't look at me Armstrong, I'm no oil painting.'* She was only a girl when she joined, but she said she quickly toughened up and learned to stand up for herself. She was assigned to 613 Battery, which was probably equipped with six 3.7in QF AA [which were similar to the legendary German 88mm]. The battery was first assigned to Edinburgh, where Maud was very impressed with the sailors she met. Then it was moved to Wales and then finally to London in time for the blitz. They travelled sometimes by 3-ton truck and sometimes by train. Maud saw her crew as a close-knit family who looked after each other but like families they would also play jokes on one another. Since Maud was quite light, they liked to lift her up and place her in the luggage compartment rack of the train!

In London, they were based at Hampstead Heath, which did not take much bombing but the battery was constantly in action against enemy aircraft. Maud's job was to cook for the officers and take tea to the gun crews, which she did under the terrifying din of bombs and artillery fire. She saw doodlebugs fly over and V2s, both of which were far too fast to be brought down by artillery fire. 'We were frightened, but we did not run away,' she said.

Maud worked 24 hours on, 24 hours off and in her spare time went into London to work in a hotel on Hyde Park Corner. They lived in tents during the good weather, but in the winter were allowed to move into evacuees' houses, which they were careful to respect and look after. Their letters were censored and sometimes they were not allowed to send any at all. The NAAFI was the centre of entertainment and relaxation, with concerts and dances, involving air and ground crew from a neighbouring fighter base.

Towards the end of the war 613 battery was waiting to be assigned to the Western front, but the war finished before they could embark. Maud was demobbed in 1946.

A 3.7in AA Battery, London

Railroaded

Dennis (Dickie) Toms

Born:	28th December 1917 Banbury Oxfordshire
Service Dates:	1938–43
Place of Enlistment:	Banbury
Units:	4th, 5th and 7th Battalions Oxfordshire and Buckinghamshire Light Infantry
Theatres:	Home Front
Awards:	Defence Medal

This account is not chronological and has been put together from anecdotes recorded on tape about 10 years ago. They refer to Dickie's time on the Home Front, mainly in the South of England between 1938 and 1941.

Training

Dickie joined the 4th (TA) OBLI in 1938. This battalion was local to Banbury, his father and uncle having been in the same regiment in the Boer War and Great War respectively. As light infantry, speed was emphasised and on parade, they marched at 148 paces per minute rather than the usual 120. He remembered endless marches carrying an ever-increasing weight of kit. This often involved marching halfway to Oxford, meeting another battalion coming in the opposite direction and then returning, a distance of 20+ miles carrying up to 60lbs.

There were also assault courses which could involve jumping down a ten foot drop. Dickie was thankful that they were issued with the old style bandage-like puttees, which gave better ankle protection than the more modern spats. He excelled at shooting with the WWI Lee Enfield rifle and won the battalion individual competition. Others were not so gifted and he remembered one man who was not allowed to shoot at targets on Crouch Hill, near Banbury, as there was a risk that he would miss the hill and kill someone in the village beyond!

When war broke out, Dickie was sent to be trained as a sniper in the Peak District. All new arrivals were paraded and questioned and anyone from a city or large town was excluded. The reason for this, he discovered, was that it was felt that city folk would be more likely to be spooked by the dark and unfamiliar sounds of the countryside – Snipers could be in an isolated rural setting for a long period whilst waiting for a target. Snipers would generally have an observer with them and because of their extra training in concealment, they could be used to spot and report on, enemy movement.

Sentry Duty

Dickie was stationed mainly on the South Coast because of the fear of invasion and spent time in Devon, Kent and Hampshire. He said that although they guarded installations, their main concern was not the Germans but the IRA. When at their post, they would be visited at a set time by the duty officer. If anyone approached either two minutes before or two minutes after this time, they were to open fire. They were ordered to shoot to kill as, *'dead men don't complain.'*

On one occasion, he recalled that one of his colleagues heard movement in front of his position and on two challenges being ignored, opened fire killing the local farmer's prize bull!

Dickie's most vivid memory was being on sentry duty on Horsey Island, near Portsmouth. Horsey was only an island at low tide. One evening his position was approached from the landward side by a crowd of men, who appeared to be soldiers from the battalion coming back from a night out. He told his mate to take cover as he stepped out to stop them. They ignored his challenges however and pushed the leading man straight onto Dickie's bayonet, causing a minor wound. The injured man was an officer and Dickie heard later that when the officer recounted the tale in the mess the CO said, 'It's good we've got a soldier who knows his job.'

Another account by Dickie illustrates that during the early part of the war it was sometimes difficult to imbue the local population with the importance of complying with military law. Dickie said that a roadblock had been set up near Islip Oxford and that all cars were to be flagged down and searched. One car ignored the road block despite the frantic efforts of the soldiers to flag it down.

The soldiers therefore, had no choice but to open fire. The driver, a vicar, was unharmed but the passenger, his daughter, was killed.

Officers

Dickie described his officers in very positive terms. He said that they were usually from the landed classes but were always courteous and fair.

As he was able to ride a motorcycle, at one point Dickie was attached to the adjutant's office as a dispatch rider. The adjutant at the time was a Lieutenant Moggs and he had access to the motorcycle as required. On one occasion, Dickie had been maintaining the bike when Moggs came to take it. Dickie said, *'Be careful Sir, it has a tendency to drop out of second gear.'* Moggs looked at him in an amused, 'you do not know who you are talking about' sort of manner and set off. He had barely travelled a few hundred yards before he went sprawling as he tried to slow down for a gate. He rode back to Dickie and said: 'Be careful Toms, it has a tendency to drop out of second gear!' and walked away.

Another anecdote concerned a Lieutenant Little who, unusually, had been promoted from a Sergeant Major. Dickie's platoon was marching through a town to join a parade when Dickie noticed that Little's straps were crossed on his back the wrong way round. He quickened his step, caught him up and told him. Little said,

> *'Thank you Toms, but what can I do?'*
> *'Just nip into that shop sir.'*
> *'Good idea.'*

A couple of days later Dickie was on sentry duty and had not cleaned his rifle. Little, the duty officer, was a stickler for detail. On his inspection, he upbraided the previous man to Dickie for the state of his rifle. As far as Dickie was concerned, it had looked immaculate. By comparison, his own must have looked like a factory chimney. Consequently he was dreading what Little would say. Little carefully inspected the rifle and announced, 'This is how a rifle should look.' Later he took Dickie to one side and said, 'I will come to see you just after stand down and if your rifle is not perfect, you will be on a 252.' (A charge).

Detention

At the outbreak of the war, Dickie was still in the TA, but worked as a fireman on the Great Western Railway out of Banbury. He explained that whether or not you were called up was based on your occupation. If you were in a reserved occupation, you could join up but could not be conscripted. If you were in key work however, you were not allowed to join up. The bureaucracy related to this was not fast moving and he had been with the 5th Battalion for 18 months before they caught up with him. One day he was approached by the CSM, who said that on the CO's parade the coming morning Dickie would be sent back to the railway in Banbury. Dickie asked how he could get out of it. The CSM replied, *'If you are not here we cannot send you.'* Thus, he went AWOL but returned a few days later, handing himself in to the gate guard. A runner was sent to the officer's' mess. He was told to do all his buttons up, because if he presented himself sober and properly dressed he would be put under open, rather than close, arrest. The CO gave him 168 hours detention, which meant being kept in the cellar of a mansion, which was being used as the battalion HQ.

He was let out for one hour a day, during which he had to double to the cookhouse for his meal. This was a two mile round trip. Inevitably his food would be cold by the time he returned. Every day five Woodbines and matches would appear through his window. He found out later that the CSM, named Cole, had sent them.

Another soldier was subsequently incarcerated in the cellar and took the option of doing work. He was given crates of Mills bombs (grenades) to clean. He had to remove the base plates to make sure that there was no fuse, before pulling the pin out. After several boxes and no fuses he got careless and pulled the pin out of a live grenade which started to fizz. He could have thrown it through the window but men were drilling outside, so he threw it to the other side of the room. The explosion seriously injured him.

Railway

Eventually the authorities caught up with Dickie, who spent the rest of the war on the Great Western. He did not like this at all and at the end of hostilities, on his last trip into Banbury station, he put in enough coal to get the engine there safely, threw the shovel in and jumped, never to return.

The North Africa, Italy
& Burma Campaigns

Since several of the army servicemen interviewed served in North Africa and Italy or Burma, we have placed their accounts under one heading. As these are people's individual stories, the bigger campaign picture is not extensively covered. In this introduction therefore, we give a brief historical background to the campaigns for reference.

There are further references to this campaign in the sections on RAF and Naval life.

North Africa

In June 1940, as France was on the point of capitulation, Mussolini took the opportunity to declare war on France and Britain, hoping for easy gains. With France's surrender, Italy looked to capturing Egypt. The Italian Army in Libya was ordered to invade Egypt in September 1940. Opposing them was the Western Desert Force, under the command of General Richard O'Connor. As the Italians slowly advanced, the overall commander in the Middle East, General Archibald Wavell, ordered a limited operation to push the Italians back – known as Operation Compass. It was initially planned as a five day raid, but developed through its success into the total defeat of the Italian forces. This lead to the capture a large part of Libya, as far as Tobruk, a key port on the North African coast. One of the supporting forces for the 7th Armoured Division was Harry Hays' 8th Field Artillery Regiment RA. As the fear of invasion declined, Britain began to dispatch more of its home forces to the Middle East. However, with the Mediterranean still controlled by the Italian navy, the safest route for these troops was around the coast of Africa. Several of the accounts describe that voyage, particularly the pleasant stops at South Africa.

The success of Operation Compass led to the Germans dispatching the 'Afrika Corps' under the command of General Rommel, to North Africa in

February 1941. Frank Harrison was probably one of the first soldiers to be engaged with the Afrika Corps when he met the advance of the German forces. The German attack soon had the British driven back to Egypt and Frank describes that retreat. The British however still held at Tobruk. If it fell to the Axis it would form a forward port for them, shorten their supply line and make an invasion of Egypt, a far easier proposition. To prevent this, what ensued was one of the longest sieges of a British force in its military history, beginning on 10th April and continuing for 240 days, until relieved by the British 8th Army. Frank describes this siege in his account, as does Adrian Grimes earlier in this book. It was to fall later in Rommel's second offensive on 21st June. Frank Harrison arrived at Tobruk just before its fall and was captured in his attempt to escape; his account goes on to cover his time as a PoW in North Italy. Leonard Dunn and his unit, the 276th Heavy AA Queen's Regiment, did manage to escape from Tobruk back to Egypt. They were later to take part in the Battle of El Alamein, 23rd October 1942. Jim Wetton was in the 41st (Oldham) Royal Tank Regiment arriving in early 1942 and going into action for first time in the Battle of El Alamein. He then participated in the pursuit of the Axis forces back across North Africa. These accounts cover almost the full extent of the British Empire forces time in North Africa.

Italy

Following the success of the North African campaign an invasion of Italy was now a possibility. The 8th Army, which included Jim Wetton in the 41st Royal Tank Regiment, formed the main part of the British contingent for the invasion. Newly trained units were also sent out to participate in the invasion, such as James (Jim) Fitzsimmons' 5th Reconnaissance unit.

The invasion began with the taking of Sicily in July 1943, followed by the invasion of the Italian mainland in September. James covers the actions in South Italy after the invasion. Eighteen year old Arthur Todd, arriving just after the landings with the 2nd Battalion North Lancashire Regiment, (Loyals) gives a short but telling picture of its aftermath. All three cover the hard-fought advance up through Italy. Just north of Florence the Germans had built a formidable defence known as the Gothic line. It incorporated the Apennine Mountains, which stretch almost coast to coast. The battle to take this line was to prove a massive undertaking involving forces even greater than at El Alamein. The toughness of the battle is well covered by Arthur Todd's account.

As the war ended, police actions had to be undertaken, particularly in Palestine, where Jews were fighting for a homeland and had organised terrorist groups against British control of the protectorate. This would be the final destination of James Fitzsimmons and Arthur Todd after the Italian Campaign.

Not all the forces in the North African campaign were sent to invasion of Italy. The Japanese entered the war in December 1941 and took Singapore, shortly after. Britain had to rush out some of its forces to India to fight the Japanese in Burma. This was the destination of Harry Hays as well as Adrian Grimes and Jack Laidler.

Burma

Following Pearl Harbour on 7th December 1941, the Japanese looked to take Singapore. The British attitude was one of complacency, as evidenced by one young officer's reputed comment regarding the newly completed defences. *'I do hope we are not getting too strong because if so the Japanese may never attempt a landing.'*

The Japanese invaded Malaya and on 11th/12^{th,} December defeated the British forces at Jitra. By January they captured Kuala Lumpur, Malaya's capital. At the end of January, the Japanese had reached Singapore and on the 8th February 1942, 23,000 Japanese, despite being outnumbered, took Singapore. The British had been caught out by the speed, ferocity and expertise of the Japanese Army. The result was the surrender of 100,000 men. Included in this was the newly arrived 18th Battalion of the 5th Loyals North Lancashire Regiment, who now faced the horror of the Burmese PoW camps. From this battalion, we have Geoff Knowles' account, a story that should never be forgotten.

Following the fall of Singapore, the Japanese turned their attention to taking Burma. They planned to capture the port of Rangoon and push up to the Indian border before the monsoon season ended the fighting. The British began to prepare defences, bringing re-enforcements from North Africa and Britain. However, as the monsoon season ended, the British found that they could not launch a major attack. Supply lines through Bengal to the Burmese border were not fully set up and many troops had to be diverted to suppress the many 'Quit India' protests, which broke out all over Bengal. (See Adrian Grimes'and Jack Laidler's account).

In 1943, the British did make two small attacks against the Japanese in Burma, one of which was by a new force known as the Chindits. This was one of the largest Special Forces used in the war and was the brainchild of Orde Wingate, who recruited and led them. The aim was to create a force able to penetrate and operate deep within Burma, supplied by airdrop, thus making them independent. There were two Chindit expeditions. Frank Anderson was in the first expedition, in late 1943. Adrian Grimes and Jack Laidler were trained for the second expedition in 1944. The Chindits proved a controversial force. Although some would regard them a success, others considered them a waste of resources, The reader may come to their own conclusions on reading Frank Anderson and Harry Hays' accounts.

In late 1943, the British reorganised their forces, including the setting up of the 14th Army. This became known as the 'Forgotten Army', as their exploits gained far less recognition at home, by comparison with armies in the West. Its commander was General William Slim, whose leadership obviously engendered a real comradeship throughout the army. They all felt themselves to be, 'One of Slim's Boys' as Harry Adams' account of his time in the 14th Army is entitled.

Following the monsoon season of 1943, the Japanese decided to invade India. The Japanese 15th Army crossed the Burma-India border on the 8th March, their objective being to capture the key supply towns of Imphal and Kohima. Jim Leach, in the West Kents, was marched up to Kohima and arrived just in time to meet the Japanese attack on the town. Jim reveals the remorseless attacks the defenders of Kohima faced. Having failed to dislodge the British in both towns, the defenders now found themselves under siege and cut off. (See also Harry Winder's RAF account of being in Imphal)

On the 15th May General Slim began the counter offensive which broke

C-in-C Louis Mountbatten arriving for a pep talk, Burma 1945

the siege. As the Japanese fell back, with units such as the Border Regiment (Adrian Grimes and Jack Laidler) operating in their rear, the withdrawal turned into a rout, utterly destroying the 15th Army. It was the first major defeat of a Japanese Army and now the British were on the offensive, driving them back through Burma to Malaya. Les Parker gives a graphic account of this follow-up action into Burma. A seaborne invasion of Malaya was planned in 1945 but did not need to be undertaken as Japan surrendered. Harry Winder (RAF section) was to see that surrender at Singapore and supplied photos of this event. We recommend reading accounts of the RAF in Burma by Bill Ray, Harry Hays and Les Parker. Finally, we are proud to present a poem by Harry Hays in remembrance of the 14th Army and of all those who served in Burma.

Desert Gunner

Harry Hays

Service Number 986015

Born:	29th February 1920, Deane near Bolton
Enlistment Dates:	May 1940–December 1946
Unit:	8th Field Regiment Royal Artillery
Theatres:	North Africa, Burma
Awards:	1939/45 Star, Africa Star with 8th Army Clasp, Burma Star, 1939/45 Medal, Defence Medal.

Harry enlisted in May 1940 at Bolton and he was sent for basic training to the Royal Artillery camp at Sunnyvale, Rhyl. As well as basic infantry training he learnt gun handling, how to ride a motorbike, drive a Bren gun carrier and a Scammell transporter. He was then sent to Woolwich and on to Glasgow, to embark on the *SS Cameronia*.

He sailed to Durban in South Africa via the US eastern seaboard and Freetown. Upon arriving, they were allowed shore leave and were adopted by local families who treated them to meats and fruits, many of which the soldiers had never before encountered let alone eaten. Some soldiers were so impressed with the life at Durban that they deserted!

From Durban they sailed on to Egypt where Harry joined the 8th Field Regiment RA, which had recently arrived from India. He had originally been trained as a driver and wireless operator but now he became a signaller, using either semaphore or a short flag that used short and long strokes similar to the Morse code.

Harry's regiment consisted of two or three battalions, each of two troops, with each troop consisting of four 25pdr field guns pulled by *quads*, accompanied by ammunition and other service vehicles. On the way to the front line, German Stuka, dive-bombers suddenly attacked them inflicting about one hundred casualties.

The regiment now formed part of the corps artillery supporting the 7th Armoured Division, known as 'The Desert Rats' due to their gerbil arm badge. In addition, they supported the 4th Indian Division, their first action was at Halfaya 'Hellfire' pass, where they shelled an enemy position prior to an attack by the Scots Guards. Harry remembers miles and miles of Italian prisoners moving back down the road with only one guard every few hundred yards. They now advanced along the coast and then onto Seewa, a beautiful oasis and Fort Jarobub where many more prisoners were taken. At night they formed a laager; a circle of vehicles, for all-round defence. Harry commented that since both Axis and Allies used captured vehicles to replace losses, there were unfortunate incidents of firing on one's own side. Harry also mentioned that the regiment would take part in duels with enemy tanks over open sights, but suffered few casualties. They also came under air attack from Me 109's, who hugged the contours to try to catch them unawares. At the first sign of such an attack, everyone would dive into the nearest trench or shell hole and often several men would be piled on top of one another.

At Sidi Rezegh they were charged by tanks from the front and orders were given to open fire, only for them to be immediately rescinded, when it was realised that these tanks belonged to a British Hussar regiment. They passed through, but were then stopped by the Scots Guards, who boarded the tanks, turned them round and sent them back into action. It was here that Harry witnessed his only dogfight, in which a Hurricane was shot down. Harry said, 'I can see it clearly now. The pilot bailed out, but then hit his own burning aircraft and they both crashed together into the desert.'

The desert war in 1941 was a very fluid affair, as one side and then the other came to the limit of their communications and had to retreat. As Harry's corps retreated they picked up prisoners at Tobruk, who told them, 'You will all be our prisoners soon!'

In May 1941 the Regiment was sent to Port Said en route to Crete, but when Crete fell to an airborne attack they were rerouted to the Far East, arriving in Bombay at the end of 1941. They undertook jungle training at Ranchi near Calcutta before moving up by road to Mondaw, where the Japanese were defending three tunnels along the road to Boothbay through the mountains. Harry's regiment formed part of the 25th Indian Division and he himself was attached to the Observation Post (O.P.) overlooking the Japanese position. The observers zeroed in the artillery fire onto the targets, but the fire had a limited effect as the Japanese were so well dug in. Harry's job was to check the cables running from the O.P. to the H.Q. and to repair any damage. Harry found being in the jungle much more trying than the desert. He was constantly bitten by insects and attacked by leeches and everyone suffered from malaria, foot rot and diarrhoea. Harry added that the Chindits, who operated behind enemy lines, suffered far more. Harry met some who returned completely wasted. He was seething at the Chindits leader, Orde Wingate, who he described as a, 'Bloody nutcase.' Harry felt that the resources that they used were not justified by their results. Not surprisingly, in 1945 when volunteers were sought for the Chindits, he declined.

Harry eventually left Burma in July 1945 after three and three quarter years and following a period of leave was sent to join the Northumberland Hussars which was a tank regiment. Harry finished his duties in Hamburg, Breitenfeld and Schleswig-Holstein Guard's depots, before he was finally demobbed at the end of 1945.

Harry supplied us with this poignant poem:

By the Road and the Hill lie scattered the seed
Bamboo Grass on each lonely grave
Shimmering Silence and Jungle Weed
Enfold and touch lightly – here sleep the brave
Not yet may the fruits of your dying be tasted
The Sun and the Rain no harvest unfold
But rest we shall see that the seed is not wasted
The living remember, the tale shall be told

Written by a solider of 14th Army, Jan 1946

With the AA in Egypt

Leonard Dunn

Corporal/Acting Sergeant
Service No 1496757

Born:	14th June 1918, Bradford
Service Dates:	16th July 1939–2nd February 1946
Place of Enlistment:	Oswestry
Units:	527th, 276th, 638th Heavy AA, Queen's Regiment
Awards:	1939/45 Star. North Africa Star. 1939/45 Medal. Defence Medal
Main Theatres:	North Africa

Leonard came from an army family. His father was a sergeant major in the Duke of Wellington's Regiment, spending a long time in India.

In July, 1939 Leonard was selected for the militia, which he said was a home defence force recruited to deter Hitler. He was sent to Oswestry for training and on the outbreak of war was immediately incorporated into the 527th Heavy Anti-Aircraft regiment, which was equipped with 3.7in calibre artillery. Bell tents were the main accommodation and the weather was so poor that the Daily Mirror sent a photographer to record the flooding. From Oswestry, the unit moved to Pembrey to act as AA protection for an armament factory. Leonard said, however, that the main fear was from the IRA, so they kept guard with rifles, though it seems the War Office could not spare the expense of supplying bullets for them.

There followed more training in Southend-on-Sea, then in early 1941 they were sent to Liverpool to board a ship for overseas service. While waiting to sail from the Mersey estuary Leonard observed a night attack on Liverpool with massive explosions and the constant rattle and flash of AA batteries.

The convoy set sail on a circuitous route via Iceland, the Caribbean and Freetown Sierra Leone, finally arriving in Durban South Africa. Here his regiment, now the 276th Heavy AA Regiment, had to wait for a week while the ship was repaired.

In his first trip ashore, he was 'adopted' by two white women, who gave him and his friends somewhere to stay and showed them around South Africa. They told him later he was the first 'squaddie' they had approached. Had he declined, they said that they would have been unable to go on to befriend any others. He discovered sometime later that they subsequently went on to look after another 100 men and they told him that none of them had in any way abused their hospitality.

Leonard eventually landed in Egypt and received further training at the army camp at Tel-el-Kebir. He remembers that the food was terrible. He then moved round Egypt, guarding camps and towns. At one time, he found himself at Aboukir, the scène of a land battle between the French and British, which also overlooked the bay where Nelson had destroyed the French fleet in 1798. While digging in that position they disturbed a large number of human bones and these turned out to be French sailors and soldiers killed in the battles. The bones were collected and re-interred in a nearby cemetery.

The desert war was a very 'seesaw' affair. Advances became bogged down and then driven back because of the lack of supplies. In one of these stages Leonard found himself in Tobruk, where the 3.7in AA gun was being used unusually as conventional artillery. The position of the German armour was radioed to them as it was out of sight over an escarpment and they bombarded the position with H.E. The Germans were surprised that the British 3.7in weapon was not used in a direct anti-tank role., as Germans had used their 88mm AA gun. Leonard explained that the barrel of the 3.7in could not be depressed to anywhere near the horizontal. In fact, on one occasion, when stationed on a height overlooking a bay, they could not fire at aircraft coming in low and so were useless to protect the ammunition ships at anchor in the bay below, which were then sunk.

Jerusalem 1943 (Leonard rear row middle)

After a few days, it was decided to evacuate Tobruk, with the Royal Engineers preparing for evacuation by destroying their facilities. One of these was the NAAFI and Leonard, amongst others, was given a carton of 500 John Player Cigarettes. However, even this bonanza did not encourage him to take up smoking.

The unit retreated east along the Qattara Depression as the coast road was occupied by the enemy. The depression was reputed to be impossible for vehicles, but the battery got through by using two vehicles where necessary, to get a gun up a slope.

The retreat eventually stopped at El Alamein where Leonard's first contact was with an Indian brigade. When someone asked him for a cigarette, he gave them 500!

The 276th were not involved in the battle of El Alamein and the need for AA declined as the Luftwaffe became less and less evident. Many units were broken up following Rommel's defeat and Leonard, now a corporal, was posted as instructor to the 638th AA regiment, at Port Said. Leonard recalls that one night two feet of snow fell – the only time it had been seen there in living memory.

In early 1943, he managed to get approval for two weeks leave in Palestine. He visited many of the holy sites and while in Jerusalem he bumped into King Feisal of Iraq, a 17-year-old young man also touring. They had a conversation and Leonard was invited to join the King's party at a ceremony in a mosque. Afterwards, the King was presented to cheering crowds that had gathered outside.

Leonard found Palestine fascinating and friendly. This turned out to be in sharp contrast with his stay there two years later with the 276th unit, where they were not allowed off camp because of the murders carried out by the Jewish Stern gang.

On his return to Egypt the 638th he was assigned to the defence of Port Said and on one occasion was involved in a 'box barrage' put up to protect the Sicily Invasion fleet from incoming aircraft. [A Box barrage is where each artillery piece is assigned an area of the sky into which it fires, without any attempt to identify or target particular aircraft].

Leonard eventually followed the 8th Army into Italy, where they were converted into infantry as part of the Queen's Regiment. He again acted as instructor with the rank of sergeant, training at Naples. He remembers he had the unenviable task at one point of arresting a man in his unit for a misdemeanour. The man had previously served a sentence for murder and when Leonard found him drinking in the NAAFI he shared a drink with him before escorting him to the lock up.

At the end of 1945, Leonard was eventually able to return to England, after six years in the army and four years abroad and was finally demobbed in York on 2nd February 1946.

Lucky Jim

James (Jim) Harvey Wetton

Sergeant Major
Service No 7906349

Born:	January 21st 1919
Service Dates:	12th December 1939–1946
Place of Enlistment:	Oldham
Units	41st (Oldham) Royal Tank Regiment TA
Awards:	Military Medal, 1939–45 Star, African Star, Italian Star, War Medal 1939–45
Main Theatres:	Egypt, Sicily, Italy.

Jim was called up at the end of 1939, just before his 21st Birthday. He reported to Earl Mill, Oldham for basic training. The 41st (Oldham) Royal Tank Regiment had originally been the 10th Battalion Manchester Regiment during the First World War, where it had distinguished itself. In light of this, the regiment was converted to a new tank regiment in 1938. Jim was one of thirty conscripts called up at that time from the Kendal, Barrow and Grange-over-Sands area.

During his basic training Jim remembers marching through Oldham and tripping over a stone; Jim explained, 'the Sergeant Major told me to pick my feet up. I told him I had tripped over this stone'. He replied,

'It's been there a long time' to which Jim responded, 'Well I've only just found it!" Jim also remembers Guard Duty, calling out. 'Friend or Foe' to anyone who approached. 'Mind you,' he added, 'if they had been 'Foe', I could not have done much, as we had been given no guns or ammunition.'

After basic training, he was sent to Otley in Yorkshire, where initial training for the tank crews took place and where they decided what role to take on – driver, gunner, etc. Jim was selected to train as a tank commander. Following Otley they were sent down to Eastbourne and then to Salisbury Plain for training in tanks. This training lasted until March 1942, when they received orders that they were to go overseas. On the 6th May, they boarded the HMT *Scythia* at Liverpool, bound for Egypt. The voyage took nine weeks and Jim was seasick for six of them. They used to say, 'Put your lifejacket on there is a German submarine about,' but Jim was past caring and replied, 'I do not care if it hits us.' They arrived in July 1942.

The 41st was part of the 24th Armoured Brigade of the 8th Armoured Division. In Egypt, they began desert training and Jim was promoted to corporal. They were also issued with new tanks, the Sherman armed with a 75mm gun and a 0.5in machine gun. This training continued up to October 1942, when they went into battle for the first time at El Alamein.

The battle began with a barrage from the big 250mm guns, set 10 miles from the front line. Under the cover of this assault, the 25mm guns were brought up to begin a creeping barrage. Under this barrage, the Royal Engineers and the Infantry, followed by the tanks, advanced. The casualties were heavy, particularly among the Royal Engineers, who had to advance first to clear the land mines. The Infantry followed and then the tanks came through. Trapped between the heavy barrage and the creeping barrage, the German casualties were terrible. As daylight broke, the sight of the dead and wounded before them was ghastly. 'You could not avoid bodies, you had to drive over them,' Jim stressed. He remembers the tank in front was forced to stop, as they had a body trapped in their tracks, which had to be removed.

On another occasion Jim remembers he had to stop his tank to ask an M.P where the 'Sun track' was. (There were various tracks marked out, 'Sun track, 'Moon track', 'Star Track' and 'Tree Track'.) He directed Jim and no sooner had Jim dropped back into the tank, than the MP stepped back onto a land mine and was blown up. If Jim had been out of the hatch, he would have been killed. Land Mines posed the biggest danger to tanks throughout the war. Jim had three new tanks, as the previous ones each had a track blown off by landmines, 'If you found yourself in a situation where a track was blown off by a landmine, you got out quickly,' said Jim.

One of the biggest problems they had in the desert was the water supply. They got one pint of water per day for everything: shaving, washing and drinking. It wasn't enough, but they also got five gallons of distilled water per day for topping up the tank batteries and this solved their water problem as they peed in the tank batteries and kept the distilled water for drinking. It did not seem to affect the tanks at all.

The men never changed their clothes They worked and slept in them. They could not undress, as they had to be ready at all times, day and night, to move out in ten minutes. Showers of course were very rare. Jim won the competition for the dirtiest vest, the prize being a bottle of beer. His vest was then dipped in petrol and ceremoniously burnt. He had to get a new one from the stores.

Whilst in the desert one day, they saw a parachutist coming down. They located the 'chute' but not the man. Parachutes were very valuable as you could sell them for £60 in Cairo. Shortly after this incident a notice appeared, stating, 'All parachutes, enemy or allied, must be handed in to stores,' and underneath this notice one of the men added – 'So the officers can sell them'.

At one point Jim contracted Sand Fly fever, which is like Malaria. He described it as having sweating bouts every few minutes and being very ill. He was taken to an Indian run hospital and treated very well but he was glad to get back to his mates. He saw some terrible things but despite this said,

> What kept you going was the comradeship. Everyone looked out for each other. Men literally put themselves at risk to save their friends. And no matter how horrific the things they witnessed, there was always a sense of humour among the men to keep spirits up – We learned to make the most of things.

After El Alamein, they pushed on to Tunis and after the Germans were finally defeated, they were sent back to Egypt to regroup and reequip, ready for the Invasion of Sicily. Jim had now been promoted to Sergeant. They had expected major opposition, but there was nothing; The enemy had withdrawn before them. He remembers the fields full of tomatoes and a farmer's wife of about fifteen stone coming out to give him a hug, declaring, 'British good, good, good,'

'I bet you said that to the Germans,' Jim remarked.

After Sicily came Italy. As they travelled up the country, they could park their tanks anywhere, usually at farms where the farmer's family would bring them food. They got on very well with the Italians. As they fought their way up to the River Po, they were sometimes so close behind the Germans that they came across their camps with their soup and tea still steaming. The infantry would be sent in to pursue and to take prisoners.

They were now fighting alongside the New Zealanders. Jim rated their fighting ability very highly, much better than the Americans or the Canadians. One New Zealand lad took Jim to where nine of his comrades had been hung from a beam. He told him that after this gruesome discovery, the New Zealanders had vowed to take no prisoners. From that moment on, they never did. On reaching the river Serio, an officer came and asked Jim to go on a 'recce,' to see if they could get troops across. He refused at first, but the officer argued that he was exhausted and he had given an order, so Jim had to comply. On moving to the river he met some Scots who suddenly grabbed him and pushed him to the ground. A German reconnaissance group had been on the verge of discovering them. He never saw the Scots again, but they had saved his life. He had been lucky.

He waded waist-deep into the river to see if the tanks could cross. He also ventured into the German lines, before going back to report. The tanks then moved forward. It was one o'clock in the morning and Jim was in the scout car leading along the road. He was not sure where he was and so he ordered the car to pull up. There, right in front of them was a large bomb crater and they had stopped right on the edge. 'Luck', Jim explained, 'is what you need to survive in war.' For four years he had slept within half a mile of the Germans and in all that time, apart from a piece of shrapnel in his arm, which was treated with a field dressing, he had been unhurt. He added, 'You learn to be cautious and a country life teaches you not to do anything daft'. Jim had been a gamekeeper before his call up.

They moved round the crater and the German guns opened up on them; but they still managed the river crossing. One point where Jim felt his luck might have run out was further north in Italy. He had gone to answer the call of nature and not taken the precaution of arming himself with a gun. Suddenly he came face to face with an armed German Paratrooper. He did not shoot though, but held out his hand and said., 'friend'. The German then threw his machine gun down and gave himself up. Jim took him back and they gave him breakfast soon afterwards, twenty more Germans came in and surrendered They were all about sixteen and had been dropped there and told on landing to kill as many of the enemy as they could.

Jim's tanks pushed north where all the towns had to be taken street, by street by the infantry. He remembers that a sniper held them up until someone saw the puff of smoke from his gun and killed him. On another road, Jim spotted a German through his binoculars. He told his gunner to fire a burst, but the German did not move. 'My bullets are going through him,' declared the gunner, but the German still did not move. When they reached him, they found he was frozen stiff.

On reaching the River Po, they were not allowed to cross the Bailey bridge as the tanks were too heavy – namely 22 tons. It was here that they received the news that the war in Europe had ended. Jim heard it from his wireless operator, who sent to him in code.

From the Po, they went on to Padua, to make it their base. Jim got a month's leave. On his return, he heard that the plan was for unit to regroup and prepare to go to Japan. In the end though, all that happened was that they handed over equipment to other regiments. There was also talk of the Eighth Army going on into Europe, but Monty refused, stating that the Eighth Army had done enough.

After the war, Jim was promoted to Sergeant Major. This was because the previous Sergeant Major had been in a motorbike accident and broken both arms. 'The lads', as Jim said, 'knew before I did about the promotion. Ronnie Brown', he said, 'whom I had served with throughout the war, came up to me and asked that since I was now a Sergeant Major could I do him a favour. He then gave me a gun and said, 'Go and shoot yourself'.' Ronnie, along with Jack Hartley, had been Jim's friends since training. Both were from Blackpool and came through the war unscathed.

As Sergeant Major, Jim had to carry out inspections of the tanks. Soldiers live by their wits and made what they could by trading. During active service, items got 'lost', no doubt sold or traded. Thus, few tanks were fully equipped. At an inspection, the first couple of tanks would be fully equipped, but the rest would all have items missing. Items from the first tanks, already inspected, would be passed along to the other tanks so they would pass the inspection. On his first inspection, Jim decided that he would start with tank number nine. The sergeant declared that he could not do that, as the tank would have nothing in it!

It was suggested to Jim that after he became Sergeant Major, he should put himself down to become a Second Lieutenant. He refused. He could not afford to be an officer due to the cost of the uniform and kit required. He added that the best officers he knew had come through the ranks and were liked and respected. Others straight from officers training were ill equipped to do their job. He remembered one such officer from Sandhurst. While Jim was training to be a tank commander, he told Jim to take his tank across a piece of land onto a hill. 'I told him I could not cross it as it was watery grass. He replied, 'You're here to receive orders, not to question them' Jim checked again, 'Are you sure, you want me to take the tank across that piece of land? 'Having received confirmation, Jim followed the order. The tank, over thirty tons, went a few yards and then sank, belly down. It took them three days to dig it out. As Jim commented, 'they knew nothing.' In Italy, he met another Sandhurst officer just out of training. There were a lot of Germans around with heavy shelling and small arms fire. The officer just stood up in full view of the enemy and Jim shouted to him, in no uncertain terms, to get his head down. He asked Jim if he always talked to officers like that. 'This is not Blackpool beach' Jim replied and then a shell exploded next to the officer. 'Where did that come from?' the officer asked as he took cover. Jim told him that there were Germans everywhere. Later the officer thanked him.

Another Sandhurst officer arrived and Jim asked help to unload his stuff. He had so much kit, even a camp bed. Jim told him that he would not need it. The officer asked. 'What do I sleep on?'

'On't blooming floor' came the reply.

At the end of the war, Jim received the Military Medal and £25 through the post. He was not told why he had received this medal. He speculated that it might have been for the time he had led a river crossing and the bridge had blown up behind him, leaving him stranded. He had to stay there and keep firing, trying to conceal the fact that his was the only tank there, until others could get across and join him. After the war, he returned to Witherslack as a Gamekeeper. He stressed again how terrible war was, but also how good the comradeship had been.

Historical Note: The 41st Royal Tank Regiment began life in the First World War as the 10th Battalion Manchester Regiment, but in 1938 was mechanized as the new 41st Royal Tank Regiment TA.

Greetings From Italy

James (Jim) Fitzsimmons

Trooper
Service Number 3190908

Born:	19th May 1921 Perth
Service Dates:	1938–May 1946
Place of Enlistment:	Castle Douglas
Units:	7th Dumfries and Galloway Battalion of the KOSB, 5th Reconnaissance Regiment
Awards:	1939–45 Star, Italy Star, France and Germany Star, Defence Medal, 1939–45 Medal, QE11 25th Anniversary Medal, Exemplary Police Service Medal, TA Medal.
Main Theatres:	North Africa, Italy Palestine, Germany

In 1938, Jim joined the 7th Dumfries and Galloway battalion of the Kings Own Scottish Borderers at Castle Douglas. On the outbreak of war, he was immediately called up. At the time, the battalion was in Edinburgh and Jim remembers being reviewed by Princess Alice, Duchess of Gloucester – the battalion marching down Princess Street with bayonets fixed.

Initially, they were trained for action in France but this was abandoned following the evacuation of the British Expeditionary Force, (BEF) at Dunkirk. As Jim was excluded from overseas service, (he was still under 18) he spent several months on coastal defence before transferring to the Reconnaissance Corps. Morecambe at the time was the main drafting depot for the Reconnaissance Corps.

After training, he was shipped to North Africa as a member of the 5th Reconnaissance Regiment. As at the time there was not much action and the enemy whereabouts well known, the regiment was not required to do much reconnaissance.

In 1942, the 5th Regiment was assigned to the 8th Army for the invasion of Sicily. They landed 20 days after start of the invasion, (D20) but for the invasion of Italy, they were selected to lead the army on D1 of the invasion, landing at Reggio di Calabria across the Messina Straits.

Jim was now a driver, as he had learned to drive motorcycles and cars before the war. Throughout his time in Italy, he drove the troop commander, Major Frederick Arthur Stephens, either in an armoured car or in a Jeep.

Jim though continued to wear his Balmoral from the KOSB, rather than the regular Reconnaissance corps beret. This did not go down well with the RSM. One day, the RSM shouted, 'Get rid of that *** hat', to which, Jim bravely replied, 'It is not a hat it is Balmoral.' Jim said that the RSM could not push it further, because of Jim's protected position with the CO, so the Balmoral stayed.

The 5th RR travelled 400 miles into Italy before being brought to a halt at the Matauro River, a position overlooked from nearby heights occupied by the Germans. The regiment occupied a defensive slit trench position, but had to be careful as one puff of dust immediately attracted shellfire from the Germans on the heights.

A couple of times a week they had to send out a patrol to capture a prisoner. This involved one man finding a safe route through the intervening minefield while the other covered him. The biggest danger in crossing the minefield was that if you made any noise, the whole area was immediately criss-crossed with Spandau German machine gun fire. Once through, the patrol took up an observation position with the hope of grabbing a careless German. This rarely succeeded but if it did, one faced the greater difficulty of getting him back quietly in order for him to be interrogated.

The 5th RR was left for some time in this position, although Jim remembers getting leave to go to Naples for a week – a city full of Americans, drink and women. Finally they were relieved by the US 5th Army and once the Americans were settled in, the 5th RR was allowed to re-join the British 8th Army, by

Jim with that Balmoral

then on the east coast. Here the brigade commander, Brigadier Lorne Campbell, who had won the VC at El Alamein, visited them. Jim said he was fearless officer, six feet four inches tall, wore a kilt, and carried a stave. Spying Jim in his Balmoral in the HQ, he went straight up to him. 'Are you Scottish?' he asked. On Jim giving the affirmative, he said, 'you will be soon home when we have beaten these ******* Germans.' The RSM, who had witnessed the exchange, came up to Jim to ask what the Brigadier had said. Jim replied, 'He said I was a good soldier.' The RSM stalked off somewhat chagrined.

The 8th Army was now transferred to the west coast for the ANZIO landings and it was here, at Pompeii, that Jim awoke at 9am to see the sky black from the eruption of Vesuvius. The unit had to move immediately driving through the ash up to a foot deep.

They landed at ANZIO on D8 or 9 and tried with difficulty to dig in on the sandy beach under the constant shell fire. They led the breakout but to their disgust, General Clark's 5th Army took over their road in order to be the first to arrive in Rome.

After 12 months in Italy, the 5th Reconnaissance Corp were given leave to go to Cairo, but instead of returning to Italy they were sent to Palestine because of the terrorist actions of the Jewish Stern Gang against the Arab population. Jim described his duties as mainly policing. They were meant to be a highly mobile unit equipped with Jeeps, Humber Snipes and Daimler armoured cars. In the Jeeps, they carried small arms and anti-tank weapons, with Vickers machine guns in the armoured cars. This policing role turned out to be futile, as each time they arrived at the scene of an incident, the Jewish terrorist gangs had long since gone. The main nuisance to Jim and the 5th RR was the Arabs themselves as, 'they would steal anything, even though we had everything chained down.' Jim said, 'They would get into compounds, naked and covered in oil so you could not get a hold of them and if you stopped in the desert, they would appear from nowhere and nick anything they could.'

By the time the 5th's stint in Palestine was over, the allies had reached Northern Italy. The 5th RR though, was landed at Taranto in the south. [The scene of the great Fleet Air Arm exploit in 1940.] It was winter and Jim remembers washing and shaving in his great coat with snow falling around him. He also remembers having to change a wheel on a jeep in two feet of snow. The regiment did not go to northern Italy as planned. Instead they were shipped to France in a brand new US troopship, the *USS General Richardson*. To Jim this was pure luxury, as he could just pick his own bed space and eat ice cream and chicken. They landed in Marseilles in a sand storm but were soon dispatched to Belgium. Here, they were addressed by General Montgomery (Monty). Monty informed them that he wanted the 5th RR to lead the crossing of the Elbe into Germany. Unfortunately, Jim developed a severe throat infection and spent the next month in the 6th British General Hospital in Brussels. By the time he rejoined the 5th RR they were on the North German Baltic Coast. He immediately got a week's leave, which he used to get married at Bassenthwaite in the Lake District.

By June 1945 the war in Europe had finished. The unit was across the Elbe, running two large refugee camps for Displaced Persons (DP) called the Vassar and Yale camps, near Salzwedel. Many of the occupants had been fleeing the Russians. At the end of June, the regiment had to withdraw as this was territory allocated to the Russians under the Potsdam agreement. After a night of drinking with the Russian soldiers, the camp was handed over at 4.00am on 1st July. It was at this time that the regiment formed the 41 Club named after the year the regiment was formed. This was an all ranks club and became a feature of the regiment's time in Germany. Each time it moved a new premise was set up. At Vienenburg, it is recorded that something like 100,000 gallons of paint was used to decorate the club premises under the eye of the regimental artist, L/Cpl Gamblin. In another premise, Gamblin created a vast map depicting the

In Palestine

incidents in the regiment's history covering the great variety of the climates, the people and the customs the regiment had experienced. It was entitled 'Never Again.'

The regiment's duties were now mainly guarding depots. After the DP camps, the 5th RR moved onto Vienenburg, south of Brunswick, on the edge of the Harz Mountains. The regiment was here for four months at the end of which it was informed that it was to leave the 5th Division without its vehicles and equipment and was to remain a regiment in name only. A farewell ceremonial parade was held at Veinenburg and the regiment was posted to Hanover. It now formed part of the 8th Armoured Brigade, its role being to guard food stores. In February, the regiment was finally disbanded and in May 1946, Jim was demobbed and returned to England. The night before he was due to go his friend Jock Aichsan (decorated with the MM) was drunk and ended up being arrested by the Military Police. Jim managed to intercept the letter of his friend's misconduct to the CO so that they could both embark together, without further incident.

On his return to the UK Jim joined the Police, serving in the Cumberland force before retiring as a Chief Superintendent.

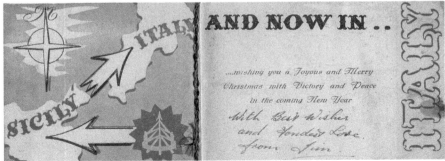

Forces Greeting Card sent by Jim from Italy

One of the Seven

Arthur Todd

Private
No. 14583538

Born:	19th March 1925, Silloth
Service Dates:	1943–47
Place of Enlistment:	Formby
Units	1st and 2nd Battalion North Lancashire (Loyals) Regiment
Awards:	1939–45 Star, Italy Star, 1939–45 Medal, Palestine Star
Main Theatres:	Italy, Palestine

Arthur's mother married his father at 11.00am, on 11/11/11 and had 11 children. Arthur was the seventh child. His father served in the RFA in the Great War and was blinded on the Somme. After hospitalisation, he recovered his sight and finished the war serving in Italy. He lived to the age of 86 with a piece of shrapnel still in his head. His seven sons all served in the armed forces in the Second World War and returned safely. His daughter however died during the war of measles. His eldest son Fred served in the 5th Battalion Borderers (TA).

He saw service in Belgium in 1940 and was evacuated at Dunkirk. Fred carried the anti-tank rifle in his platoon, but when he used it, he found its projectile just bounced off the enemy tanks. On his return from Dunkirk and in preparing to go to North Africa, a medical discovered that he had an operation on his ear as a child which made him unfit for military service, much to Fred's chagrin. He returned to Silloth to work on the docks where he was hurt by the accusations of some of his fellow Dockers that, 'he had worked his ticket out.'

Arthur's brother Bill was also at Dunkirk but in the Navy. He was part of the force sent into sink ships in Dunkirk docks to deny their use to enemy. He spent most of the war though in the Channel serving in Motor Gunboats (MGB). Bill told his brother that the worst moment for him was not an action, but being present during the bombing of Portsmouth.

Of Arthur's other brothers, John was in Army Medical Corps, first in Greece and then Palestine, while Eddie was in the Catering Corps and the Royal Scots. Roy was also in the Army Medical Corps in Tunisia and finally Ronnie, the youngest, was in the 1st Borderers involved in the reconstruction of the German cities after the war.

At the start of war, Arthur was 14, working as a caddy on the golf course for 6d. a day. He remembers seeing bombers taking off from the nearby RAF airfield and flying over the golf course. One, crewed by Czechs or Poles, crashed on take-off just beyond the golf course. It turned into a fireball, with tracer bullets firing out in all directions. Nothing could be done for the crew.

In 1943, at the age of eighteen, Arthur travelled to Formby to join up. He was assigned to the North Lancs. (Loyals) and they sent him to join the regiment in Sussex. He thought at the time that this was an artillery regiment but discovered his error on arrival. While he was at Shoreham doing his basic training, his brother Bill came up coast in his Motor Gun Boat (MGB) to visit. One of the problems Arthur found in his training was that he could not swim, so on leave back at Silloth, Fred taught him in the 'guts' (the docks) .

Arthur was in the 2nd Battalion and after training, it was sent to the Clyde to board a troopship. They thought at first that they were heading for the Far East but in fact, they were being dispatched to join the American 5th Division at Anzio. They were the last full battalion to be sent there. Arthur remembers the voyage in the troopship across the Bay of Biscay. It was so rough that he thought the ship would capsize. He also remembers the escorting Corvettes dropping depth charges onto U-boats, which was very reassuring for them all.

They arrived at Naples, where they saw ships upside down in the harbour. Some were used as ramps to help to get the men off the troopships. They marched through the city to the camps beyond. The 1st Battalion had taken such heavy losses at Anzio that the 2nd Battalion was now to be used as reinforcements. Arthur said that that there were heavy casualties due to men having to dig in soft sand and then being smothered as the trenches collapsed under shell-fire. From the beachhead they moved onto the Gothic Line where there was more stable soil.

From Anzio, they moved to Rome and when the battalion sent a Bren carrier forward, it found no opposition and brought back a milestone. Rome had been declared an open city, but much to the chagrin of the Loyals, they had to stand aside to let the Americans through as they wanted to be the first in. The Loyals were pulled out to what they called 'Dusty Valley' for a visit from King George VI. They lined the roadside and gave him three cheers. Arthur remembers that the King wore make up, presumably for the photographs.

The battalion then entered in to the Po Valley and on to Florence, which turned out not to be the open city as had been claimed. While near the railway station, a woman approached Arthur and said, 'Bomba, Bomba.' She then took him to a house nearby and in the back was a large shell. Arthur, undeterred, picked it up and put it in the nearest ashes dump. Another woman called to him for help, 'Bambino Bambino" she called. Arthur knew no Italian, but Bambino sounded like 'babbie' – Cumbrian dialect for 'baby'. He followed her to a part of city that the Germans had been shelling from their positions beyond. There was a lot of street fighting going on between partisans and Mussolini's men, with the latter often firing from the rooftops onto British troops. One had to move carefully, but finally reached their destination and Arthur found not a baby, but a child, (the woman's grandchild) lying wounded and bleeding.

Back at the railway station position, while looking over a wall, Arthur saw a, 'beautiful lass', like a film star but her parents came out and made all of them swear not to touch their daughter. Later, on a return visit to Florence, he saw the same 'lass' again at the NAAFI with the officers – obviously she was for officers only.

Moving out of Florence, they met partisans at a stately house just beyond the city. Arthur and his comrades were in slit trenches when the partisans came up to them to talk through the gates. Suddenly the Germans opened up and the partisans, still in the open, were badly mauled. Arthur remembered one partisan with blood spilling out of him.

From here, they moved up to Mount Chico. At the bottom of the mountain was a 'string bridge' and they had to wait as stretcher-bearers came by, carrying the wounded and dead down from the mountain. One pair of bearers passed with a lad minus his head – which shook them. Arthur remembers one of the sergeants, Sergeant Pendleberry, turning very grey at the sight of it. Arthur felt then that something was going to happen to the Sergeant, as normally he did not react that way. Later, he heard that Sergeant Pendleberry had been shot in the neck. Luckily, while serious, this did not prove fatal and he was demobbed.

They then proceeded to the top of the mountain, which had been taken by the Duke of Wellington's (DOW) Regiment, their dead still lay everywhere. The Loyals took over the DOW slit trenches, finding used grenades littering the bottom. Arthur rolled them away. The Germans were so close that they could hear them talking. As Arthur looked out of his forward slit trench, a bullet from a sniper hit the ground in front of his face spurting dust and dirt into his eyes. Arthur told a lad, Neaves, to take the sniper out but as Neaves looked out, a bullet from the sniper hit him just under the helmet lid, giving him a 'good trim.' The injured Neaves was pulled out. Arthur decided to take out the sniper with a Bren gun but his position was too close and the sniper would get him before the Bren gun could be fired. The Bren gun had jammed, so taking another off a dead DOW man; he asked his platoon officer if he could move to a slit trench that would give him both a better chance to stay alive and to take on the German sniper on equal terms. Permission was granted, but even from his new position, the sniper remained elusive. The sniper, who was a crack shot, was proving to be a deadly problem for Arthur. A brigadier came crawling into Arthur's trench. 'Where is the enemy?' he asked. '10 yards away,' replied Arthur. 'What am I doing here?' added the alarmed brigadier. Before he quickly withdrew, he promised to have Arthur relieved from that position as soon as possible

During a truce called to bury the dead, a young German soldier, who could not have been more than 16 years old, approached them. He was crying, so they took the youngster away down off the mountain. Just as it was getting dark, Arthur asked a comrade when the truce would end, at which point it did end – with all hell breaking out. Under the bombardment and gunfire, Arthur decided to get some sleep, as he knew no one would be in the open around them while it was going on. It then went very quiet. In the silence, they heard someone shouting, 'Komrade' Arthur informed the officer and asked if should bring him in. 'Yes', was the reply, so in the dark Arthur crawled out into the open and found a German, who was literally, 'square-headed'. He was also 'bomb happy', (shell-shocked), so Arthur took him prisoner and brought him in.

The brigadier kept his promise to have Arthur relieved from his forward and precarious position. His relief came but was shot in the heel just as he lifted his foot above the trench. The sniper had shot him. Arthur felt that if he tried to move from his position the sniper would have him too. He did notice though, that the sniper respected stretcher-bearers. Therefore, when they came up to take the injured lad away Arthur assumed the role of one of them and thus made his escape. He felt that the brigadier had probably saved his life.

When Arthur got back, his officers promised him he was going to be recommended for the Military Medal (MM) but nothing came of it. This upset Arthur, particularly as his comrade, the injured Neaves, received the MM for holding that slit trench with him. Arthur was informed that he was to be made a sergeant but he turned it down, as he was worried that if he had more money, his mother's allowance back home would be reduced.

They now moved against Mount Grandee, another height on the Gothic Line that had to be captured. They were to take over from the Yanks. Arthur remembers being taken there up by a black American, who drove, 'like a bat out of hell.' They relieved the Yanks, but found that they had been very relaxed and not even bothered to dig in which meant that the Loyals had to dig in for themselves. The Americans had left a wooden structure which was dangerous, as the Germans could use it as a target. As two lads were digging right by it, it was hit. One of lads was killed and the other was shell-shocked and had to be taken out of the line. He came back a few months later and Arthur asked, 'Why did you come back – you could have been back in Blighty?' The lad replied that he had felt he had lost his nerve and had to come back to face his fears.

The troops were issued with white linen suits to camouflage them in the snow, although they failed as protection against the cold. The battalion had two snipers, a 6ft cockney, Benson from Woodford Green and Arthur's Cumbrian friend, Sergeant Bannister, known as 'Todd Hunter'. 'Todd Hunter' had been awarded the Military Cross at Anzio and had the cottage where he was injured named after him. He rejoined the battalion on Mount Grandee. He and Benson would wrap up their guns in white bandages and with their white linen suits would simply vanish into the snow.

Arthur remembers seeing some Canadian tanks, Shermans, stuck in the snow one day. He and another lad (from Southport) were sent down to a slit trench nearby to protect the tanks from any enemy patrols. The snow was deep. The German artillery opened up on the tanks as they struggled to get out of the snow. The tanks were not hit but the noise of the shells screaming by frightened the lad from Southport so much that he panicked and climbed out of the trench. Arthur managed to persuade him to get back in.

Arthur talked about supplies. One real treat in the trenches was 'choc duff' which was water from a shell hole, biscuits and chocolate. One officer, inspired possibly by the naval tradition of giving out rum as ships went into action, distributed rum to them before sending them over the top but as Arthur commented ruefully, 'he only gave them a spoonful each! '

Bringing up supplies was always hazardous. A Sergeant Hedge, 'a great bloke' Arthur commented, was sent on leave. On the way back from his leave, he brought up supplies with some mules. As he came up the mountainside, the Germans opened up on him. Panicked by the shells, sadly, the mules trampled Hedge to death.

December of 1944 found them at a farmhouse. Dead bodies surrounded the farm and the chickens were eating the corpses. No-one ate the chickens! Arthur remembers one dead German on the path with a 'tatty masher' (grenade) still in his hand. They did their best to convince the Germans that the farm was unoccupied by not lighting fires despite the cold and ignoring the chickens. They only went out for patrols. Arthur remembers that on one patrol, the snow came up to his waist if he stepped off the path.

They were relieved by the 'Buffs'. Soon afterwards, the Germans did shell the farmhouse and the Buffs were slaughtered. Arthur wondered if the Loyals had just been lucky or if the chickens had been the key. As the chickens had not been eaten, the Germans would have been convinced that the farmhouse was not occupied.

For Christmas 1944, they were in a farmhouse near Bologna. Arthur recalls hearing the Germans singing 'Silent Night' from their positions. Orders came down from the officers that there was to be no action on Christmas day and there was none.

Life on the Gothic line consisted of one-month in the line and then one month rest. As Arthur commented, 'it became just a job!' When just coming out of the line, they were once treated to a war film starring Errol Flynn. The men were in hysterics at his antics and lines such as 'if anyone thinks this war should be fought let them look to Norway'. It was a strange choice of film to show to men just out of the trenches. On another leave, they passed a farm-house and looked in. There was a couple inside, dead but with no marks. It was felt that shells had landed on each side of the house, creating a vacuum, which killed them.

Arthur was now a 5-star private. He could fire any infantry weapon which meant he earned extra money as well. He had also become blessed by the battalion with the nickname 'killer Todd.' He was not sure he liked that. Arthur was delighted when his friend Todd Hunter, from Whitehaven, was awarded the MM.

Arthur described mountain warfare. Attacking was exhausting as they were always going uphill and then when they took a position, the Germans just withdrew back to new positions further up, meaning more uphill attacks. He mentioned the 'moaning mini'. This was a 6-barrelled mortar that the

Germans used, fired electrically. It was not much of problem as you could hear the shells coming as they 'moaned' through the air. The real worry was the 'quiet' mortars, which could catch them unawares while in the open. He also commented that the American battalions who relieved them were twice the size of the British and thus struggled to fit into positions held originally by a British battalion.

With the ending of the war in Europe, the Loyals were taken south, past Monte Cassino, to Puglia, where they played some soccer. They then boarded transports and were taken across the 'Med', to Haifa and onto Gaza. There they were to police Palestine. One job was to turn back Jewish refugee ships and send them to Cyprus, until room could be found in Palestine for the refugees. They also had to search Tel Aviv for weapons and ammunition being hoarded by the Jews. They got on well with the local Arabs, drinking sweet coffee in their houses. On the other hand, the Jewish terrorist gangs, such as the Stern gang, made it very rough for them. He remembers that three soldiers were taken by such terrorists, hanged and booby-trapped with ammo in their stomachs.

While in Palestine, plans were made for the battalion to train as a Chindits unit to serve in Burma and Malaya against the Japanese. The feeling in the battalion was that they would not take any Japanese prisoners. They never felt that way towards the Germans, but there was great anger at the way the Japanese treated their prisoners. The war in the Far East ended before anything could come of this proposed training.

Arthur was in Palestine until 1947. He was then demobbed and worked at Flour Mills in Silloth. He remembers with admiration the Southern Irish who signed up with the battalion to fight in the war. For their own protection, they had to leave their uniforms at the depot in England whilst on leave in Ireland.

What upset Arthur was the issue of his medals. He was told he would have to pay for them but didn't see why he should have to, after serving his country. He did get his Palestine Star after a long wait. At the time of the interview for this book, he still had not received his Italy star, his 1939–45 medals or the Military Medal promised to him on Mt Chico. On Armistice Day, he proudly wore his brother-in-law's medals on his behalf, as he was killed in North Africa.

Arthur described his whole experience, as doing a job and surviving. Arthur supplied us with these Battalion songs, which kept the troops' spirits up,

Captain went to the Zoo

Captain went to the zoo
Nothing better to do
Saw a mole
Digging a hole
Therefore, he thought he dig a hole too
This hole was 6ft by 4ft 6in by 2
Now we like moles
Digging our holes
To hide ourselves from you.

And I sing you one oh, green grow rushes oh

I sing you one oh, green grow rushes oh
What is one oh?
The one is Captain oh
Always drunk on vino

Other verses being:
Two oh, is second in command
Calls him sunray minor oh

Three oh is RAP oh
Four oh for gallant major oh
Five oh is for rifle companies oh
Six ho is for six-barrel mortars oh
Seven oh is for Day privilege oh
Eight oh is for policemen on the gate oh
Nine oh is to ask MO for a number nine oh
Ten oh is for company orders oh

The battalion song is the Scottish song *'Love is like a red, red rose'*

Burma Railway POW

Geoff Knowles

Corporal
Service number 3858367

Born: 29th July 1918, Morecambe
Service Dates: September 1939–March 1946
Place of Enlistment: Bolton
Units: 5th Loyals North Lancashire Regiment, 18th Battalion Reconnaissance Regiment
Main Theatres: Singapore

At the start of World War Two, Geoff was studying law in Manchester when he was immediately called up. He joined the 5th Battalion of the Loyals. He was sent to Bolton and then onto Tarporley for his basic training. By the time he had completed this training, the 5th Loyals had become the 18th Reconnaissance Regiment and as such, they were entirely mechanised in Rolls Royce armoured cars, scout cars, Bren gun carriers, Jeeps and motorcycles. Geoff was made a driving instructor. Any soldier who was not sufficiently flexible to deal with the new unit's demands had to leave. Geoff remembers one man who contracted V.D. and had to leave the unit for the hospital. His wife lost army pay as he was not fit for service.

By early 1940, his unit was stationed at Tonbridge Wells, where they took an active part in the Battle of Britain. Their Brens were used as anti-aircraft protection for farm workers who were being strafed by enemy fighters. They also rescued downed allied pilots and returned them to their units or hospital as necessary. The regiment was also involved in apprehending Luftwaffe crew and on one occasion Geoff, by now a corporal, watched one of his men chase a German round a haystack. Geoff ordered the man to stop, at which point the German ran right round into the soldier. The battalion was now attached to the 20th Guards Brigade and they began their training in preparation for action in the Middle East.

Whilst on embarkation leave in Morecambe, dressed in civvies, Geoff was annoyed by some RAF personnel who lived in a house near his parents. They were waving white feathers at him! Geoff visited them the next day in full uniform with a pistol at his side, letting them know that he knew how to use it!

The 18th RR joined a convoy to Halifax, Nova Scotia, where they were transferred to an American ship, which took them to Bombay via Rio de Janeiro, the Antarctic and Cape Town. While continuing their training in Bombay, they heard that Pearl Harbour had been attacked and that the USA had entered the war. The Japanese invaded Malaya, sinking battleships *HMS Repulse* and *HMS Prince of Wales* off Singapore. The Army decided to reassign the 18th Division including the 18th RR to Singapore. On arrival and before they could land, Geoff's ship, the *Empress of Asia,* was attacked and set on fire by Japanese aircraft. The ship was abandoned and the survivors picked up by other members of the convoy. Thus, they landed in Singapore without any equipment and found a scene of total chaos. The Japanese had already crossed the straits from Malaya, by apparently using bamboo poles as floats. The water supply from the mainland was cut off and despite heavy casualties being inflicted on the Japanese, General Percival, (Commander of Singapore) felt no option but to surrender.

Geoff was now a prisoner of war and was kept in Changi jail for several weeks before he volunteered for pineapple planting in Malaya. This turned out to be bridge building in Siam. He was one of the first parties to work on the infamous bridge on the River Kwai hauling teak logs by rope.

Geoff was transferred to the Burma railway, to a camp called Kanachaburi. The guards were a mixture of Japanese and Koreans and their behaviour was brutal and uncompromising. Prisoners were slapped to the ground on any pretext, or hit in the stomach with rifle butts. For trivial infringements, a man could be locked in the 'oven'. This was a hole in the ground, where you spent the day under the baking sun with no water, after which you were taken out at night, beaten up and put back. One guard in particular, nicknamed 'the under-taker', often killed prisoners by hitting them in the abdomen with the butt of a rifle, rupturing the spleen. They could be vicious with their own men too. Geoff recollected a Korean guard who showed his sergeant the stock of his rifle, which had been broken by hitting someone with it. The sergeant immediately knocked the guard unconscious with a monkey wrench.

Geoff had a sense for survival not shared by all the prisoners, some of whom gave up washing and looking after themselves and died unnecessarily from sores and disease. Geoff made friends and he was put in charge of the cookhouse where he was in charge of supplies. This enabled him to smuggle in vitamin pills, which he gave to particularly sick prisoners. He also got to know American Japanese who acted as his interpreter and arranged for his brother who was at a different camp to come for a three week 'holiday'. He also met a 'Hollander', a Dutch man from Java, who taught him Japanese that enabled him to get on more cordially with the guards.

The prisoners' diet consisted of rice and pumpkin and if they were lucky, ghee – a sort of butterfat. They could wash in a nearby stream but cholera was carried in it and they had to disinfect themselves as they came back to camp. Red Cross parcels arrived at the camp regularly but only got as far as the guards, who were particularly keen on the medical supplies. Geoff's only luxury was the occasional shower using a perforated 40-gallon oil drum.

Finally, the war was over and the camp was paraded for an officer, who had parachuted in, to receive the Japanese surrender. The prisoners remembered how, when they had first arrived at the camp, the Japanese officers had taunted them for surrendering, suggesting that they should instead have committed 'hara-kiri' (suicide.) The Japanese believed in the concept of Bushido – that it was totally dishonourable to surrender Therefore, when it was time for the Japanese to surrender the prisoners retaliated, chanting, 'hara-kiri, hara-kiri' as the Japanese commander surrendered his sword. When it was handed back, he was greeted with derision from the prisoners, as he had not taken the opportunity to follow the Bushido code.

A Dakota flew Geoff and the others out to Rangoon and into quarantine. He looked forward to being reunited with his brother Don. However, the US forces were still attacking Japanese positions, which presumably did not know that the war was over. Don's PoW camp was mistaken for a Japanese supply depot and US bombing killed Don along with sixty-seven other prisoners.

At the time of his capture, Geoff weighed nine and a half stone. At the time of his liberation, he weighed five stone and four pounds. Geoff returned to the UK via Ceylon where there was a rapturous reception. On arrival in England, he was still in the army but was allowed a long leave to recover his health. This he did partly by living on a family farm in Monmouth where he had the novel experience of watching German POWs working in the fields. He was finally demobbed in March 1946. He continued his law training and was pleased to give evidence against war criminals including 'The Undertaker' who as a result was executed. At the time of this interview Geoff was a treasurer for the Burma Star Association and lead the Armistice Day parade.

A Morecambe Chindit

Frank Anderson

Private
No 3715360
Kings Regiment (Liverpool)

Born:	24th August 1914, Morecambe
Service Dates:	March 1940–end of 1954
Unit:	5th Bn, King's Own 1940–2, 6th Bn Kings Own 1942–45
Place of Enlistment:	Lancaster
Awards:	1939–45 Star, Burma Star, 39–45 Medal and Defence Medal
Main Theatres:	Burma

Frank enlisted into the 5th Battalion of the King's Own at Bowerham barracks, Lancaster in March 1940. He was immediately transferred to the 21st company Traffic Control, a branch of the Military Police based at Penrith and covering the A6.

When the fear of invasion had passed some two years later, this organization was disbanded and Frank was sent to join the 6th Battalion of the King's Own.

In June 1943 he arrived via convoy, at Doolali near Bombay and because of his A1 fitness classification was selected for the Chindits – a special force being recruited by Orde Wingate to operate behind enemy lines in Burma. They were named after dragon-like mythical beasts, statues of which guarded pagodas in Burma. Frank commented on the influence of Wingate on his men. The Bible was at the heart of Wingate's outlook and he issued each man with a small black plastic cross with the inscription 'Death Felt One Lost'.

A Chindit

Frank underwent six months of very rigorous training with the 1st King's Liverpool near Jhansi, south of Delhi, where he learned river crossings, night marches, working with mules and managing on meagre rations. Frank believed that Wingate's philosophy was that men could force themselves far beyond what they would normally have believed to be their limits.

They were being prepared for the 'Thursday Operation'—the second Burma campaign – and with the 1st King's Regiment, replacing the 13th Kings Regiment, they were now part of the 77th Brigade under Brigadier Michael Calvert. However, Frank knew nothing of this at the time until they paraded one day on an airfield with Dakotas, gliders and miles of nylon rope. Operation Thursday was underway, 5th of March 1944.

Frank had never seen a glider before and his first flight was not encouraging. The tow rope broke and they crash-landed. The very skilled U.S. pilot managed to find a small lake, which fortunately proved to be shallow, but they were still in India. Next day, they set off again and this time they were successfully flown to 'Broadway', a base behind the Japanese lines. His parent Regiment had already marched off, so Frank was attached to the number 81 Column as a Vickers machine gunner.

The gun was carried on a mule, while Frank, carried a 70lbs pack of equipment plus a canvas water carrier. Rations consisted of K-Ration packets. Each person carried 15 packets, 3 a day for 5 days. Aircraft dropped new rations, but as Frank commented, the time came when the Japanese prevented this and they had to live off the jungle as trained. Frank described how leeches quickly led to 'jungle sores'. The only way to remove them was to applying salt or a lighted cigarette. Frank added that their strength was severely sapped by the jungle but their sound training showed that they could continuously find the extra effort.

The Column's job was to draw the Japanese forces against them and then disappear into the jungle. They moved everywhere in snake file, often through

15 feet high grass. If not toggled together men could just lose the route and never be seen again.

Unknown to Frank high command decided that a solid block on the Japanese communications was needed. The 111th Brigade, commanded by John Masters was to call in outlying posts and columns, including the 81st column. They were to form a new stronghold on the road and railway leading to Mogaung, near Hopin, codenamed 'Blackpool'. The idea was that this would be such a threat to the Japanese that they would divert major forces from the front to deal with it, thus relieving the pressure on the Japanese siege of Imphal. When the Japanese discovered their position, fierce fighting ensured. For three weeks Frank manned his machine gun on the perimeter and was under constant attack. Frank said that the sound of the Japanese, 'yelling and going mad was frightening for a while, as it was meant to be, but you soon got used to it.' Their attacks were fanatical but once you got a line on them they were mowed down. Some of the Japanese appeared to be members of the Guard as they were over six feet tall. Some got through and one bayoneted his friend George Charnock, who operated a mortar. Frank tried to stop the blood flow with his silk escape map, (which at the time of interview he still possessed), but it was to no avail.

During his time there, the monsoon broke and he and his sergeant had to tie themselves to trees because of the ferocity of the wind and the rain.

Eventually it was decided to withdraw the garrison and Frank was involved in the unenviable task of burying 200 dead in a shallow grave. Weapons and stores were destroyed and a textbook retreat was organised by the commander. The original columns went their separate ways, Frank with the 81st to Mogaung from where

Frank in Burma

they eventually left Burma. Here they were assisted by the ingenuity of the Americans who adapted Jeeps to run on the narrow gauge railway lines.

He returned to India having lost over a stone in weight in six months and classified B1 for fitness, as oppose to A1 Plus when the campaign started. He was suffering from malaria, ear problems and post-traumatic stress and was in hospital for weeks. This was the case, as Frank commented, for most of them. He fortunately had the opportunity of recovering in the cool hills of India before returning to England in Sept 1945.

The operations and even the existence of the Chindits were shrouded in controversy. Clearly, the disruption of enemy communications and supplies affected the ability of the Japanese front line troops to operate at their full potential. Some thought however that taking the fittest men away from British units, the enormous resources needed to keep them in action and not least the severely debilitating effects of campaigning, were not justified by the results.

Not long before being interviewed for this book, Frank returned to Burma on a pilgrimage to see the places where he had lost so many friends. He went to the Commonwealth Cemetery in Rangoon to visit George. He eventually found his name on a pillar for those with no known grave.

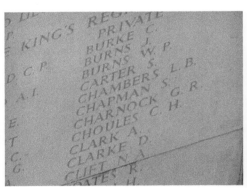

George Charnock's name on pillar of those with no known grave

Frank Anderson

One of Slim's Boys

Harry Adams

Sergeant
Service No 3711325

Born:	13th March 1921, Lancaster
Service Dates:	April 1938–April 1948
Place of Enlistment:	Carlisle
Units:	2nd Border Regiment, Kings Own TA
Awards:	1939/45 Star, Burma Star, 1939/45 Medal, Defence Medal, LSGC
Main Theatres:	Burma

Harry was fifteen when he joined the Kings Own TAVR as a drummer. Two years later (1938) he tried to enlist into the 1st Kings Own but they told him that there were no vacancies. His older brother Jack had joined previously but had died at the age of 18 after falling out of bed. Their father attended the inquest and accused the regiment of negligence and Harry felt that this may have caused him to be excluded. He therefore went to Carlisle to join the Border Regiment on the Supplementary Reserve, which meant that he would be trained and then leave – but be paid, 30 shillings (£1.50) per quarter on the Reserve.

On the outbreak of war, he was quickly called up and eventually assigned to D Company of the 9th Borders at Egremont.

In 1942, they transferred to Blackpool to be kitted out with tropical gear and were then shipped out to Bombay in the *Duchess of Richmond.* Harry was now in the 2nd Battalion of the Borders. On arrival in India, they spent a short time at Meerut, north of Delhi. This was the scene of the outbreak of Indian Mutiny in 1857 and the garrison church was still fitted with rifle holders at each pew. In addition, armed guards stood watch at each service so they could not be surprised as had happened in 1857.

Jungle training followed in Ceylon for seven months. Here they were introduced to mules and unconvincing cardboard cut-outs of Japanese soldiers. In September 1943, they were transferred to Danapore in North Burma and then to Kabaw valley and Sun le Chaudhry. The CO said that from here on it was bandit country. On Harry's first sentry duty at night, he heard a rustling from behind him. He turned and came close to bayoneting his CO who was doing his rounds.

The 2nd Borders with the 14/13 Frontier Force Rifles and 4/10th Ghurkha Rifles formed the 100th Independent Infantry Brigade of the 20th Indian Division of Scoones's IVth Corps. As the Japanese fell back under the assault of the 14th Army, Harry was involved in a number of patrols. One of his first was with a very new lieutenant and it involved following the noise of bells, known to be worn by elephants used by the Japanese. Nothing was found however and the patrol got lost because the lieutenant had not taken any bearings. They had to wait until dawn to find their way back.

Reconnaissance patrols consisted of two men and their job was to watch and note enemy movements, in order to prepare for an attack or artillery bombardment. Fighting patrols were from a platoon up to a company in strength and they would put in major attacks supported by mortars, artillery and sometimes aircraft. Following one such patrol, they took a village after a bombardment and found wounded villagers who had been hiding underground.

Retiring patrols could be ambushed and on one occasion, Harry's patrol was surrounded and they only broke out as a result of a daring bayonet attack.

Harry had a lot of respect for the Japanese. 'They were bloody good fighters. They would fire their last bullet and then come at you with a stick if they had one.' They could also tag on to the end of an incoming patrol, which led the

Borderers to count men in. Harry recalled a squad of seven men and an NCO bringing up ammunition. The NCO was challenged and was asked, 'How many?' 'Seven,' he replied. He should have said, 'Seven plus one,' and as a result, the 8th man was shot dead. He was Harry's friend, Ginger Holden.

The Japanese also had a remarkable capacity for digging in. They took a position called Nippon Hill and were underground in no time. They beat off continuous attacks from the brigade, which included one from the Ghurkhas. Harry observed it while sitting next to the Ghurkha colonel. The colonel was almost in tears as the Ghurkhas were badly mauled. Eventually the position was bypassed.

Normal practice every morning was to, 'stand to' just before daylight, as this was the most likely time for an attack. If all was clear, they stood down and then dismantled their weapons for cleaning. As this was happening one day, they were amazed to see someone wandering around beyond the wire. They brought in a dazed Japanese solider who had buckteeth and thick glasses just like the cardboard cut-outs in Ceylon! The soldier was a source of much curiosity and was keen to show pictures of his wife and family, before he was sent down the line for interrogation.

As time went on, armour in the form of Stuarts was introduced into the fighting. Sometimes they had to be winched up steep slopes but they were invaluable in subduing strong points. The tanks had external telephones so an infantryman could talk to the commander to indicate the target.

Eventually Rangoon fell to the 2nd Division and the 100th Brigade reached Meiktila from where Harry flew to Poona to be repatriated. On returning to England, he joined the TA.

After the war, he was employed on the railways and when General Slim, the commander of the 'Forgotten 14th Army' got on a train in Lancaster, Harry was asked if he could load Slim's luggage, as he had carried loads for him for the three years in the jungle. General Slim acknowledged this by turning his wife and saying, 'Eileen, my dear, this is one of my boys'.

Defender of Kohima

Jim Leach

Corporal
Service Number 6344954

Service Dates:	193?–1946
Place of Enlistment:	Maidstone
Units:	4th Battalion, West Kents
Main Theatres:	Burma

By the time, he was eighteen years old Jim had been working as a fisherman for five years but he wanted a change, so he joined the army. He went to the local recruitment office where he was shown a catalogue of the possible units he could join. He was attracted to the White Horse badge of the West Kents and so enlisted with them.

He went to Maidstone for his basic training, which consisted of drills, marching, keep fit classes, weapons training, polishing and cleaning. He was not allowed to leave camp for three months or more precisely until he could keep his swagger stick exactly horizontal. He completed his training at Shorncliffe, where alertness was encouraged by the use of live ammunition!

He then returned to Maidstone as a Physical Training Instructor (P.T.I.)

As a garrison town, Jim said that the soldiers were not popular. Many had enlisted to avoid prison and they were all tarred with the same brush. They had to form a separate queue for the cinema and could only sit in the front seats. Eligible civilian women would have nothing to do with them but he did meet a woman from the ATS whom he married. When the war started the depot became overwhelmed with TA battalions and reservists reporting for duty. Jim's job was to try to get them into shape with P.T. on the parade ground.

Jim was then transferred to the 4th Battalion of the Regiment and after various moves around the country, he arrived in Blackburn where they received more training. Following this, they entrained for Scotland and since this was at midnight, they were ordered to march in plimsolls so as not to wake the populace. At the station, however they found a big crowd waiting to see them off.

From Scotland they sailed via Freetown and Cape Town to Bombay and then onto the principal base at Doolali. Here they joined the rest of the battalion, which was training for jungle warfare. Jim was part of the guerrilla platoon (G.P.) which consisted of only one officer and thirteen other ranks. The battalion itself consisted of four companies A, B, C and D, plus an HQ company, which controlled the heavy weapons. The guerrilla platoon was attached to H.Q. and was held in reserve. If any of the rifle companies was held up by enemy action the G.P. were to move onto the flank and force the enemy to withdraw.

The 4th West Kents with the 1/1st Punjabis and 4/7th Rajputanas formed the 161st Brigade of the 5th Indian Division. In early 1943, they were ready to move to the front. They initially moved through the day but the heat and humidity made it hard going. Their CO 'a little Irish bloke called Laverty' rode a horse, but during one rest stop, someone drove his horse off into the wild. Laverty took the hint and marched with the men. From then on, they marched at night with a silk worm attached to the man in front so they could see where they were going. At the Mandor Pass, they had a skirmish with the Japanese Imperial infantry. Jim was impressed with the Japanese. They looked strong and smart and were chivalrous allowing the West Kents to bring in their wounded.

On reaching Chittagong – which is in modern day Bangladesh – they were transported by Dakota to Dinapor and then by truck to Kohima. General Slim had marked Kohima as a position of major strategic importance because it was the last pass into India from Burma. The territory to the east was so inhospitable, by virtue of its numerous ridges covered in jungle, that Slim thought the Japanese would struggle to get as much as a battalion through it.

When the 4th West Kents arrived at Kohima they found it quiet and thus they returned to Dinapor. Almost straight away news of a major Japanese advance on Kohima was reported and they were sent back. They had only just started to dig in when the Japanese attacked and so began one of the pivotal battles of World War Two. The Kohima position occupied a ridge looking north and east. Jim was entrenched in the northern sector near the Commissioner's bungalow. All the battalion transport had been captured in the first Japanese attack including a supply of mortars along with their ammunition. The garrison was effectively surrounded but the divisional artillery was on a hill two miles to the west and able to shell the Japanese positions. The main attack came against the east side. The fighting was at very close range and it was here that Lance Corporal Harman won a posthumous VC for taking Japanese positions single-handed.

Jim described his own involvement, modestly, as skirmishing. They were subject to continuous mortar fire from short range but did not come under serious attack. The only source of water was in front of their lines and getting supplies at night was a hazardous exercise. Tinned food was rolled down the hill into their trench line. They opened the tins with a bayonet and then later used the empty tins for their ablutions before throwing them over into the Japanese lines. The commissioner demonstrated more sang-froid than judgement by daily walking his dog around the lines. The Japanese could have easily killed him and Jim suspected, much to his disgust, that the Japanese thought that the commissioner was better alive, as he would insist on coming to 'chat' to the British soldiers thus pin pointing their position.

Provisions quickly dwindled and had to be supplied by air. RAF Dakotas flew so low that they could see the crew kicking supplies out of the plane. The USAAF flew so high that those on the ground could barely see the aircraft and a high proportion of those supplies fell into the enemy lines. The Japanese supply line was stretched to breaking point and they could not adequately supply the major force that they had in the area. The West Kents held the ridge for sixteen days under remorseless pressure but were eventually relieved by the 2nd Division. The battle of Imphal and Kohima continued for weeks and completely drained the strength of the Japanese. When they retreated, the 5th Indian Division was involved in the pursuit. It covered the left, eastern flank and this meant that it had to hack its way through jungle, occasionally coming to major towns like Meiktila and Mandalay. The guerrilla platoon furnished many of the patrols. The commander was not as gung-ho as his rhetoric would have suggested and as Jim put it, he often got a bout of 'actor malaria' if danger threatened. Patrols would for example, lay up close to the enemy's Line of

Jim today

Communication (LOC.) They would time enemy movements down a trail and report it back to the artillery. On this information, the artillery would bombard the area at the right moment. They also undertook fighting patrols that would set ambushes, or attack unsuspecting groups by throwing grenades at them.

The Japanese could be extremely ingenious in their defensive arrangements. A hill could be tunnelled from the back with only a small fire slit at the front. The West Kents' brigadier, 'Daddy Warren' was familiar with this tactic as he had been in Japan before the war. He showed the Kents how these positions could be attacked from the rear.

Jim suffered the typical range of maladies including malaria, dysentery, cholera and prickly heat, but he rarely left the line. Food in the jungle was not plentiful and Jim had to rely on K rations. One of his 'treats' was the army biscuit crushed into condensed milk to make a biscuit burger. Often they would stop where the enemy dead had been buried. The corpses would have an arm left protruding from the ground and pointing to the sky. If they had time and with grim humour they would sometimes put a biscuit in the hand. Most men smoked but tobacco was in short supply. Jim's wife sent him a tin of Senior

Service every week but it was never received. The men smoked cheroots and sometimes dried tealeaves. Towards the end of the war Jim, as a corporal, was sent with a man whose nerves had been shattered to Secunderabad in Southern India. He had to wait a fortnight and so he went to the army postal sorting station to see if he could help in any way. There he found thousands of tins and packets of cigarettes that had not been sent on to the troops. Jim reported this to the colonel in charge and as a result, the postmaster was immediately posted to the front!

When the Japanese surrendered following the atom bomb drops on Hiroshima and Nagasaki, Jim found himself in Rangoon. As he had been a peacetime soldier, he was not demobbed immediately as he had anticipated, but instead was posted to Ramsukh in the Khyber Pass. Here he joined the Wiltshire Regiment. The regiment had already reverted to peacetime 'spit and polish', which Jim found very irksome and he made his feelings very plain. Eventually he was allowed to return to England and was demobbed in June 1946.

Reconnaissance in Burma

Les Parker (in 1941)

Sergeant
No. 3858015

Born:	15th August 1918, Heywood Manchester.
Service Dates:	1939–1945
Place of Enlistment:	Bolton
Units:	6th Loyals, 2nd Reconnaissance Regt
Awards:	1939–45 Star, Burma Star, Defence Medal, 1939–45 Medal
Main Theatres:	India and Burma

In 1939 Les Parker, before he was called up and much to his family's disgust, decided to volunteer and enlisted with the 6th Battalion of the Loyals with his friend Freddie Chaloner. The 6th Loyals were then a motorcycle battalion and Les got a driving job replacing a man who had thick spectacles and could not see where he was going.

In 1942, Les joined the 2nd Reconnaissance Regiment as part of a draft from the 6th Loyals and he was given the distinctive lightning badge illustrated in his picture.

In March he embarked on a Dutch liner for 'God knows where' as part of a convoy of 92 ships. They first sailed to Freetown, zigzagging to put off the U-boats, then onto Cape Town and then finally arrived in Bombay. After disembarkation they were sent to Poona where they trained in Daimler armoured cars. This consisted of teaching them to scout enemy positions and to escape danger as quickly as possible. They carried short-range small arms, mainly submachine guns and pistols. This was for self-protection as it was not part of their job to get involved in prolonged firefights.

In early 1944, they were sent by train to the Burmese border as far as Dinapur. Les described how from that point they had to proceed on foot, 'From now it was walking and it came as rather a shock.' They were still a reconnaissance unit however and preceded the British 2nd Division as they advanced into the jungle. 'Snipers were the main problem' Les commented, 'We lost three officers early on because they had pips on their shoulders and carried binoculars and map cases. They soon learnt though, although it was now – 'Bill. Carry my binoculars!'

Sometimes they brought up Lewis guns to spray the trees. 'On one occasion we found four Japs hanging dead from the trees by their straps.'

Below is an account of one action he described graphically in a letter to the Morecambe Advertiser published on 21/7/1944.

A certain Saturday in June had been full of excitement, mostly unpleasant trouble from snipers etc. When our unit, which was leading the division in pursuit of the fleeing Japanese along the Manipur road, took the first bridge not blown up by the enemy, everyone was well satisfied with the day's work. The divisional commander decided to call a halt. Less than a mile forward of the bridge was a Nagar village known to be in Japanese hands... Our own little troop of 28 men strong was given a position a few hundred yards to the rear of the bridge on a high jungle ridge. As darkness fell we prepared to make ourselves at home in newly dug Japanese positions.

However, about one o'clock in the morning the troop commander received orders to move down to the road and take up defensive positions around our tanks. Grumbling and

SECTION 1: ARMY

cursing we trooped down a jungle track to the road and several of us took falls as we tripped over the roots and the under-growth in the dark. At last, we heard the boots of the forward section on the road and as we walked along in single file, we were surprised to find ourselves intermingled with a body of men coming up from the opposite direction – about thirty of them. At first, we thought they were not natives as their feet made no sound on the road, nor did they come in any regular formation. Then someone in the leading section said, 'What a smell of blasted Japs.'

It suddenly occurred to use that the supposed natives were Japs as the former were never seen within miles of a battle area. Therefore, we began to sit up and take notice and a casual suspicion became an alarming certainty. Straining our eyes we noticed the small stature and picked out packs, capes, peaked caps, etc. We were actually rubbing shoulders with the enemy!

It all happened so quickly that no one had time to be alarmed, but the excitement was terrific as we waited for our last sub – section to get clear. 'Firing positions' rang out and in a second, volleys of shots filled the air as we gave them everything we had. A single grenade was the only reply and that did no harm.

BLOOD AND DUD MONEY

At dawn, we went to the spot. Pools of blood, items of kit, a large wallet containing dud money, with which the Japs used to pay and bribe the natives, drugs and valuable documents told us that several more sons of Nippon had been gathered unto their ancestors.

On a further occasion, Les and his patrol spotted 20–30 Japanese in a hollow some yards below them cooking a meal. He suggested to his officer that they attack them with grenades but he declined saying that it was their job only to report back. He said 'The Durham Light Infantry put in an attack and got plastered. Probably a Jap lookout had spotted us and was waiting for them.'

When not on 'recon' duties Jim had other tasks like taking supplies up to the front by mule. He named his mule Gregg after the War Minister. He was quite attached to it until it kicked him in the face nearly blinding him.

Another duty was escorting Forward Observation Officers (F.O.O.'s) to their observation points (OPs). On one occasion, they climbed a ridge to see Japanese troops moving down a parallel ridge. The F.O.O. immediately radioed back 'Fox 20' or a similar map reference to bring artillery fire directly down on the enemy. Les could see shells bursting all along the trail.

Les Parker's main memory of the Burma campaign was the discomfort and the misery.

> I was down to eight stones, I had malaria, dysentery and ring-worm. I was constantly wet – socks rotted on your feet, my boots were in tatters and we could not get them replaced. You were constantly annoyed by anything that could fly, bite or slither. I put grease on my feet to keep out the leeches, but they still got through and every evening I would have to burn them off with a cigarette. Everyone had sores that would not heal properly and the food was poor: spam or bully beef, sometimes with local vegetables.

Badge of Reconnaissance Corps

All through the war, Les had been trying to get into the Army Mobile Cinema Unit, as he had been a projectionist before the war. After a stinging letter to a journalist who had written an article saying troops in Burma were well entertained he was posted to the unit. Ironically, this was just before his own unit was due to be repatriated. He went back to India and between running his own shows he got to see at another cinema, 'The Green Berets' starring Errol Flynn about how the Americans had won the Burma campaign. In the cinema there were a number of Scottish soldiers. They were so incensed by the film that a riot and mass fight broke out between them and American servicemen.

Jim finished his service in Rangoon. 'Life suddenly became more enjoyable. I could wash daily and wear clean clothes.'

After three years and ten months, Les was returned to England on the *Pelix St Adegone*, returning via Suez. Back in England, he was finally demobbed at Catterick. He found it difficult to settle back into life in Morecambe and for some time continued to suffer from the diseases he had contracted while fighting with Slim's 'Forgotten' 14th Army.

SECTION 1: ARMY

Other Professions

It is easy when talking of army experiences to assume that one is referring only to the fighting soldier. This section has been written in acknowledgement of the fact that there is more to the army than a man with a gun.

As well as fighting soldiers, the army could only be fully functioning through the support it had from a whole range of other professions, many of which were far less in the limelight than those on the front line. We interviewed four such soldiers to hear their experiences and from their stories we have put together accounts covering four areas which are key to the successful functioning of the army: These are morale, maintaining roads and bridges, communications and air transport.

Len Henson, of the 1st Highland Light Infantry, was possibly the only English Piper to serve in a Scottish regiment. His story covers the early actions in France, the retreat to Dunkirk, his return to France and the invasion of Germany 1944–5. His role was a vital one in terms of maintaining a good level of morale.

The second account is about an Engineer. It would be true to say a 20th century army cannot move without its engineers. Major Russell Theobald OBE describes his time building bridges across Europe from the Normandy landings to the invasion of Germany. He commanded the 613th Field Park Company, which included heavy equipment such as bulldozers. The latter were essential for clearing the debris of wrecked vehicles following frontline actions, in order to allow the rest of army to follow through.

For a modern army to operate it must have skilled, specialised technicians, for example the Signallers and we have an account of Signaller John (Jock) Wilson.

Finally, Len Wright's account describes a lesser known role in the army as an army pilot. During World War Two, army personnel were trained as pilots for the army's Air Corps to fly gliders. Wright's story can be compared with Leslie Kemp's experiences (found in the RAF section), although trained as an RAF pilot, Kemp was loaned to the Army to operate as an Army glider pilot following the large loss of Army pilots at Arnhem.

An English Piper

Len Henson

Piper
1st Highland Light Infantry
No. 3310743

Born:	23rd January 1914 Hulme, Manchester
Service Dates:	2nd February 1932–28th January 1946
Place of Enlistment:	Bath St, Glasgow
Units:	1st Highland Light Infantry (HLI)
Awards:	1939–45 Star, France and Germany Star, War and Defence Medals, Normandy and Dunkirk Medals
Main Theatres:	France (Dunkirk), Normandy, Germany

Len grew up in Morecambe and became fascinated as a teenager by the bagpipes, which he had learned to play in the boy scouts. In 1932 he decided to join the Army and travelled to Glasgow. He enlisted with the Highland Light Infantry (HLI) on 2nd February 1932 so he could to become a piper. Immediately after enlistment, they told him that since he was a Sassenach he would not be entitled to become a regimental piper. Len was, not surprisingly, indignant about this and when the regiment called for volunteers for the RAF, along

SECTION 1: ARMY

with others, he put his name forward. He passed the tests but his commander Lieutenant-Colonel Telfer Smollett refused him permission to leave.

He was trained at Maryhill barracks and became a signaller in 'A' company where, on the intervention of the pipe major, he was allowed to play the bagpipes after all. 'C' company at this time had a 2nd Lieutenant David Niven the famous actor. Len said that Niven was very popular with the men. He was kind and gave them cigarettes on route marches, but he did not appear as popular with the CO whom, Len said, pushed Niven out.

Len stayed in the HLI until 1935 and then went into the reserve. He married in 1938 and the following summer he was called up for two months reservists training near Inverness. It was while there, that he heard the news that the war had broken out and he knew he was in the HLI for the duration.

On the 20th September, the 1st HLI was sent to France to the port of Cherbourg via Southampton on the *S.S. Duke of Rothesay*. From Cherbourg, they moved to the Belgian frontier just as the Germans were entering Holland. What followed, Len said, was a game of cat and mouse where the HLI was the mouse! The battalion was always on the defensive and found itself split up into small groups. His group was about twenty men under an officer and Sergeant Maguire. They fell back trying to avoid the much more powerfully equipped enemy. He heard that another group of HLI had surrendered and whilst awaiting transport for Germany were found by another group who rescued them. They also heard of atrocities committed by the S.S. One in particular was of a hundred men of the Norfolks who, although that they had surrendered, were still lined up against a wall and machine-gunned. One officer escaped. Two men, who were left for dead, were found by villagers of Le Paradis and nursed back to health and later returned to England.

Close to Dunkirk, Len's group passed the C-in-C General Gott who was full of praise and good will. Finally, they reached Dunkirk and Len's persistent memory of this was the beach with long lines of single file men snaking out into the sea waiting to be picked up. He was hauled aboard a powerboat still in his Greatcoat and with full equipment. The powerboat took him to the minesweeper *HMS Salamander*, which was standing out to sea. He clambered aboard via the scramble nets and immediately fell asleep on the hot deck. He awoke later bone dry.

For the next few years, Len was moved around the U.K. undertaking training in preparation for the second front. It was at this time that he was introduced to General Montgomery, during one of the General's inspections of the South coast. Len's colonel singled him out as the only English piper in the battalion. Len described Monty as a, 'remarkable looking man with steely blue eyes'. It was at this time that the 1st HLI joined up with the 1st East Lancs.

Regiment and with the 1st Oxford and Bucks formed a mixed brigade within the 53rd (Welsh) Division. In 1944, the division set sail from Dover under a naval smoke screen with Len playing his bagpipes as they left the harbour. On the 15th June 1944, they came ashore from their landing craft at Sword Beach, Normandy.

The area was under heavy shellfire as the HLI moved quickly inland towards the German positions. Their attacks were supported by fire from the Corps and Divisional artillery as well as close support from the Manchesters – a heavy machine gun regiment. Sometimes battleships joined in and Len could see the muzzle flashes followed by the screams of the shells overhead before they exploded on the German positions. Night attacks were aided by 'Monty's moonlight' (searchlights) whose aim were to both the vision of the attackers and blind the German defenders. Prisoners were coming in on a regular basis; however this could be tricky as Len explained. Major Kindersly, his Company Commander, accepted the surrender of a soldier who said he knew of others who were keen to surrender and he offered to bring them in. Major Kindersly was suspicious, suspecting an ambush. He was proven right when as he anticipated, the soldier returned with armed men. The Major was ready and all the Germans were promptly killed.

The HLI then took over from the Royal Scots Fusiliers on Hill 112, the ground still covered with their bodies. Here a friend, found a set of bagpipes next to a dead fusilier and presented them to Len. Len would use these pipes through the rest of the war and long after. From Hill 112, they advanced into the German trench line. They were constructed with a highly sophisticated network of tunnels and bombproof shelters. This was the start of the breakthrough and Len was relieved to get away from the stench of corruption into the wide-open country as they raced towards Antwerp, reaching it in nine days.

Len was now appointed Battalion Transport Sergeant because of his uncanny ability to acquire vehicles. As a result the 1st HLI was one of the few units to maintain a full complement of vehicles.

The 1st HLI remained part of Montgomery's 21st Army Group, and became involved in bitter fighting in the Reichswald. In atrocious weather, they took a series of chateaus and strong points. This was by the Corps 25pdrs putting down a barrage, which the battalion would advance behind. If they met strong Germans resistance, then more artillery was zeroed in, backed with battalion mortars. This was usually enough to induce the defenders to surrender.

Len's battalion suffered significant casualties from machine gun fire, from German 88mm cannon fire and from antipersonnel mines. Mines were feared the most. Crossroads were especially hazardous with mines laid in the corners to catch anyone taking a short cut. On one occasion, a Bren gun carrier driver declined to go down a forest track until it had been checked for mines. Len, who by this time had been nicknamed 'Mr Fix-it', volunteered to check it. Len had gained a knack for detecting disturbed ground, caused in the burying of a mine and thus was able to find a safe passage.

The Division now moved into Germany. At Alsdorf his company was marching in loose formation down the village street, when it was ambushed from a nearby wood. They came under a hail of machine gun fire, small arms and mortar bombs. They immediately dug in and later were able to drive the Germans away but they had taken many losses in the ambush. However in driving the Germans away they captured a badly wounded German soldier. Len was keen to get him looked after and found a local doctor called Goebbels (!).

Len approached the CSM, Sergeant Pearson and his Company Commander, Major Nesbitt for help but they were not interested. Eventually Len and Doctor found a jeep and they took the German to a dressing station. Dr Goebbels put a sign on the back of the jeep with the words DOKTOR. On leaving the soldier at dressing station, he saw the soldier force himself to sit up in order to wave his thanks. There were many different ways soldiers treated prisoners. Len was one of those whose hate for the enemy disappeared once he was no longer a threat. Len thought, 'it was putting something in the bank' by being merciful if not generous and he saw it as prophetic that both the CSM and CO were both killed a few days later.

After the German surrender, the 1st HLI was reequipped for transfer to the USA with a view to intervening in the Pacific Theatre. Montgomery assured them that he 'would not sacrifice one soldier until the enemy had been thoroughly demoralised by bombardment'. In the event, the atom bombs brought the war in the East to an end with the total demoralisation of the enemy. The 1st HLI was now earmarked for Palestine, but Len with other soldiers were transferred to the 1st Glasgow Highlanders and returned to the U.K. Since the war Len has continued his piping and was eagerly sought out for ceremonies, memorials and funerals, as well as regularly playing the pipes on Armistice Day. He taught the pipes to many in Morecambe and remained an active member of the Dunkirk and Normandy Veterans Associations. In 2010, Len sadly died the only English piper to serve in a Scottish regiment.

Building Bridges across Europe

Major Russell Theobold MBE

Date of Birth: 25th June 1924, Karachi
Service Dates: November 1938–October 1974
Units: Royal Engineers,
Theatres: West Europe, Palestine, Egypt, Iraq, Aden
Awards: MBE, 1939–45 Star, France & Germany Star, 1939–45 Medal, Defence Medal, GSM Palestine & Aden.

Russell enlisted in the Royal Engineers in 1938 training at Chatham initially and then Chepstow where he became involved in specialist bridge laying in preparation for the D-Day landings.

When the landings began, Russell was in the second wave with the Third Canadian Division on Juno beach. He remembers the bombardment of the beach, which included rockets and *HMS Warspite*'s 16in guns. Russell was in a tank landing craft with his engineer company – the 613 Field Park Company that included bulldozers and heavy plant gear. In the end, they did not land on the assigned beach, as it proved too shallow for the heavier craft. However since their map showed only the narrow strip of the beach they were meant to land on, they were lost. Russell waded ashore and dug in firing his Bren at enemy aircraft. His unit was bombed and Russell was slightly wounded, his hat riddled with shrapnel. Later he asked for a replacement hat from the Quarter Master, but the QM wanted him to pay for it. He believed that Russell had damaged it deliberately!

Russell's main assignment was to repair the Power Plant at Caen, but he was prevented from doing so, as Caen did not fall on the first day as planned. In fact, it did not come into allied hands for some weeks by which time, there was nothing left of the power plant to repair. Russell and his unit were assigned to a rock-crushing machine in order to supply hardcore for repairing the roads. While they were working with this machine, General Montgomery stopped and asked what they were doing. He then gave out cigarettes to them – courtesy of the Daily Mirror.

For the following few weeks, Russell's 619 Field Park Company was used as a reserve rifle company but was not brought into action. Russell was then called on to supply his bridging skills and was transferred between corps as required. The bridging, Russell explained, has four operations;

- 1/ Assault the far bank with fast plywood boats to form a bridgehead.
- 2/ Take over armour on rafts. (Russell's job here was to keep repairing the split pins which held the raft's engine in place.)
- 3/ Lay out the folding bridge
- 4/ Replace it with a more permanent Bailey pontoon bridge.

Donald Bailey, a civil servant in the War office, Russell explained, invented Bailey pontoon bridges. Their design was highly successful as they could be assembled with minimal aid and without heavy equipment. This made them ideal for advancing forces. As the Allies crossed France and into Germany Russell worked constantly on producing the bridges. Once in Germany, his unit was the first to reach the Belsen concentration camp – it was a shock! It changed Russell's view of the Germans radically. Beforehand, he felt they were, 'gentlemen' but Belsen changed that opinion. His colleague who had driven a bulldozer all the way across France and already seen much horror in clearing the battlefields, found Belsen beyond compare. In newsreels of Belsen, he can be seen bulldozing the dead into pits – 'he was never quite the same again', Russell emphasised.

After the war Russell did Engineer duties in Palestine, Iraq and Egypt, followed by ten years in Kenya digging water wells. In this, he became an expert and wrote the Army textbook on the subject. In 1965, Russell was in Aden on his way to a meeting when he was caught in a skirmish with Arab guerrillas. In ensuring fight, the Land rover he was in was blown up. Russell later received his MBE for his services there. In 1974, Russell retired from the Army to become a metalwork teacher at Morecambe High School. In 1986, he retired from teaching and sadly died in 2006.

A Bailey bridge, the kind of bridge Major Theobald constructed to help the British Army traverse France and Germany

Technician in War

John 'Jack' Wilson

Service Number 2601066

Born:	1923, Grasmere
Service Dates:	1942–6, 1947–74
Unit:	Royal Corps of Signals and Royal Observer Corps
Theatres:	U. K. Egypt
Awards:	1939–45 Star, Defence Medal, General Service Medal, ROC Long Service Medal

Jack was born in Grasmere Westmorland in 1923. In 1939, he applied to join the RAF as a boy entrant, but with the advent of war they stopped recruitment of boy entrants into the RAF, so Jack was turned down. On coming of age in 1942, he went into his local recruiting office in Kendal to try to join the RAF. He was told that he would have to go to Carlisle to do so. Jack thought about it and decided to opt to join the Royal Signals right there and then instead.

He completed his basic training at Catterick as a wireless operator and was posted to the Orkneys as part of the defence force. He stayed there until March 1944 and then was sent to Huddersfield to train as a line mechanic with telephone equipment. While there, he broke a wrist playing football and thus missed a draft for the Middle East.

Instead he was sent to S.E. London to help in a factory that was testing a new form of communication, the first to use parabolic disks to enable transmission and reception without cable. He arrived in time to be a target for German rockets. He saw a V1 'Doodlebug' flying over at tree top height and on hearing the engine cut out, he and his mate 'hit the deck' before the explosion. Later he also heard and felt a V2 explode a few miles from the factory.

Initially, the women working at the factory were hostile towards him, because he was regarded as being on a 'cushy number' while their husbands were abroad. Cordial terms were finally established before Jack received his own posting to the Far East.

He was dispatched to a holding station at North Walsham ready for his embarkation. It gave a little time to visit his wife in Newcastle-upon Tyne. However, two days of heavy snow delayed his return and when he did eventually arrive back it was to receive a letter sending him straight back to Newcastle to wait for a ship!

In December, he boarded the *Samaria*, a fast liner, with mainly soldiers and RAF personnel. They sailed without escort to the Mediterranean. On expressing his concern about U-boats, a sailor told Jack, 'The buggers won't catch us. We are one of the quickest ships in the P&O.' – and so it proved. He arrived in Cairo where he remained for two years. This was longer than he had expected, but his specialist knowledge of the new transmitters was too important to let him go sooner.

Demobbed in January 1946, Jack joined the Royal Observer Corps based in Grasmere, his hometown. Because of the Cold War, his main training was in relation to nuclear warfare. In his underground bunker, his job was a) to plot 'ground zero' of any explosion by means of triangulation, b) to measure the force of the blast by a pressure meter and c) to measure the level of radiation using a Radiac Survey Meter. This information was passed on to a regional centre, although Jack was not clear how this was to be accomplished 'with all the power lines blown to bits.' He stayed with the Corps right up to 1974 due largely to the lifelong friendships that he had made there.

Glider Pilot

Len Wright D.F.M

Staff Sergeant
Service Number 1890104

Born:	1920
Service Dates:	26th March 1939–1946
Units:	244 Field Company, Royal Engineers, C Squadron 1st Glider
Awards:	Distinguished Flying Medal 39–45 Star, France-Germany Star, Defence Medal, Victory Medal and Long Service Medal.
Main Theatres:	North Africa, Europe (D Day, Arnhem and Germany)

Len was 19 years old when on 26th March 1939 he became 'Pte. 1890104' in the 244th Field Company of the Royal Engineers. He had been an industrial chemist before his call up. Before the war Len had always wanted to join the Civil Air Guard but was prevented by being in a 'reserved occupation.' They assured him though that once he was in the Army it would be quite 'easy' for him to transfer to the RAF. He then spent the next three years in the Engineers, training in bridging, demolition and bomb disposal. During his training, he missed what turned out to be a suicide mission for at the time he was out with his girlfriend in Burnley. In this he was twice blessed as the girl, Vera, would become his future wife and lifetime companion. In 1940, he was promoted o Lance Corporal, but his chances to transfer to RAF remained elusive. Then in early 1942, Len at last saw his opportunity to fly, by volunteering as an Army glider pilot. He was blissfully unaware of what that entailed. Transferred to the Glider Pilot Regiment, Army Air Corps, he was sent to RAF Booker Elementary Flying Training School (EFTS) to learn to fly with Tiger Moths and Magisters. After learning to fly, he was sent onto the No. 1 Glider School at RAF Croughton. Here he leant to fly Hotspur gliders. Hotspurs were small gliders designed to carry eight persons, including the two pilots. It was not roomy particularly for the pilot. Getting in and out has been described like getting into and out of a 'go kart.' They had proved a failure operationally so were utilised for training purposes.

After training on Hotspurs, he moved onto Heavy Glider Conversion at Brize Norton, learning to fly the Horsa glider. This was much bigger glider built in three sections and bolted together, consisting of the pilot's compartment, the main fuselage and the tail section. The tail section was designed to break off easily on landing, to allow a rapid exit of troops and equipment. It had capacity for 15 troops and was a successful and manoeuvrable heavy glider. It had 'barn' like flaps which when down gave the glider a very steep and high rate of descent allowing pilots to land in constricted places.

Len had maintained an 'above average' assessment throughout. Despite this he still had to attend another course at Chilbolton, which was then followed by more glider training at Netheravon and Holmsley South. Here he learnt to fly the American heavy glider, the Waco, built to carry much heavier loads. It had unique floor construction of honeycomb plywood that meant it could carry loads heavier than the glider itself (4060lbs). Thus it could carry vehicles such as: Jeeps, or 75mm pack Howitzers with crew, or even a small bulldozer and its operator.

Training finally ended with a ten-hour tow around Britain behind a Halifax bomber. This was in preparation for 'Turkey Buzzard' – flights to North Africa. Len joined 'C' Squadron of 1GPR. He flew two trips from Portreath. On one, Len recollects that, as they were towed, the Halifax tail-gunner kept trying out his guns!

On his third trip to North Africa, his luck ran out and they had to ditch off the Portuguese coast. Portuguese interned them for some weeks before allowing them to be flown back to RAF Lyneham as 'civilians.'

From October to November 1943, he was at Tarrant Rushton for a Hamilcar conversion course. The Hamilcar was the largest of the heavy gliders, in fact the largest wooden aircraft that saw service for the British air services. It was designed to carry light tanks, 40 troops, or various artillery pieces. On the 6th June 1944, Len took part in the D-Day invasion, his wedding to WAAF Corporal Vera having had to be postponed for this more pressing engagement. By this time, Len was a Staff Sergeant. He took part in Operation Market Garden, the ill-fated landings at Arnhem. He fought his way out receiving shrapnel wounds and having to swim a river to safety. He arrived back to convalescence in Leicester Royal Infirmary; and once recovered he finally 'tied the knot' with Vera on the 14th November 1944. Len then got back to flying competency with various courses. He took part in the crossing of the Rhine, Operation Varsity, on the 24th March 1945 and again fought his way back safely to the UK. Of 880 pilots in Operation Varsity, 175 were killed or missing and 77 wounded.

Back in England, while Len was enjoying a well-deserved break he learnt that he had been awarded the Distinguished Flying Medal for his part in 'Operation Varsity.' Len left the service in 1946, becoming a Physical Education Teacher. His service as Army pilot had included over 500 hours in Tiger Moths, Magisters, Halifax (as the 2nd pilot) and more important, Hotspur, Horsa, Waco and Hamilcar gliders. General William Westmoreland of US Army said of Glider pilots

> Every landing was a genuine do-or-die situation for the glider
> pilots. It was their awesome responsibility to repeatedly risk their
> lives by landing heavily laden aircraft containing combat soldiers
> and equipment in unfamiliar fields deep within enemy territory,
> often in darkness. They were the only aviators during World War
> Two who had no motors, no parachutes and no second chances.

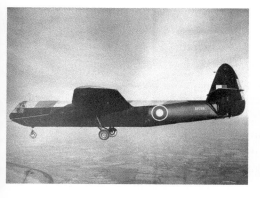

Airspeed Horsa

Hamilcar at Arnhem

Post War Army Life
National Service

During World War Two, conscription was introduced called 'Military Service'. Following the war and demobilisation, peacetime conscription was established through the National Service Act, 1948. From the start of 1949 every healthy man between 17 and 21 was expected to serve in the armed forces for 18 months. After this, they were put on a reserve list for four years. During those four years, they could be called upon to do up 20 days service or training, however not more than on three occasions. Men in reserved occupations such as mining, farming or merchant marine were exempt. Anyone claiming conscientious objector status could decline National Service but on the same tribunal procedures as operated in the War. With the outbreak of the Korean war, 1950, National Service was extended to two years although in compensation being on the reserve list was cut to three and half years.

Basic training for National servicemen could be very hard. Unlike volunteers once they were called up, they could not change their minds during their basic training. Thus, they were a captive audience and faced far harder treatment than the volunteers did (see Fred Hudson's account in particular).

By the 1960s, youth culture was in rebellion against doing National Service and in addition, the country was aware that in the pursuit of a more highly educated workforce, National Service got in the way of pushing more people into Universities and higher education establishments. So in 1960, National service was ended with the last National Servicemen leaving in 1963 (Alan Hill being one of last of them).

National Service could be just surviving the boredom of two years in a military base before one could get back to one's life (see naval experiences of Don Potter and Robert Dix). However, in this period, the British Empire was in still existence and although the sun was setting on it there were was still many police actions to be undertaken. For many national servicemen it gave them the opportunities to see something of the world. It would be a generation before young men could have this opportunity again through cheap air travel and overseas holidays. As can be seen the experiences here cover a considerable range of overseas posting including Germany, Italy, Korea, Hong Kong, Malaya, East Africa, Aden, Egypt, Sudan and even Christmas Island. We enclose Alan Hill's account of his time on Christmas Island here, although he was Senior Aircraftsmen, his account adds more to this section on the experiences of the National service than on the RAF per se.

The downside was that overseas postings could mean combat. Many of these postings were police actions against insurgents of a fading empire and with case of Korea it was to serve in a war. (see Bob Hayton's account)

Many of those interviewed served in the Canal Zone. In a treaty of 1936 with Egypt, Britain insisted on maintaining an armed presence in the area around the Suez Canal (Canal Zone) until 1956. In 1951, Egypt unilaterally abrogated the treaty and insisted on taking over the Zone. The British with 10,000 troops present refused to accept the abrogation. The Egyptians began an armed harassing operation and rapidly a 'Suez Emergency' was declared, with Britain sending in up to 80,000 men, including many young National Servicemen into the zone. 54 servicemen were killed and many more including family members were to lose their lives through disease and adverse conditions before Britain finally pulled out in 1954. The operation was soon forgotten, possibly overshadowed by the Suez Crises of 1956. It attracts only a few lines in the various histories of the Canal; but if officially forgotten it was not by the young men who were sent there. They formed their own association, 'The Canal Zoners' and campaigned hard for a service medal. To their disappointment, official response was that the Canal Zone was only an 'Emergency' of the post war period, thus they were not entitled to a medal not even a General Service medal. It was perceived officially as 'non active service' despite that more died in the Canal Zone than in any other similar actions. Finally after 50 years and much effort by the 'Canal Zoners', a Suez Canal Zone Medal was finally struck and awarded.

We have several accounts from this forgotten emergency, thanks to the Cumbrian branch of the Canal Zoners. Included are stories of Brian Warmsley, Raymond Gill and George White (under Grenadier Guards). The problem of the Canal Zone was not just the fighting of Egyptian insurgents, but also the highly hostile climate of a very dry dusty desert or salt flats. In summer, temperatures could reach as high 48 C, (120F) and 38 C (100F) was the average, although night temperatures will drop to freezing. It was described as 'a very hot sand box ten miles wide and 100 miles long with a ditch running down the middle' and for many, accommodation in this environmental hell was a tent. With the heat, came the flies that covered everything. Almost all came down with 'Gyppy Tummy' caused by the flies. For those who wish to know more, we recommend John Hunt of the Canal Zoners booklet 'Suez The Hidden Truths' and 'White Knees Brown Knees – Suez Canal Zone 1951–54 The Forgotten Years' by Douglas Findlay. We also refer the reader to Jack Fletcher's account in the Naval Section). As a Royal Marine he served in the Canal Zone. He was also to serve in the Malaya Emergency, a guerrilla war, fought against the Malayan National Liberation Army (the military wing of Malayan Communist Party) from 1948–60. It would take the lives of over 1800 servicemen and women before its conclusion. We have three accounts from this campaign, all of whom were to serve at the same base in Malaya, two in the same battalion, although none of them met or knew each other. The accounts complement each other. Rueben's account describes life at the base while Tony Parnham's account covers the jungle warfare. Fred Hudson allowed us to précis some of his book 'Loyal to the End' which covers his time in Malaya. In this book, he covers in depth the training for Malaya and its jungle, which bridges well Reuben and Tony experiences. Together they give us a very rounded account of National Service life in Malaya.

After National Service, service personnel were placed in reserve for 18 months and during this time they could be called up for further active service. This is what happened to Chris Hill, called up months after his service ended to participate in the Suez Invasion 1956. Chris had one of those most vital roles in army life – the army cook – and not an easy option by any means.

The one recurring theme throughout all National service accounts was the deep sense of comradeship it created, whether against the adversity of basic training, the rigors of military life or from active service. We were moved by the strong friendships that it created, which have lasted decades. Many who served talked of the advantages; it gave them in later life, from learning a trade to a greater sense of humanity through comradeship and experiences. On the downside it did leave deep lifetime scars particularly those who faced combat.

It's Christmas

Alan Warwick Hill

Senior Aircraftsman MTDH
Service Number 4235036

Born:	13th November 1935 Liverpool
Service Dates:	October 1957–October 1960
Place of Enlistment:	Gloucester
Units	RAF (MT)
Main Theatres:	Britain, Christmas Island

Alan had already trained for four years as a journalist before being one of the last to be called up for National Service. Before enlisting at Gloucester, he had to have a pre medical and intelligence assessment at Hornchurch. Alan had put in for the RAF to be a pilot. However Hornchurch showed he had a lazy eye and his maths was not up to scratch. Disappointed, they told him that if he volunteered for an extra year, he could have some choice of what he could do. So he volunteered to be a Motor Transport (MT) driver for the RAF.

He did his basic training at Bridgenorth. In each flight, there were 24 men, billeted in a wooden hut. As it was winter and extremely cold, it was a grim experience. They had just one bucket of coke per day for fuel. Thus fuel was always on their minds. They found an air raid shelter full of coke but after three nights, they had used it all up. Then they had another idea. As part of their fatigues, they had to draw a wheelbarrow and spade, fill it from the coke bunker and take it to the officers' mess. Since their billet was next to the officers' mess, every other load ended up in their billet. As Alan explained, a serviceman with a wheelbarrow is like one walking around with a clipboard it is always assumed he is doing something official, so no one stops him and no one asks him any questions. Fuel problem solved.

Basic training was hard but Alan enjoyed it. He was a keen mountaineer and was very fit when he joined up. He added that after basic training he found he was less fit than when he started! The only hard part of basic training for Alan was that it was six weeks before they got any leave.

After Bridgenorth (which is now a nature reserve), Alan was posted for further training at the major driving centre at Weeton, Blackpool. There were now eight of them in a training group although still in a wooden hut. The cleanliness of the floor of their wooden hut was their Corporal's 'big thing'; so they walked on felt pads to ensure the floor remained clean.

The driving instruction began and Alan really enjoyed himself, driving cars and 3-ton Austins around Preston and Garstang. The problem with the Austins was getting used to their height and width. Once the instructor took him down a lane and then told him to stop. Alan asked why and the instructor pointed out the bridge ahead and asked him whether he knew its height and whether the truck would fit underneath. Alan's thought was 'why did he bring him down this lane if it could not.'

After Weeton, Alan was posted to Wellesbourne, Mountford, near Stratford upon Avon. Wellesbourne was a base for an airfield construction unit with earth moving vehicles. These were parked in the hangars and seemed little used. Wellesbourne was also a RAF Photography Centre with Dakotas and Ansons, again little used. Alan acted as driver for the photographers doing road field trips.

Alan's main duty was transporting parts in particular to Stranraer, where they were shipped on to St Kilda for the construction of a radar station. He also acted as a 'taxi driver' for the officers.

With his keen interest in mountaineering, Alan kept volunteering for Mountain Rescue (MR). He also saw it as a way in keeping in the UK. His persistence paid off and he was posted to Harpur Hill, Derbyshire where there was an active MR team led by Sergeant John Stead. Unfortunately, Alan was retained as a driver at station so he could only be involved in the MR team when he was free from his other duties. An opportunity did arise for him to train with MR Team at

Langdale in the Lake District. An MR team consisted of a one-ton Austin radio truck, a Land Rover Ambulance, a three-ton truck for equipment and a Land Rover. However, as a driver Alan had to stay with the vehicle all day so he did not get much chance to get out onto the hills. Desperate, one morning before breakfast, he persuaded a friend, Hutch (Hutchinson), to go with him up the Holly Tree Traverse on Ravenscragg. On their return, the sergeant was not impressed but at least he had got onto the hills. Despite these restrictions, he did enjoy his experience with the MR team.

Harpur Hill was an ammunition depot, which included everything from large shells to 9mm bullets, stored in underground tunnels of an old mine. (Today Harpur Hill is a Mine Safety unit.) Alan's duties would include shipping this ammunition to the docks at Liverpool, London and Portsmouth, or other RAF stations for air transport. Trips could be lengthy but as he was on his own, after dropping the load, he could as Alan put it, 'drift' on your way back.

Harpurs Hill was also a fuel dump, part of a network. One of Alan's more enjoyable jobs was to act as chauffeur to the officer who had to inspect the other dumps. This meant he had the opportunity to see many different places, officially.

One of the more unusual trips he undertook was to go the London Science Museum to pick up a load of stag heads for the officers' mess. He remembers getting back very late and it was foggy. His instructions were to deposit the load at the Armoury. Alan knew that the lad on guard duty at the Armoury was nervous of the dark. This seemed an opportunity not to be missed, so getting one of stag heads and he banged it on the window – the lad jumped out of his skin.

Life in the service was about such jokes. Alan remembered that on one occasion he was in the guardroom cleaning out the cells and getting a lot of hassle from the MPs. After an hour, Alan asked if he could leave, but they told him he could only leave if he made them laugh – so Alan did a complete joke routine for them.

One of the more unpleasant duties for drivers was to be the duty driver at the camp, which lay up the hill isolated from the main quarters. The latter were purpose built barracks and mess, (now a college for Buxton and High Peak (Derbyshire) University) and it had a great village atmosphere. The camp however, isolated on the hill above, was a lonely posting. In addition, if an MP, a Telephonist, the Medics or Ammo workers at the camp needed anything even just a bacon sandwich the duty driver would be sent down the hill to the camp mess. The driving could be hard in the winter because of the snow and even though they had a big snow blower, it would leave just a one-track road. One day, Alan had been up and down the hill several times on various errands and was tired. He rang up his friend, Mac the telephonist and asked him to hold any calls for a while so he could get a kip. After a few minutes, the phone rang.

'What the Hell do you want now?' Alan exclaimed down the phone,
'Who is it?'
'Your CO.'

Alan said he was out of that bed and standing to attention in a second, while his friend Mac who had been unable to prevent the call was 'killing himself' with laughter. The CO however did not put him on a charge but did make him walk back up the hill from the barracks to the camp.

Later Mac informed him that Alan was to be posted overseas to Christmas Island. It was August 1958 and Alan had heard some publicity and service rumours mentioning Atomic Bombs having been tested there; Alan would be part of the cleanup operation (Taskforce Grapple) sent in after the tests. First, though he would need a medical in order to test his blood count, a requirement for radiation exposure. If it were negative (i.e. too low a blood count), to his relief he would not be going. However, all that happened was he was sent to Wilmslow for another test. This also proved negative so they sent him to a tropical medical hospital for yet another blood test. This proved positive so they sent him.

On arriving at Christmas Island, they met the personnel who had been involved in testing the A bomb moving out. The clean up and running down of the place was now underway. Alan found it an idyllic situation, a coral island in the Pacific with an ideal climate – shorts and sandals all the time. For an outdoor person like Alan it was perfect but for others such an isolated posting was very hard. There were no women, except visiting airhostesses. They remained within confines of the hospitality of the officers' mess. For other ranks, there was only the consolation of a black-market in lipstick stained cigarette butts after airhostesses' visits.

The main airstrip and camp were in the NE of the Island near Manulu Lagoon. The atomic bomb tests were held off the south end of the island. The southern end, where a small airstrip had been built, was only connected by single tarmac road to the main camp – about a half hour drive with priority to those going down to the airstrip, halfway between the camp and this southern airstrip was the Bay of Wrecks – a great place for fishing. The port, Port London, was in a lagoon near Cook Island, at the northern tip of the island. This was also were the indigenous islanders lived.

Accommodation was tents in rows with electric cables to supply power for one single light bulb. The more enterprising men soon adapted this, connecting bedside lights, radios etc to that bulb socket. One adaptation was known as the 'Grapple heater', named after Taskforce. This consisted of two wires connected to the light, while the other two ends were attached to two nails in a piece of wood. The nails were then placed into a drink to heat it. These adaptations did reduce power and at certain times fuses blew. The worse culprit was the heating of soup. Soup was the worse liquid for resistance. If a fuse did blow, the usual solution was to place a nail across to restore power. Inspections were carried out to stop this activity but the men soon became adept at hiding their 'adaptations'.

Alan had not been there long before he was assigned to be an ambulance driver and sent to share a tent with three medics. He went about 'modernising' their tent for them with bedside lights etc. One day there was a heavy downfall. The tent had internal guy ropes attached to the outside ones that in turn were linked to the aerial. Alan's 'modernisation' had been a little amateurish and as David, one of medics, strolled in, taking a damp towel off the outer guide rope, he fell immediately to the floor screaming. 'Ah well,' Alan added, 'it was just 110DC, he was not too worse for wear.'

One hazard of tent life was the land crabs. These were semi nocturnal cannibalistic carrion eaters who lived in burrows. They were big creatures a foot across and 'grotesque' to look upon. 'Alan remembers being asleep in his tent when he was awaken by a clinking noise. On opening his eyes, he espied 'a huge, horribly green land crab' climbing up the side of the tent and trying to get into bed with him – ugh. He also added there were big spiders to fill your nightmares, but much sweeter were the Jerboas (Kangaroo Rats). These small creatures were such pretty little things and some lads made pets of them.

The tents were near the sea and it was so tempting to go for a swim. However, with sharks, dangerous tows on the coral reef and the possibility of coral poisoning, it was not surprising that swimming was banned with heli-copters on patrol to enforce it. Some men did go for a swim in order to commit suicide because of the stress of being away from home. They would let them-selves be swept over the reef into the deep waters beyond. Others who swam got 'strange sores' and were shipped out immediately to US facilities in Hawaii.

For Alan the island itself was great. He would borrow a vehicle, stock up at the NAAFI and go camping for the weekend, (There were no weekend duties.) He could go anywhere on the island with the exception of the SE corner, near the bombsite. He would go spear fishing, walking, or just exploring. There were sharks, stingrays, puffer fish and spiny urchins in the lagoons. He would collect eggs from frigate birds, boobies and fairy terns and all very tame as few people went there. He remembers crossing a channel to an island and as he came back, the tide swept in. The channel was much deeper now and halfway across he

Alan outside the Accommodation in 'relaxed' uniform

looked round to see a large manta ray curiously looking at him. He admitted that he was not sure who was more afraid.

At the time of the Bomb tests, there had been 4,500 personnel on the island; this was now reduced to 2,500. Thus, there was lots of equipment surplus to requirements. Vehicles were mothballed, the engines filled with oil and sprayed with a kerosene based mixture to protect them. Alan stressed that there were rows and rows of vehicles, all left parked. There were whole toolkits and welding kits and unless 'liberated' by the men, the RAF left them abandoned, simply not inclined to ship them away. Alan added it would not surprise him if they were still there today.

After a short time as an ambulance driver, Alan was enlisted to be the CO's driver. He remembers the officer who interviewed him for this role. As Alan left, the officer told him, 'by the way stand near a razor in the morning.' Discipline concerning general appearance on the Island had become very lapse, Alan explained.

Being the CO's driver was an easy job as his CO drove himself. Alan's role was to prepare the car in morning, clean it, check the oil etc and have it ready for the

Alan (CO driver) and car

Alan on exploration of the Island fishing on Bay of Wrecks, Christmas Island

CO at 8.00am. The CO then took the car and Alan was left to his own devices for the rest of the day. One of the benefits of the job was the opportunity to go in the CO's mess and order a 'super breakfast'.

A warrant office concerned at Alan's lack of work asked him if he would like to drive a motorcycle. On obtaining a resounding affirmative, the officer took Alan to a hangar that was full of stored motorcycles. His job, the officer explained, was when the CO did not need him, to look after all these motorcycles. That meant that Alan had to ensure that each motorcycle had ten miles on the clock each month. 'What a job!' Alan explained, motorcycle heaven and he could go anywhere on the island. He particularly loved driving the 500cc bikes used by the MPs, so he could pretend to be an MP himself. As he drove around the island on them, people immediately got out of his way.

There were occasions when the CO did need him to drive such as functions where the CO was expected to drink. It was on one such trip that Alan saw that the road was full of land crabs. With expert driving, Alan managed to avoid them all and the CO complimented him on his concern for the crabs. Actually, Alan was worried about the mess he would have to clean off the car if he hit any.

On another occasion Alan was to drive the CO for the visit of the Royal Yacht Britannia and the visit of Prince Phillip. Three cars were to be used to ferry the party from the port. Alan was the driver of the third car; Prince Phillip went in the first, a Humber Snipe. This was the official VIP car and had a sunshine roof. However, having been long on the island the roof had seen better days. As they

Photo of the Vulcan that Alan took.

left the port they were hit by a downpour, the roof leaked and Prince Phillip got very wet. So after the visit, a new car was ordered out from the UK. The ships were unable to get into the lagoon to unload, so lighters had to be sent out to bring the cargo into the Port. As this new car was loaded onto a lighter, two of the chains broke and car gently tipped into the sea and sunk into the vast depths below – not a great loss many felt.

Another time Alan drove his CO, was to see the arrival of the Vulcan bomber, landing at Christmas Island on its long distance test flight. Even though he was told that photographs were forbidden he took his camera anyway, (see his photograph).

Leave for men on Christmas Island was ten days in Honolulu. Alan went with his friend Chris from Whitby. They flew by Hercules to Honolulu – the Hercules did regular trips to Honolulu to collect pineapples and fresh vegetables. They stayed at the YMCA at the back of Waikiki beach – 'where the action is.' They hired a car toured the island for a couple of 'fantastic' days enjoying the splendid mountain scenery. Once they stopped for lunch at a beach when a man approached them asking for directions. At the end of the conversation, he confessed that he knew the directions, he was in fact a local and he just wanted to hear those 'lovely British accents'.

Finally, his duties on Christmas Island ended; he had thoroughly enjoyed it. He added many others did not. He mentioned that a few years later while he was in Scotland at a Youth Hostel, he met Gerry who had also been on Christmas Island. Gerry told him, he hated it. His duties were being a waiter

Alan and friend Chris with car they hired to explore Honolulu

in the officer's mess and unlike Alan he did not get much chance to get out and explore.

Christmas 1959 found Alan back in Britain at a Flying training station, RAF Valley near Holyhead. Much to Alan's delight, he got the opportunity to be attached, although only part time, to a mountain rescue team. The MR leader was Sergeant Johnny Lees, a pioneer in Mountain rescue techniques and foremost in developing MR equipment. For Alan it was a real privilege to work with him, he was brilliant mountaineer and rock climber. Lees died in 2005.

Returning to driving 3-ton trucks about the country, he of course had opportunities again to 'drift' back to the station. Alan took the opportunity to drift to see his girlfriend (his future wife). On one occasion following such a 'drift', when he did finally get back, he was informed that they had been trying to trace him, as North Wales, where he was suppose to have been, was covered in bad weather. 'Had he deviated off the route? Did he have a secret girlfriend anywhere?' they asked. Alan would not to admit to anything. Bad weather Alan noted could be really bad in those days. He remembers being caught in snow on Ham Hill in his 3-ton, with is no heating in the cab, it was not at all pleasant!

On his discharge, he got his HGV licence. The RAF did try to persuade him to stay on, but he knew that 'Transport' did not hold good career or promotion prospects. The pay was not much good either, therefore, he left and pursued a career as an industrial writer. At the time of the interview, he was retired living in Kendal.

A Hong Kong Dollar

Walter Rowland Hill

Private
Service Number 23044839

Born:	25th March 1936, Lancaster
Service Dates:	April 1954–1956
Place of Enlistment	Carlisle
Units:	Kings Own Royal Regiment
Awards:	National Service Medal, clasps KORR, Hong Kong 1954–56
Main Theatre:	Hong Kong

Rowland was called up in 1954 to do his two years National Service. He expressed an interest in joining the Royal Military Police, but instead he was sent to join the Kings Own Royal Regiment. The basic training was at Carlisle Castle where they were joined by drafts for the King's Liverpool Regiment and the Border Regiment. Rowland's basic training was in small arms. This included the Lee Enfield .303, the Bren gun, the Sten gun and the Mills grenade. Drill was emphasised and groups were released from the parade ground only when the six-foot five-inch Sergeant Major, known as 'Tiny Shaw', felt they had demonstrated competence. Once, one man remained alone as he could not co-ordinate his arms and legs while marching, Shaw eventually got two corporals to march beside him and move the soldier's limbs like a marionette. Despite even this, he still could not get it right and Sergeant Major 'Tiny' Shaw gave up in despair.

Once their basic training was over, Rowland's group 54/13 were dispatched to Southampton to be embarked on the *Empress Orwell*. Rowland remembered them sailing out passed the towering mass of the liner *Queen Mary*. Six weeks later they were at Hong Kong, via Gibraltar, Cyprus, Colombo and Singapore. Rowland joined 10th platoon D Company 1st Battalion King's Own Regiment, which had just moved there from Korea. The battalion occupied three camps; Rowland's was 'Bea Stable' camp. '

Rowland was made batman to his platoon commander, 2nd Lieutenant Ian Bishop. The base was within a couple of miles of Communist China and part of their duties was to patrol the border and occupy lookout posts alongside the Hong Kong police. They were told not to shine their searchlights into Chinese territory as they might be shot at!

Rowland was also involved in manoeuvres and mock attacks from section to battalion level. Rowland remembered the colonel took the battalion into a valley, only for the umpire to inform him, much to the colonel's chagrin that

*Rowland Hill and comrades at
Bea Stable.*

Hong Kong 1954

the 1/17th Ghurkha Rifles had occupied the surrounding heights and had wiped out his whole battalion.

An important part of garrison life was the weekly pay parade at which Rowland received £3 5s. 6d. Immediately on receipt he had to pay up his weekly debts to various wallahs who supplied tea, sandwiches etc, a necessity Rowland pointed out, as rations were meagre.

His tour ended in 1956 and he returned by ship, docking briefly at Limassol, Cyprus where the EOKA troubles had erupted. There he was put on sentry duty with a loaded Sten gun and was instructed to kill anyone attempting to board the ship.

Eventually Rowland got back to Lancaster two weeks prior to his discharge date and since he lived close to the Bowerham barracks, he was allowed to sleep at home. One morning, while returning to the barracks, he cut across the corner of the parade ground just as new recruits were being drilled. He was immediately confronted by the drill sergeant', who then 'bawled him out' and put him on a charge. The following morning he appeared before the depot commander, a major, who seeing that he had a clean record and only a few days to go, dismissed the case. The sergeant went purple with rage; but there was little he could do about it.

Hong Kong Dollar

Rowland in Hong Kong

Life on the 38th Parallel

Bob Hayton

Born:	18th November 1930, Crosthwaite, Westmorland
Service Dates:	2nd December 1951–December 1953
Place of Enlistment:	Brancepath, Durham
Units	S Company, Assault Platoon, 1st Battalion, Durham Light Infantry
Main Theatres:	Berlin, Korea, Egypt Suez Canal
Awards	Korean Medal, UN Medal, Canal Zone Medal and Queens LSGC for the Fire Service

Bob's national service was deferred because he had trained as a technician but on his 21st birthday, he received his call up papers. Despite passing tests for the Royal Corps of Signals, he was instead assigned to the 1st Durham Light Infantry (DLI). They sent him to Brancepeth County Durham for his basic training and after a mere six weeks, he was dispatched to Berlin. Here he was involved in internal security using Jeeps and Bren gun carriers. A frequent problem was the Russians moving their barbed wire barricades forwards to grab a piece of land. The RSM told his twenty-year-old recruits to look fierce while he gave the Russian soldiers a dressing down, in English, for their unshaven faces and scruffy boots. If Russians still did not to move the barricade back the RSM got a pot of white paint and poured it along the proper line and in the process, over the feet of the Russians.

On May Day 1952 crowds gathered shouting 'Tommy go home, your liberation hour is here'. At first, water cannons were used to quell the crowds. Then placards in Russian, German and English were held up reading 'Disperse or we will fire'. Then came the order to load, with the instruction 'if ordered to fire to make sure you killed your target – we don't want people screaming on the ground, it will get the whole crowd going.' This threat was always sufficient to quell the crowds.

While in Berlin, Bob received training in mines, booby traps, demolition, field engineering and river crossings. This was at the Olympic Stadium. They also had ceremonial duties and were responsible for guarding Spandau prison, which contained a number of high-ranking Nazis. The battalion returned to England in June 1952 to receive more training. The colours were laid up in Durham cathedral to which a large crowd turned out. Spectators greeted the NCO's barked orders with 'Don't shout at them they are only bairns'. Older people, had much to Bob's embarrassment, put half crowns in his pocket.

After the ceremony, they were put on 'line of march' and informed they were now considered to be on active service. There were roll calls every hour and, told if anyone was missing they would be charged with desertion in face of the enemy. They embarked on the captured German liner *Empire Trooper* at Southampton. There were 850 men of the DLI plus others. They had three tier canvas bunks where at any moment they could be ordered to 'lay at attention for inspection'. The soldiers themselves did the duties on the ship and Bob found himself on kitchen fatigues having to wash up for 1000 men. They sailed through the Mediterranean to Port Said where the locals tried to sell them food and trinkets from boats. The soldiers also took pennies wrapped in silver paper, threw them into the water and watched the children to dive for the money. They then sailed through the Suez Canal, only to be greeted by the not so friendly locals raising their djellabas to display their equipment! In Aden, the battalion went ashore for a two-hour march in the midday sun, before returning to the ship. They were then allowed two hours shore leave only if immaculately dressed. Anyone going down the gangplank with so much as a crease out of place was turned back by the RSM 'Batter Edwards'.

They crossed the Indian Ocean, to Colombo, onto Singapore and Hong Kong, where at each port they were made to do more route marches. The heat was stifling and they found it hard to breathe. There was no sympathy for sea sickness. It was regarded as a self-inflicted wound. Many of them slept on decks but in the Bay of Bengal, they faced a Typhoon, with wave after wave breaking over the decks, soaking everything. From Hong Kong they continued on to Pusan in Korea where they landed at night to be greeted by an US Negro band playing 'If I Knew You Were Coming I Would Have Baked A Cake.' The whole journey had taken six weeks. It was September 1952 and they had now reached their place of active service – the Korean War.

The battalion moved up to the front line by train. It had wooden slats rather than seats and had a standing guard ready to return fire at any bandits. Now and then, the train stopped to allow the crew to rest, at which Colonel Jeffreys organised a run up and down a nearby mountain for the whole battalion. After a couple of days, they reached Britannia camp and moved up to the Imjin River and Gloucester Valley for a week's acclimatization. Bob was one of a small group that went forward to join the Australian Battalion (1st RAR) to prepare for the arrival of the whole of the 1st DLI at the Naechon position.

Emphatically told that they should not show any light, talk, or make any sound as they moved up, they were surprised to arrive at the frontline to find the Aussies sitting around campfires loudly singing and drinking. The Aussies greeted Bob with 'Come and see the gaffer mate,' meaning their CO and added for good measure, 'You shouldn't have left your mothers apron strings lad.'

Bob shared a 'Hutchie' with three Aussies. A hutchie is a deep trench for protection from artillery fire and was built on the reverse side of a hill away from the enemy. The deeper the hole the safer the occupants. Bob was thus a little alarmed therefore that the one he was to share was not deep. He was reassured with the words 'Don't worry mate it will be deep enough in a week.' The floor was covered to a depth of a couple of feet with boxes of beer!

Bob went out on a listening patrol where they went up to a forward position to be the early warning of any enemy advance. His Aussie companions were curious about what Bob had in his pack and his reply of bootlaces

Bob with warning sign at 'Little Gibraltar'

(amongst other things) caused great ribaldry. The Australians had different priorities; one had a loaf with a bottle of drink in it, and another had a gramophone that he proceeded to play to the enemy. Some days later, 25th September, the DLI arrived to begin a three week stint in the line followed by three days out in reserve. They were shelled and mortared severely through the coming year, more intensely during daylight hours if any movement was seen or heard by the Chinese. Their closest position to the Chinese lines was just 35 yards!

Bob was part of the assault platoon of S Company, which also controlled the guns, mortars and anti tank weapons. He was involved in a number of patrols. This could involve taking an enemy position, which was nearly always empty because the enemy disappeared down tunnels. Later pole charges

'All the comforts of home'

were used to blow them in. On another patrol, they avoided walking into an ambush because they heard the Chinese communicating by bird sounds. If a patrol was ambushed Bob said the Chinese would kill any wounded using the butt of a rifle and then later bring mortar fire on the position to catch anyone recovering the bodies. They often negotiated minefields by prodding with a bayonet to create safe routes across. While the patrol put in its attack, a separate new path was marked out with white cones for them to return through, as the Chinese would always shell the original path. Getting back to the lines was difficult in the dark, so allied tanks would obligingly shine a light into the sky as a marker. They also had a password that would change every six hours. They were always nervous of approaching a US position, as their soldiers were jittery and trigger-happy. Bob remembers that while on sentry duty a dark figure approached through the gloom. Bob gave half the password inviting the response, but as it was not forthcoming he was just about to fire when an Aussie voice came out of gloom, 'don't shoot you pommie bastard... we don't bother with this password stuff!'

When in the trenches they all 'stood to' at dusk and slept during the day, as the Chinese attacked at night accompanied by trumpets and cymbals. They would pass through the barbed wire entanglements by throwing rush matting and their own dead on to them. Listening patrols often gave early warning of the approach and Bob said that they could often smell the rancid clothing of the Chinese who carried garlic and fish in their pockets. He also added that you had to develop a sixth sense for danger. If they spotted anything or even suspected a movement, they could bring in divisional or corps artillery fire down onto a pre-designated position. Colonel Jeffreys had a number of

Bob on 38th Parallel

epithets, one of which was 'We are here to stay so we will dominate the area!' A second was 'dig or die', thus every available hour was given over to improving the trench system, in particular the communication trenches with the fighting area at the front of the hill. This would have to zigzag to avoid shell blast and 'fighting pits' stuffed with ammunition and grenades. The living area was at the back of the hill where comfort was more of a priority. They made beds out of poles and canvas machine belts arranged in a bunk system.

The temperature in the winter dropped to forty degrees below, they therefore rigged up a chimney using artillery shell cases and an ingenious kerosene stove to keep off the chill. They never undressed in the winter and so got body lice. They were treated often with DDT and other chemicals, which Bob believes may have contributed to subsequent ailments. Bob himself caught malaria. He would suffer from this for the next fifteen years with near fatal results.

South Koreans were recruited into the Army and termed KA Com. (Koreans attached to the Commonwealth,). They were well liked. Other Koreans acted as porters bringing up water and ammunition from the rear.

The Chinese had a surprisingly detailed knowledge of the allies. A woman known as 'Wailing Hannah', broadcasted to the allies from a megaphone or from an aircraft and she seemed to know when a unit had arrived or left and could even know if a relative of a soldier was ill in England and offer to repatriate him! When artillery was directed at her suspected position, she expressed her disappointment and play back a gramophone played 'Don't Throw Bouquets At

Me'! During their time in the line, the DLI lost twenty-seven killed or missing and one hundred and four wounded from an original strength of eight hundred and fifty. Finally, they were taken back to the 38th Parallel for the cease-fire on 27th July 1953.

Bob saw there a battered Australian position with 5000 Chinese dead in front. The Chinese were allowed to collect the bodies and cremate them a few hundred yards away. The war was now over and at 6pm a mass of Very lights was fired into the air and numerous spotlights switched on.

In September 1953, the battalion re-embarked on the *SS Empire Orwell* and left Korea. It was disembarked at the Suez Canal zone and was involved in guarding installations there until December. As Bob and another eighty National service men, had finished their service, they were returned to England to be demobbed. Bob and others flew back in a converted Lancaster bomber. On Bob's arrival in Durham, he was taken to a dilapidated hut. There he was immediately charged one shilling and eight pence for a broken window. Welcome back! They were also ordered not to talk to new recruits. They did not want to argue with this, for even at this stage they well were aware that they could still be detained in a punishment centre for six months. After the demob on December 1953, Bob remained as a reserve in the TA for another three and a half years, which he completed without mishap. Bob then served in the volunteer fire service for 26 years, being promoted to Sub Officer. He also served as the chairman of the Korean Veterans Association.

Bob Hayton in Egypt 1953

Following Father & Grandfather

George James Parker

Service No. 22343049

Derek Austin Parker

Service No. 22335617

Both Born:	7th October 1931 Lichfield Barracks, Staffordshire
Service Dates:	1950–1952
Place of Enlistment:	Carlisle
Unit:	1s East Lancashire Regiment
Medal;	GSM Suez Canal Medal – clasp Canal Zone
Theatres;	Sudan, Egypt

Derek and George Parker came from an army family. Their grandfather was a sergeant major with the Lancashire fusiliers in the 1890s on the North West frontier and their father was a Regimental Sergeant Major of the 2nd Battalion Kings Own Royal Regiment (KORR) stationed in India from 1923 to 1941. The brothers were to spend much of their youth on the subcontinent.

SECTION 1: ARMY

Derek and George as boys with Bengal Lancers

They remember their arrival in India, with many natives rushing forward offering to carry their luggage; however they had been warned only to use War Office Government Servants, identifiable by their armband with a crown and the initials WOGS.

They were particularly proud of their father's competence and status. One of his skills was in relation to punishment. If a man transgressed, he would give him the option of appearing before the CO or to take the RSM's (their father's punishment.) If a soldier opted for the latter, he was taken round the back of the huts for a fight. The defaulter was invited to throw the first punch only to be nearly always knocked out by the counter punch. In 1941 when the 2nd KORR went from India to Tobruk the brothers returned to England and moved to Lancaster. After the war, their father who had become the Lieutenant Quarter-Master at the barracks was able to join them. In 1950, they received the call up for National Service and sent to a depot in Carlisle for basic training. From there, they moved to Chester, opting to move from the KORR to the East Lancashire Regiment, so they could serve overseas. While in Chester the battalion was paraded to receive new colours and Derek relates how he was next to 'an old sweat' called Chipping. He was a '22-year veteran' of World War Two and had won the Military Medal. While at the slope, his lieutenant came up and told Chipping to move his hand and then little later to move it back. This proved too much for Chipping and he flung his rifle to the ground saying, 'How the f...ing hell do you want it.' Chipping was naturally arrested and Derek, who could not stop laughing, found himself also on a charge. When they were arraigned before the Company CO, everyone laughed so much that the charge was dismissed. George emphasised that he never came across any bullying in his national service, even 'poking' as physical contact was forbidden. When a corporal roughly repositioned George's beret and cut his forehead George agreed to hush it up as the corporal could have been

George with his Bugle in Khartoum

demoted. He also remembered a barrack's corporal making a disparaging remark about a picture of a recruit's girlfriend; he was immediately reduced to private. George stated a typical defaulter's punishment was to be called by bugle to the guardroom every half hour and then told to return next time in a completely different kit. This would take the whole of the intervening period to organise. Their battalion contained many NCOs who had seen service in World War Two, including one who had been in the French Foreign Legion. Many had spent years abroad and were angry at another foreign posting where it would not be possible to take their families.

Derek was embarked on the *Empress of Australia* as part of the advance party. They landed at Port Sudan, Suez and entrained for Khartoum. During the heat of the day, the train would slow right down as the rails became distorted by the heat. The company then had to get out and walk alongside it. Sometimes, when going at reasonable speed the local tribesmen would jog along with the train for ten miles apparently just for the fun of it. On their arrival in Khartoum, they took over the barracks from the Buffs and prepared for the arrival of the rest of the regiment, which included George.

Before leaving Chester, George had been assigned to the HQ Company to become a bandsman. He used the journey out to Africa to learn the bugle. When he got to Khartoum, despite his youth and inexperience, he won a bugle competition. Much to the annoyance of the regulars this youngster was made the Colonel's bugler playing in ceremonials and for the officer's mess. He said he never learn to read music but remembered the calls by rhymes. For example:

> For the quarter of an hour call he used 'the little dog weed on the square ha ha the little dog weed on the square!' For the 'Officers Dress' call, he used 'Officers' wives get pudding and pies, corporals' wives get nothing,' and for the defaulters call 'You can be a defaulter as long as you answer the call.'

As the main part of the battalion marched into Khartoum, any men who were not sweating were removed and sent back to England. This was because the ability to sweat was vital for a soldier to avoid possibly fatal heat exhaustion.

Soldiers viewed Khartoum as a punishment station but the brothers enjoyed it. The Sudanese were clean, polite and tough. Sudanese stevedores were thin as rakes but could carry a box up a gangplank that would take four soldiers to carry. The battalion did a lot of desert training in Sudan, learning how to support each other and work in conjunction with heavy weapons. They would march for long periods often with insufficient water. On one occasion, while on a manoeuvre, George felt he had no other option but to steal the 'chuggles' (water bags) from the back of an umpire's Jeep.

While in camp, they were not let out much, but occasionally they were allowed to go to the cinema in Khartoum, although they were separated from the natives by a wall topped with barbed wire.

Both brothers were involved in guard ceremonies at the Governor's palace, which was at the confluence of the Blue and White Niles. George was a drummer in the band and Derek was one of the armed guards. Their march to the palace was preceded by a chain gang whose job was to sweep the road – no easy task in the desert! Church was attended with weapons, a tradition established since the massacre of soldiers in a Meerut Garrison church during the Indian Mutiny of 1857.

Whilst on manoeuvres George found himself in the Wadi, taken by the 21st Lancers at the Battle of Omdurman 1898 and the saw the plaque to commemorate the action. They also managed to visit the Mahdi's tomb and Derek got to visit the village of Omdurman itself.

Then as now, there was constant unrest in the Dhofur region of Sudan with fighting between the Christians and Muslims. Both sides deferred to the holy men. Their apparel was green from mould, as they never washed. These holy men as they walked down the road would not deviate for anyone and if any curious soldier stood in their way, they would be threatened with a knife. George was convinced if a soldier did not move he would have been killed. Traffic also always gave the holy men a wide berth.

Egypt was gradually becoming antagonistic towards the British occupation and in consequence, in November 1952

Band before Governor's House Khartoum

the battalion was sent up to Egypt. They went by ship to Tel El Kebir, disembarked via scramble nets on to the quay before coming onto parade. George then sounded the last post as it was Armistice Day. British forces in Egypt were subject to a series of attacks at the time by the 'Muslim brotherhood' and the 'Sisters of the Nile'. This took the form of sniping, road side bombs or in the case of women, throwing grenades at patrols or throwing acid in the face of soldiers. George and Derek did their share of patrols and were involved in supporting an action in Ismailia. This took place on Friday 25th January 1952. Here the local police had apparently released local criminals, armed them and then jointly occupied the police barracks. British troops were immediately called in and shooting took place. The Egyptian commander in the barracks was invited to surrender; apparently, he had trained at Sandhurst. He declined and the British brought in tanks to shell the barracks. The occupiers took heavy casualties before they finally capitulated.

George emphasised that despite the unrest he never saw maltreatment of Egyptians even when they were being aggressive. In the spring of 1952, both brothers returned to England. Derek flew back on a Dakota with inebriated airborne soldiers while George had a more sedate journey working his passage on the returning emigration ship, the *SS Georgic*.

Band on route

The Colour Sergeant

Raymond Noel Gill

Service No. 22861503

Born:	25th December 1934 Kendal
Service Dates:	April 1953–1955 National Service, 1962–1986 Regular Army
Place of Enlistment:	Carlisle 1953, Preston 1962
Units	1st Border Regiment, 1st Kings Own Royal Border Regiment
Awards:	GSM Canal Zone, GSM South Arabia
Main Theatres:	Canal Zone, Bahrain, West Germany, Cyprus, Northern Ireland

Ray got his call up for National Service in April 1953. He was assigned to the 1st Border Regiment and undertook his 10-week basic training at Hadrian's Camp near Carlisle. He said that this was very intensive as the normal 35-week basic training would eat too much into their 2-year National Service.

Training consisted of the use of the standard small arms of the time, the Lee Enfield .303, the Sten gun and the Bren. He also said it felt like they were never in the same clothing for more than two minutes at a time. At the time, they all thought the NCOs were very harsh, but they later realised than it was necessary to be able to turn raw civilians into soldiers in such a short space of time. Afternoon training would often take the form of coming back to base over very muddy ground. As they did so, the NCO would shout, 'Under Fire' and they would all have to sprawl face down into the mud. 'Everything got filthy' of course, which meant the whole evening, would be spent getting clothing and equipment clean'.

After training, they were immediately sent to Egypt. He remembers his first sensation of Egypt. 'As the aircraft doors opened, we were met by a blast of hot air and a swarm of flies.' He joined the vast garrison camp at Tel El -Kebir. He was talking to other soldiers when he got there, when he heard a shot and immediately 'hit the deck', only to find they had taken no notice. They informed him that Egyptian dissidents fired the occasional shot from outside the perimeter, but this was more of an irritant than a lethal threat.

One night Ray had cause to reconsider this. He left his tent and headed to the latrines. The latrines were a massive pit, ten feet deep dug into the sand with telegraph poles across them. A hessian screen surrounded them. Relieving yourself meant a case of balancing on poles although during the day the excrement attracted so many flies, that it looked like smoke rising from the pit. Therefore, it was best if possible to go at night. As Ray balanced on the pole, a shot rang out passing through the hessian screen and whistled right past his ear. Although not recommended as a cure for constipation Ray found it effective and was quick to finish.

Ray was moved from his battalion to the HQ of the 19th Brigade. He was appointed as the Motor Transport Clerk. An officer joined him and they set about completely overhauling all the vehicles, as they had been totally neglected. This involved ordering and collecting spare parts from an RAOC stores at Moascar. This proved hazardous because of the possible sniping and roadside bombs you could face en route. Particularly worrying was the wire stretched across the road about 5 feet up which had decapitated men on motorcycles and in Jeeps. The REME had counted this last hazard by attaching an angle iron pointing vertically from the front bumper to cut the wire.

Ray was not impressed with the behaviour of the local population, they were poor and malnourished and treated their animals appallingly. He remembers they passed a camel that had totally collapsed under its burden and was

The Camp at Tel-El-Kebir

being beaten and kicked by its owner. One of Ray's friends shot it immediately to put it out of its misery.

Ray pointed out that the Arabs were known as expert thieves, (as have other contributors in this book) and even though depots were heavily guarded with wire, patrols and dogs, the Arabs still got in and stole. They even stripped a vehicle and took it away in bits. One British patrol raided a local village, which was so full of stolen equipment, that it became nicknamed '5 Base Ordnance depot.'

Although HQ based, Ray still took part in manoeuvres. On one patrol, he remembered, they were without water for three days in the searing heat as their water 'bowser' did not arrive. They used camp rations while out but never touched the hard tack, which Ray said was less palatable than a dog biscuit. The biscuits though were a hit with the local children, so they kept them to hand out to the children in the local villages.

In their camp tents, they had two bare electric lights with a wire stretched between them and if they could, they would find a chameleon that would happily live on that wire hunting the flies attracted by the lights.

Ray's national service ended at the end of 1955 and he returned to England with the 19th Brigade HQ. He left the army and married in 1957, but then decided to rejoin in 1962. He had to do basic training again this time at Fulwood barracks, Preston. Since leaving the Border Regiment, Ray found it had amalgamated with the Kings Own Royal Regiment of Lancaster and was now in the Kings Own Royal Border Regiment.

He trained with the new SLR and SMG, the latter being a great improvement on the Sten gun, which could go off if jolted in any way with fatal consequences.

On Patrol with Highland Light Infantry
Ray on the 2nd right

Ray was 29 and was seen as a father figure by some of the recruits whom he helped as much as he could. He went with the battalion to West Germany for a year before returning to England and commencing a 3-year Foreign Service tour, starting in 1966. This took him to Bahrain, which was a 'partially accompanied station', that meant that only a proportion of the wives could go. Points were awarded for rank, length of service and length of marriage to determine which wives could go. Ray had enough points to bring his wife.

They did find some antagonism from the locals due to the Israeli-Arab conflict and Ray at one point had the full time job of guarding a section of the married quarters armed with a pistol.

Ray was very impressed with the ruler of Bahrain, Sheikh Ahmed Bin Salman Al Khalifa. He would invite married NCOs with their families to his private beach at the weekends and made a point of talking to everyone. He had been educated at Harrow and Sandhurst and was a definite anglophile.

When the Army and Navy put on a Gilbert and Sullivan opera, he came with his retinue and was the first to stand for God Save the Queen. He also bought all the actors, presents, which he gave personally after the show.

After Bahrain, Ray was in Cyprus where the EOKA troubles had more or less died out, although there was increasing tension between the Greeks and the Turks. Now Ray was 'The Unit Families NCO', this meant he took on the role of welfare advisor to families dealing with anything from unexplained skin rashes to full-scale matrimonial disputes and on one sad occasion, he had to deal with a suicide.

In 1969, he moved back to England and became a recruiter in Lancaster for three years before going to Northern Ireland with his battalion as Officers' Mess Supervisor, which involved a period of training at the Army Catering Corps in Aldershot.

While in Belfast, the army took over many of the civilian jobs such as for example as a 'lollipop lady' – school-crossing patrol. A friend of Ray's was shot dead by a sniper while doing this job supervising the children across the road.

After Belfast Ray did another stint in West Germany before completing his time as Orderly Room Chief Clerk with the 4th Kings Own Border in Lancaster. He final left in 1986, but he found it hard to get employment in civilian life. This was a time of high unemployment, but eventually he became storekeeper for B Company of the 4th Kings Own Border in Kendal. This job he had until he retired in 1999.

In 2002, Ray joined the Canal Zoners a nationwide ex service organisation for all who served in the Canal Zone. He was the local organiser and founding member of the Cumbria and North Lancashire Branch from 2003 to November 2005. He is also supportive of the local branch of the Border Regiment Association.

Defending Your Ordnance

Brian Warmsley

Corporal
Royal Army Ordnance Corps
Service Number 23231579

Born:	16th November 1936 Blackpool
Service Dates:	15th February 1955–Christmas 1957
Place of Enlistment:	Donnington
Units	Royal Army Ordnance Corps
Main Theatres:	Egypt, Libya

In the 1950s, Brian was working for the M.O.D. However, this did not exclude him from National Service. He discovered that if he was to be called up he would be paid 10*s*. 6*d*. per week however if he enlisted in the regular army instead he would get £2 per week. Brian enlisted.

He was first sent to the ordnance depot at Donnington where the Crimean cannon, for which all VCs are made and kept. After Donnington, he was sent onto Blackdown Camp, Staines to join the 1st battalion RAOC. Here he found a great deal of violence and intimidation and he found it wise to gain the friendship of one of the 'hard men.' As his education exempted him from some of the 'education courses', he used the time to help others in their courses including a private Palmer who in consequence acted as his protector.

Having finished his basic training, (1955) Brian was posted to 5-Base Ordnance Depot at Tel el Kebir in Egypt as a store man and clerk. This vast base was much run down as the British were preparing to leave Egypt for good. Perimeter cover was gradually withdrawn and Brian had to sharpen his small arms practice for self-defence. The camp had a seven-mile perimeter with a minefield outside, but as soon as the British began their operation to pull out, the Arabs tried to get into the camp. They would drive animals over the minefield and consequentially the night was filled with flashes and detonations. Brian stated that his unit and the Salvation Army were amongst the last to leave and towards the end, he was sleeping with a loaded rifle.

His unit was transported to Tobruk, the scene of the siege of the North African campaign of 1941, before moving onto Benghazi where Brian joined

Brian in Egypt

the Transport District H.Q. While he was there, he remembers a mass sale of army surplus; all World War Two equipment.

There were two main dangers at this posting. The first was that the RASC troops beat Brian up on one occasion and the second was from the rats who climbed through windows at night and jumped onto the mosquito nets over the beds. There were a number of German civilians on the base, who were making loud protests on the square. Brian was part of a detachment that lined up at the one end of the square and ordered to fix bayonets. They advanced on the protestors who did not wait to find out if they were prepared to use them!

Whilst in North Africa the army tried to limit the extent of venereal disease in the troops by licensing prostitutes. MPs would get them medically checked and if they found them to be clear of infection, they were given silver badges. This was undermined as the prostitutes just shared out the silver badges, so many of the prostitutes would have one whether they were infection free or not. Brian spent his time in Benghazi playing hockey and cricket.

At the end of 1957, Brian boarded the troopship *Dilwara* bound for England, to be demobbed. Brian is now an active member of the Canal Zone Association and carries their standard on parade.

Three Accounts
from Malaya

All Based at
Ipoh Perak Province

Colombo Camp, Iboh, Perak State
Malaya is made up of 12 federated states, each with its own Sultan

Up the Jungle

Tony Parnham

Sergeant
Service No. 22820761

Born: 20th March 1936
Service Dates: 28th May 1957–30th September 1959
Place of Enlistment: Sheffield
Units   Royal Lincolnshire Regiment
Main Theatres: Malaya, Aden.
Medals   GSM Malaya, Aden. M.I.D (twice – 28th May 1957
                         and 30th September 1959

Tony grew up with a love of camping and shooting and took the earliest opportunity to join the army. He joined the boys' service at sixteen and then joined the Royal Lincolnshire Regiment. After his ten weeks basic training, Tony was sent onto join the regiment which was in Berlin sharing a barracks with the KOYLI. He was now seventeen, but peacetime soldiering did not appeal to Tony. Therefore, he put in for a transfer to join the SAS, then operating in Malaya against the communist insurgents. His CO persuaded him to stay with

On route   *In the Jungle*

Handling the Weaponry

POST WAR ARMY LIFE

the Lincolnshires as they were going there soon. In the meanwhile, they gave Tony a stripe and sent on an NCOs course and a snipers course.

Following an embarkation leave, Tony joined the regiment's advance party who flew on a DC6 via Athens, Cyprus, Karachi and Bangkok to Singapore.

On arrival they began jungle training in order to train the rest of the battalion when they arrived. When the rest of the battalion did arrive, it was found to be without the 7th Platoon Sergeant, who had been arrested en route. Then CO, Colonel Innis, decided to interview applicants to replace the sergeant. Tony was selected and, because he had O-levels, he was excused the army exams necessary for such promotion. He also found himself senior to older and more experienced NCOs and as Tony was extremely self-confidant did not smoke or drink, he found himself resented and suspect by several of his fellow NCOs. On completing its training the battalion's companies were distributed around the state of Penang in Malaya

This was the time of the communist insurgence in Malaya. Britain and the USA were concerned about the 'domino' effect and keen to stop the communists becoming established in Malaya. Tony with the 7th Platoon, of C Company was sent to Kerdos, where the Communist uprising had begun.

They arrived by train and established an open area around the camp – a 'cordon sanitaire' as it was called. This was to ensure they could not be surprised. Lt Davey the 7th Platoon's commander was missing because of an ear infection, so Tony had responsibility for the whole platoon. He had virtually no experience of command but he had heard that you had to keep the men moving so he took them on long marches and drove them hard. Several, including the second corporal, complained over Tony's head. The CO heard the complaints, which Tony acknowledged were valid. The CO's response was to invite the corporal to transfer to another unit with loss of rank or to support his sergeant. He chose the latter. However afterwards the RSM 'bawled out' Tony with the special grasp of English vocabulary that seems peculiar to that rank and Tony thus concluded that he needed to ease off a bit.

The 7th Platoon consisted of three sections each commanded by a corporal, plus an HQ section. Tony had also in his platoon, a signaller, a patrol dog, (a Labrador), a tracker dog (an Alsatian or Labrador) plus their handlers. They also had two Ibans who were headhunters from Sarawak. Tony described them as having ears elongated by weights, holes in their teeth filled with coloured glass and tattoos. Tattoos were made by hammering nail covered pieces of wood into their bodies including the neck and mixing black ink with the blood. As trackers, they were superb. They could distinguish between tracks made by rubber soles (communists) from those by bare feet (natives) and whether or not the person had been trying to hide the trail. Tony tried to pick up tips from them but could hardly see the signs even when they were pointed out to him. The country in which C Company operated was made up of isolated small villages often attached to rubber plantations, owned by companies such as Michelin and Dunlop. Beyond these plantations, it was mostly very thick jungle. Once inside it was permanently dark and humid. Often it was so dense that 1000yards was a hard days march. When it rained, the noise was such you could not hear a rifle shot 15 yards away. Constant patrols were the order of the day and could consist of five men to a platoon. The objective of these was to try to find enemy camps to kill or capture small units or to drive them out of an area. There were also sweeps that would consist of anything from a company to a Corps. The blocking platoon would normally be landed by heli-copter and then take up position at a bottleneck or other terrain feature that the 'terrorists' would have to cross. The company would then advance with approximately 15 yards between men and push the enemy before them. All very well in theory, but a company took up a frontage of about a mile and no one could see anyone else through the dense undergrowth. Thus, rates of advance could vary, anything from a mile to 50 yards an hour and thus the whole company ended up in scattered bunches. The enemy was thus rarely ever encountered and the process was so imprecise that on one occasion Tony recalls the advancing force walked clean through the blocking force without

Artillery Support for Larger Sweeps

either noticing. For larger sweeps, artillery would be used in support, shelling suspected camps or position.

There was also air support available in the form of Venoms armed with rockets and from Lancaster bombers who were nearing the end of their operational life. Patrols were typically five days and they were transported to their starting point by lorry or helicopter. The local population, mainly Chinese, disliked both the British and the Malays. They made a living by tapping rubber trees for latex and when a patrol entered a plantation, a tapper banged his tin. His fellows for miles around would take this up thus compromising the patrol. If they saw a tapper doing this they would knock over his tins and sometimes rough him up, as he was deliberately threatening the safety of the patrol.

Camps in the jungle followed a set pattern of design (See diagram A). In addition, in setting up the camp they would try to disturb the vegetation as little as possible. Strips of rotan were used to link the HQ, the sentries and the latrine. Since it was pitch black and no lights this allowed the soldiers to find their way round. Tony said that sentry duty at such a camp could be one of the most frightening experiences for a young soldier. You felt isolated, unable to see and listening to a variety of jungle noises coming from all around. Booby traps were set up beyond the sentries often a trip wire attached to a grenade. In camp soldiers would sleep in a hammock with a waterproof covering above it and their rifle just above his head in easy reach. Just before first light and just before dusk, everyone would have to 'stand to' with weapons facing outward.

Following the killing of the governor, Sir Henry Gurney many villages, which were seen to be supporting the terrorists were destroyed and the inhabitants concentrated into bigger encampments protected by the Malay police (see Diagram B). Even from these encampments, the civilians supplied the terrorists by throwing food over the perimeter fence in the middle of the night. Sometimes a platoon could be deployed surrounding the village all night to try to catch the people red handed.

In 1957, Tony was involved in an action that resulted in him receiving a mention in despatches (see Diagram C). He advanced from the north along the game trail with two other soldiers and two Ibans. This was a fast moving patrol to making contact with the enemy. Not finding anything, they cut across the hills to the west to go home, when they heard of an ambush on C Company further down the trail. They quickly joined the company and then led a small patrol to track down the communists. They came across their abandoned packs and then located, mainly thanks to Ibans, the enemy camp lay across the river to the hills to the East. Tony went back to report to the second in command, Captain Walters, who then instructed Tony to report to the hospital as Tony's arm was in a sling because of an

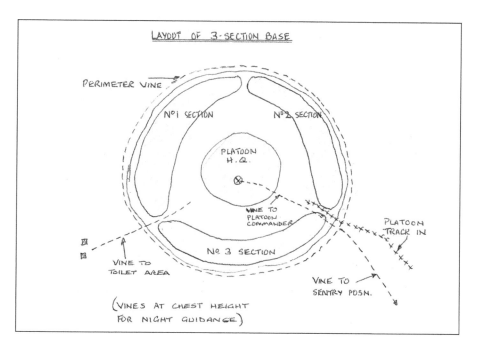

Diagram A

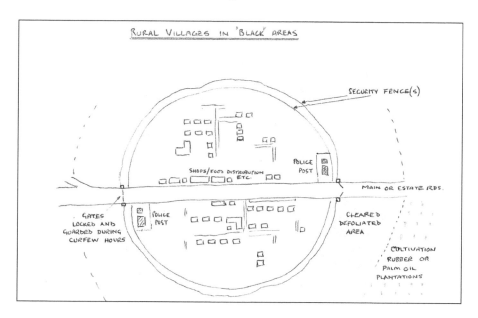

Diagram B showing the organisation of purpose built encampments for the villages

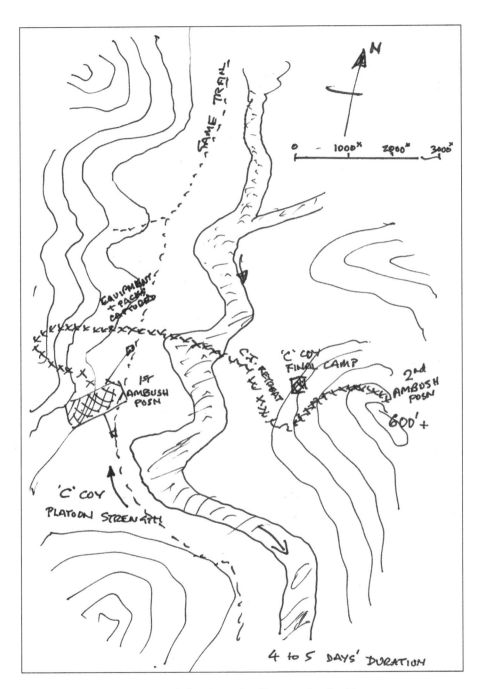

Diagram C showing action Tony was involved in

SECTION 1: ARMY

Co Rifle Team Winners, Wittlogg 1959
'The CO's wife had to laugh as it was the 8th time I was called forward'

infected finger. They subsequently attacked the enemy camp; both the Ibans were wounded. They joined Tony to recover in hospital.

The enemy Tony emphasized was rarely sighted but on one occasion, they captured a wounded woman. They treated her very gently until the Malay special branch collected her. CEPs (Captured Enemy Personnel) were given the chance to give information about caches, enemy camps etc and if they did so they would be re-designated SEPs (Surrendered Enemy Personnel). It was possible for civilians to collect large rewards (see illustration) if important leaders were captured. At the end of patrols, Tony would inspect all his men for injuries and disease. He also checked their weapons although he gave them a chance to clean them first. Ammunition was never in short supply; the same amount arrived at regular intervals irrespective of how much had been used. These included anti tank rockets despite the nearest enemy tank being in China! The excess was fired at trees or blown up. One officer, much too every ones amusement, was wounded by white phosphorous from one such explosion.

1958 saw the Lincolnshire's tour come to an end and on their way home many of the troops ritually disposed of their kit over the side of the ship. However, after a few days they were rerouted to Aden because of a worsening political situation in the Yemen. After two months duty there they did finally return to the UK only then almost immediately to be sent out to Minden in Germany to take part in corps size North European Manoeuvres. In 1959, Tony won eight prizes in the shooting competition at Wittlog, the best shot of several thousand competitors. While in Germany, he was involved in a vehicle accident that resulted in a ruptured liver. It was touch and go and his parents were flown out to be with him. He recovered but he was informed that he would never be fully well again. They offered him a pension, but Tony turned it down. A year later, he decided to accept the offer, mainly because he was courting. On leaving the army, he embarked on a career in teaching.

Rewards offered to Information on the Communist Insurgents

Loyal to the End: a Jungle Volunteer

Fred Hudson in Malaya

Born:	29th June 1936
Service Dates:	25th July 1957–25th July 1959
Place of Enlistment:	Ladysmith Barracks Ashton-under-Lyne
Units	1st Battalion Loyal Regiment (North Lancashire)
Awards:	GSM, PJM (Pingit Jasa Medal) , VM
Main Theatres	Malaya

Like many boys and young men in the 1940s and 1950s, Fred was apprehensive about doing National Service. Besides growing up through the war, he had also heard tales from ex soldiers. He was not unduly worried though, as his doctor had informed him that a perforated eardrum he got, when he was one-year-old child when he pushed a sharp pencil in to it, would certainly class him as Grade 4 in an army medical and thus he would not be eligible for National Service. Therefore, it was much to his surprise, that when he was called up for an army medical in 1957, he was declared A1. He was told his eardrum was healed (this was not true). Even so, as A1 fit he was ordered to report to Ladysmith Barrack, Ashton under Lyme.

The first thing he did was to marry his girlfriend Betty, whom he had met two years before on 'a warm autumn Saturday evening in the Winter Gardens Blackpool'. They had already decided that if by any remote chance he was to be called up, they would marry. Thus if anything happened to Fred, she would be treated as Fred's next of kin by the army. They married on 20th July 1957 at St Nicholas's Church, Wrea Green and five days later, he was walking through the gates of Ladysmith barracks.

Fred was initially called up to join the Manchester Regiment, much to his chagrin, as he had put as his first choice as the Loyals. His grandfather had been in the Loyals during the First World War, where he was wounded, gassed and was the only survivor of his platoon. He died in 1945, as the result of the long-term effects of those wounds. Fred described him as a great and loving man and Fred could not understand anyone wanting to hurt him, nor him wanting to hurt another human being, he was a 'real gentle man'.

His grandfather's regiment was not the only reason Fred wished to be in the Loyals. He was in the Loyal Cadets for three years while a pupil at Kirkham Grammar School. After leaving school, he asked to join the Kirkham Home Guard, which was affiliated to the Loyals. Its commander, Major Lawson, an old farmer from Weeton, knew him to be a crack shot and Kirkham Home Guard had a good rifle team, winning local shooting competitions. He joined the Kirkham Home Guard at 8.30pm and by 7.00am next morning the Government announced the disbandment of the Home Guard with immediate effect. Fred reckons he was thus probably the last person to join the home Guard. As the Kirkham Home Guard was affiliated to the Loyals, Fred wanted very much to continue with them.

On his arrival at the Ladysmith barracks, he was met by a Lance Corporal, who directed all new recruits to the large stone barracks on one side of the Parade ground. "He was," Fred said, "a big nasty natured type of person and I am being polite when I say a person. He was there as your first culture shock, the first of many" Fred comments that after a few weeks, he was visited by a friend, who was already a corporal. Despite being a friend, being a corporal still made Fred feel nervous in his presence. "That is what infantry training does to you," Fred added. The physical side of training he could manage as he was a non-smoking ex sportsman, but the psychological games that they played 'really did dehumanise a person'.

Shortly after arriving at Ladysmith, Fred's father had telephoned the CO at the barracks, asking whether Fred could have leave, as he had just got married. The CO replied he would think about it, but Fred heard nothing. Therefore, with trepidation he approached the sergeants about the leave pass, mentioning at the same time that the CO had said he was considering it. At the mention of the CO, Fred says the sergeants returned to a normal colour and in normal voices, instructed him to go to the Orderly office. He expected at any moment to be suddenly called back to be denied leave, but the sergeant there said it was quite normal for men just married to get a pass. Fred commented that he realised for the first time that the whole place might not have been the madhouse he initially felt it was; there were normal people about – 'soldiers maybe, but normal'.

One week later, he was back at Ladysmith Barracks and now things did not seem so bad. He had begun to realise that British Army life is a 'series of wind ups, some true, most not, but the send ups do seem to have a way of somehow keeping everything and everyone normal in times of stress'. Fred added that when in Malaya in charge of a section, they were surrounded by communist insurgents, bullets flying at them from all directions. As they lay there, one member of the platoon said, 'Do you think this is a wind up?' Immediately the stress was released and they began to think clearly about how to get out of the situation.

What particularly delighted Fred was that on his return to Ladysmiths Barracks, he was fitted out in the Quartermaster's stores with a Loyals Cap badge – he was going to in the Loyals after all. This would mean overseas services as the Loyals were in Malaya, but that did not worry Fred, as he just wanted to be in the Loyals.

He now joined his training platoon, named the Somme platoon. The Platoon NCOs informed them that if they survived training, they would survive Malaya. National Service training Fred emphasized was hard and some soldiers died in training. One of his fellow intakes died seven weeks into the training. He stresses it is hard to put into words what it was like, but it left you both physically exhausted and torn apart mentally. Unlike the regulars whom could leave if they wished after 6 weeks, or buy themselves out, National Servicemen could not – for them to try and escape from the training meant only prison and a criminal record. The one pleasure in what Fred described, as 'the nightmare of Ladysmith' was his trip to the rifle range on Saddleworth moor. He proved to be a crack shot putting five shots in a space under the size of a penny, much to the delight of the RSM.

The three months training came to end, as Fred again emphasized, an absolute nightmare that remained with him and many others he knows, for years to come. He received 3 weeks 'embarkation leave'. On his return, he joined the

The Somme training Platoon at the Ladysmith Barracks, Ashton-under-Lyne, September 1957. Fred Hudson is stood next to the lad on the right hand of the middle row.

Embarkation Company. While they were sitting down to a meal and waiting to be sent off to Southampton, Fred was told that he was to be sent to the Army Administration Training Centre on the South coast instead. Thinking this was a wind up he sought conformation from the Orderly Office. It was true and on his return to the company, he said his goodbyes, as they were off to Malaya in one hour's time. He, the platoon's crack shot, was off to Chichester to train as a clerk! The good news though, was he would be still around for Christmas and be able to be with his wife. His sister June lived in London and he would be able to visit her as well. On one visit, he passed the scene of the Lewisham Rail disaster that had happened that very day. He completed the course and was home for Christmas.

When he returned to Ladysmith Barracks, he was concerned that he might be rebadged back to the Manchesters. He was glad to discover he would remain a Loyal to the end of his Service. He worked in the office, which he did not enjoy and after three weeks, he was informed he was off to Malaya. He got a week's leave, which his sergeant advised him to make most of, as he would probably be in Malaya for the next two years. First he was sent to the transit camp at Woolwich Arsenal, which he described as quite a modern barracks with 'first class' army food (even a choice of ice cream!). He handed in his UK battle dress uniform, packing only boots, berets, cap badge, underwear and socks into the kit bag. He then put on civilian clothes for the journey to Malaya – apparently, some of the countries they would be landing while in transit would not be keen on having British troops on their soil. He flew from Stanstead in a four-engine plane with massive propellers – a far smoother take off compared to modern jets. They flew to Malaya via Ankara (Turkey), Baghdad (Iraq), Karachi (Pakistan), New Delhi (India), Calcutta (India), Rangoon (Burma), Bangkok (Thailand) and Singapore. Some of the airports were nowhere near the standard of today, for example, Rangoon was just a small wooden shack at the side of the runway.

On arrival in Singapore, Fred's first feeling was that he would never get acclimatise to the heat. Rapidly united with his luggage (Army personal always got priority) he was soon off to a transit camp for those to be posted up country. He was soon to learn 'jungle habits' the preparation of mosquito nets, including tucking its edges under the mattress – not just to keep the mosquitoes out, but also the other creepy crawlies. In addition, you learnt to always shake out your boots before putting them on. A habit, Fred adds he still does today; one does not forget survival habits, even when they are no longer required.

The next day Fred, with others, set out for the station to catch the train to Ipoh. They were still all in civilian clothes, but each carrying a loaded rifle over their shoulder. It felt strange to be so attired, but no one seemed to notice and it soon felt just normal. It is funny, Fred comments, "How quickly one's accepted attitude to a satisfactory civilized way of life changes and the abnormal suddenly becomes the norm."

As they walked up the platform, a British soldier leaned out and called them over. 'Get in here,' he said, 'you do not want to be at that end of the train. If the CTs (Communist Terrorists) blow the track it's that end of the train that gets it.' As Fred said, 'one of the goods things of army life was that no lad would ever leave you to find things out the hard way. They would always help you out to avoid trouble and that includes from complete strangers. You always, from the beginning watched each other's backs, without fail!'

At Ipoh, they were driven up to Colombo Camp. It was a contrast to the town of Ipoh, with its modern buildings and cinemas. The camp was a mixture of corrugated iron sheets and grass (attap) huts and looked more native Malay than anything Fred has seen on way up from Singapore. It was good though to hear friendly Lancashire accents. The next day they were kitted out and in contrast to camps back in the UK, were shown in a relaxed manner around the camp by the sergeants. When he was informed he would be working in an

Colombo Camp, Ipoh. The Loyals main base from 1957–1959
Freddy Hudson took this photograph from a Wessex helicopter

office, Fred insisted he wanted to be in the jungle. They thought he was mad and tried to talk him out of it. They told him horror stories about the Malayan jungle to dissuade him. It was just a most unusual request. Usually soldiers requested to be out of the jungle and into HQ work not the other way round. It was decided that Fred could undertake jungle training for three days in an operational area and then if he still insisted on it on his return, his request would be granted.

Training began, not too intense as the heat was unbelievable. For the first few weeks, it was hard to walk properly as the skin on the back of his legs was stretched so tight – an effect of the heat. The only air conditioning to be found was in the American owned Cinema in Ipoh, which brought the temperature down to cool 75F! Fred says he went twice to the cinema and wore a blazer the second time, he felt so cold in contrast to the heat outside. The Perak valley that they were in was particularly hot. It was rich in tin and iron ore and this tended to hold in the heat overnight. In fact, it was so rich in iron ore, that when it rained the ground would turn to rust, covering everything in a red dust.

Training consisted of first covering the differences between European and Jungle warfare. They would then march to a plantation next to the camp, then sit in the shade and discuss what they could see in the jungle and what they would or should do in different situations. Ants were discussed. One always found long columns of ants coming from nowhere and going to nowhere, guarded by large solider ants, the size of walnuts. Then there were Tailor ants, which would pull leaves together and then stitch them to make a nest. You did not get to close to them; they had a bite far worse than wasp sting. The Ibans used them to stitch up body wounds by nipping the head so the ants' pincers closed over the cut. They had training on the use of razor blades for dealing with snakebite poisoning and cutting out ticks. Fred was beginning to think about the office job. They then looked to weapons and there was a difference between the ones they used back in the UK and the ones for the jungle in Malaya. Some of the latter would have been illegal in other theatres of war. Of the standard weapons, they used an Mk5 Lee Enfield, which had a much shorter barrel than the standard Enfield, to make it easier to carry and use in the jungle. It also had a flash eliminator in the form of a funnel fitted to the end of the barrel. The Bren gun was also used, but with a pistol type handgrip fitted to front of Bren near its legs. It was clumsy weapon for jungle use, but with the grip, it could be fired from the shoulder like a rifle. Bren Guns were also used on top of the scout cars, in pairs and fired by remote control. Another European weapon used in Malaya was a 2in Mortar, but only to fire parachute flares when night ambushing. Hand grenades were used but only on the edge of the jungle or in the plantations, never in the jungle itself. Smoke grenades and flare guns were used for signalling for supply drops. The special weapons for the Malayan jungle, were the Remington and Winchester five shot repeater twelve bore shotgun – devastating at close range. Scouts, some officers and NCOs most often used this but the main weapon was the FN SLR (Fabrique National Self Loading rifle). Fred's choice of weapon was the Pachet sub machine gun, which was easy to use for an NCO as it had a shoulder strap, which allowed it to hang round the neck while he consulted the map and compass. One interesting adaptation undertaken to rifles was a torch fastened to the barrel to act as an aiming beam – a forerunner of the laser sighting used today. If so, was this a first for the Loyals?

Finally, they came to Jungle initiation. They spent an afternoon packing everything they needed. They were issued with three food boxes, one each for each day of the operation. They contained: Malaria tablets called a Paludrine tablets, toilet paper, a small flat tin opener, a bag of 12 barley sugar sweets, a packet of chewing gum, one oxo cube, a packet of sugar, 2 tubes of condensed milk, a packet of tea leaves, a small tin of cheese, 3 hard biscuits, a small box of nuts and raisins, a tin of Heinz baked beans and pork sausages, a large tin of Swifts steak and onions, a small packet of curry powder and a bag of rice. There was though some variety of these items in the food boxes, so if there was something you did not like, you could swap it with someone else. You also got a small fold up metal cooking stove with a pack of 12 Hexamine blocks inside and a tin of sterilizing tablets for drinking water. To this Fred added, two boxes of matches, a book for quiet moments (if any), his mess tins and eating irons. His cup was in the bottom of a pouch, which also carried his water bottle, both made of alloy and in a green canvas bag clipped to one's jungle belt. The bottle held two pints. There was also a machete clipped onto your belt, with a sharpening stone. Finally there was the water bag, jungle green and about the size of a pillowcase. It was made of a rubberoid material and in the jungle one would fill it at the water point and carry it to your Basha (Shelter), tying it to a convenient tree. The bag would hold water for a couple of days. Then there were the clothes, including a poncho that could also be used as the roof one's Basha.

Beside his individual needs, he had to pack his share of the group's needs. These included three spades, eight large batteries for the radio, four water bottles with 100% Navy rum, ammunition magazines for the Bren guns, parts of the radio and a medical bag with a tin of salt tablets. Fred took one of the spades and a radio battery. He tied these on his belt and pack. He could not believe the weight he was carrying, until someone told him not to forget his rifle and ammo as well! This amounted to 100lbs altogether. 'You really felt the weight as you went up and down hills in temperatures well over 100F – it could be absolutely torture.'

Packed, they set off to the NAAFI and at 0330hrs, Fred woke for his first trip into the jungle. They reported to the MT Park and boarded a truck and set off north in the dark. There was a strict curfew enforced, which meant nothing else moved. The only sounds were the trucks and the constant buzz of insects. Soon, in middle of nowhere it seemed the lorries stopped and they climbed out. Suddenly there was a loud crash from the next lorry. All the insects around them went suddenly silent for a fraction of second, then restarted, just like someone turning the light on or off. It was only someone dropping his rifle as he got off, but it certainly got the adrenalin going. The trucks left and the platoon set off up the track. Dawn comes suddenly near the Equator and it was now light. They made their way up a track through the tapioca plantations, men all trying to shift their packs to make them more comfortable. Each man followed the other, about five yards apart. Soon they turned off the track and into the jungle.

After a while, they stopped for a break and a drink. The platoon sergeant came round to explain to them that they had turned off the track early and had

Fred Hudson's dreaded jungle backpack just dropped off his back after his patrol. Note the Patchet sub Machine gun and the four Mills hand grenades. This denotes this is a Jungle edge camp. Hand grenades, were never used in the jungle itself. The load, all-up weight, was 95lbs (45kg).

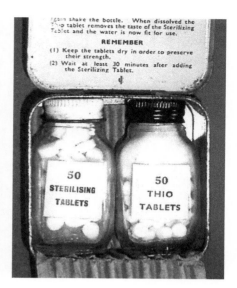

The diabolical water purifying tables. They were useless because the water was undrinkable after using them. All the soldiers on patrol did was boil their water.

cut into jungle as a regiment before them had been ambushed further up the track with six men killed

They moved on and after ten minutes, had another break. One lad found a leech on his leg and soon everyone was searching for leeches. Fred discovered he had drunk half his water bottle, a pint and it was not surprising that most of the men's jungle greens had turned black with sweat. It was literally running down off in streams.

As they continued into the jungle, Fred noticed the trees became, steadily larger. Some had large sweeping roots, which went 20 to 30 feet out from the trunk and roots where like solid brick walls which stretched up 15 to 20 feet to merge into the tree. They were the largest trees by far that Fred had ever seen. Everywhere, vines, some as big as your thigh, were hanging down from the trees. Above was a tangle of dark greenery of the jungle canopy, a hundred feet up – a green ceiling that allowed through the odd beam and chink of sunlight. The bright beams that did break through were like many

Jungle base camp, built by a convenient jungle clearing by 4 Platoons, B Company,
1st Battalion, The Loyal North Lancashire Regiment

theatre spotlights and some beams were broken by the buzzing and humming of a multitude of flying insects – busily getting on with their lives, totally uninterested in the human race below. Where the light did come through the canopy one could see trees growing branches with long green leaves and some, so big, one could hide under a single one. Fred looked at the jungle on each side of the track and just wondered how anyone got through that impenetrable tangled mess. Every bush and branch seemed to grow nothing else but long hard sharp spikes or ragged leaves with sharp saw like cutting edges. Everywhere around them the jungle exuded an over powering hot damp rotting musty smell that was always present and always around you like a fine mist. Soon the smell was part of the background, but one would notice immediately any change and see it as a sign something was wrong.

They soon set off again and being at the back of the line of men was not so bad, as the front cleared much of the path. Even so, Fred and his nearest comrades decided to try out their machetes. They were amazed how easily they cut through the vines and the bush. The problem was that it also disturbed the dirt and dead leaves and with the sweat, they soon found everything was stuck to them and they looked like a group of prize scarecrows. They proceeded down a hill to a stream and then moved along its banks, until called to a halt. Here they were to camp for the next 3 days. They set up their Bashas. Each Basha was shared between two. Fred shared his with a lad called Pete. The first thing they did was to brew tea, which gave some normality to the situation and then turned to making the Basha. Fred and Pete looked round for the flattest piece of ground they could find and cleared the scrub. The ground had two small trees, which they were going to use to form part of the Basha. Fred sought out lengths of vines, the thickness of a washing line, to tie between the trees. There were plenty of vines, but suitable ones were going fast as others claimed them for their Bashas The best way to collect them was to swing on them and hope the whole lot came down from the canopy. Using the vines and the ponchos, they soon formed a respectable Basha. Next, they had to dig their rubbish pit and fill the 'water bag' from the stream. The sergeant then came round to inspect everyone and then sorted out the perimeter vine. This was an important part of the camp. The perimeter vine marked clearly the boundaries of the camp and prevented anyone straying out of the camp and getting lost in the jungle, which was easy to do, even in the daytime. A second vine was attached to the perimeter vine and led out into the jungle for about twenty yards – this was the latrine vine. The toilet was a hole in the ground (to last for the length of the operation) with a toilet seat made up of three-wooden stakes with suitable branches tied to the stakes to form a triangle about two feet above the ground.

The camp was divided up into an inner and out sectors. The outer sector was split into three, each occupied by one of the platoon sections with their NCO's. In the centre, the inner sector was the Platoon officer, the Platoon sergeant and the radio operator, who is member of the Signals regiment. Also in the centre were the two Iban trackers attached to the unit, (Sarawak rangers from Borneo) and a Chinese Liaison officer Interpreter, usually a local policeman or civilian. There could also be a Dog section. Their handlers were members of the Loyals and the dogs were usually Alsatians or Labradors. At the bottom of the camp was placed at a convenient spot on the stream, a drinking water point and naturally the washing point was located downstream.

Each day two platoon sections went out on patrol, while the third remained at the camp carrying out all the work to improve the camp as well as guard duty. This was two hours on and four hours off, from 'stand-to at dawn to stand-to at dusk. Stand-to was when the entire platoon stood at the perimeter with weapons ready to repulse any attack, as this was the often most likely time. On the evening stand-to, the platoon officer and sergeant would walk round to check on the men, for injuries and sickness and to give out a tot of Navy grog (half-rum half water). This was Fred's first taste of Navy grog, which was to help digestion and nerves. All Fred could say about it, was it was strong and nice. After that they settled down to the evening meal and then retired to sleep, wrapped in a thin blanket, desperately trying to keep the creepy crawlies out. They did not need mosquito nets, as the jungle was higher up than Ipoh and cooler. During the night, there would be one guard, two hours on, standing at the centre of the camp.

After it fell dark, they were treated to what Fred described as one of the real wonders of the world – swarms of fireflies, giving out a mystical green light all around. Fred found his first day in the jungle fascinating and was looking forward to exploring and experiencing a lot more in the coming days. However, he admitted that it was not a feeling shared by all his comrades. Although he was a non-smoker within three days of Jungle life, he soon found that there were distinct advantages of cigarettes. First, it curbed your sense of hunger, second it kept the flies off you and finally having a lighted cigarette to hand it was the best thing for the instant removal of leeches.

The next day was to be Fred's first patrol. They set off after breakfast, starting with the corporal checking all rifles were loaded, safety catches on and ammunition in pouches. He then checked on who was to be the tail end Charlie and remind him that he had to have eyes to the rear as well as the front. They set off, four yards apart into the jungle. Within a minute, the jungle closed around them and the camp could have been miles away. They kept on the move for two hours and as Fred stressed he was soon ready for a drink. The signal came to stop and they all sat down. They immediately got down to looking for leeches. Fred found his first leech on his ankle. Although he could not feel it, he could see the jet-black slimy slug like creature, its head buried deep into his leg and its neck throbbing as it pumped blood out of Fred's body. It was so disgusting he began to panic inside, while he tried to appear calm. No one had a cigarette to spare, as they were using them to get rid of their own leeches, so Fred had to get out his matches and while still keeping calm, he lit the match, blew it out and put the hot head of the match onto the leech. There was a pause where nothing looked like it was going to happen, then the head of the leech popped out and Fred brushed it off, squashing it under his foot. To his relief he found no other leeches on him. The Corporal came round with advice not to drink any water until late in the morning, that way the water would last all day, good advice that Fred kept to throughout his stay in Malaya.

On his return to the camp, Fred noticed the Corporal's Basha had a hammock type bed made of silk. The Corporal explained that when there was an airdrop in the jungle, the parachutes were to be taken back if still intact. Any damaged one were no longer suitable for re use and these were cut up into panels and shared between the men of the platoon. The corporal admitted some intact parachutes had unfortunate accidents after retrieval.

They had another advantage, for mosquitoes could not penetrate silk, thus these panels formed an excellent protection from these torturing pests while on ambushing duty; but then they had to be green ones, which are rare, as the usual yellow or white parachutes would stand out in an ambush position. You could get such a 'special Malayan kit', from old sweats leaving for Blighty. There was a tradition to pass them on to newcomers who were called Joskins. He was not sure why they were so called unless it comes from the word to josh, to tease someone one and certainly, newcomers were teased.

The second day again saw Fred out on patrol. At one point, they entered a bamboo grove. The grove was about the size of ten football pitches and to a newcomer it is an amazing site, like something out of Arthur Conan Doyle's 'Lost World'. Each bamboo plant was about the size of four houses with shoots going out in all directions. Most are not like the thin ones you see at garden centres, but as thick as dustbins and around 50 feet in length. As they passed through, climbing over bamboo branches or shoots there was a sudden bang like the sound of a grenade going off. One of the lads was thrown two feet into air. They all dropped down, looking for Commies. Fred was looking desperately around for someone or something to shoot at. His senses were as he said, at an unbelievable height with fear pumping adrenalin through his body. He was listening so hard for a sound that would give the Commies away that it actually hurt. Then he realised he had forgot to breath, so he slowly let his breath out, then breathed in again slowly. All he could hear was the lad who been thrown into air, moaning in pain on the ground nearby. He said that he never had felt so frightened before or since. Then someone called out, that it was only a branch that had broken. The lad had climbed over the branch, which held down by its enormous weight had suddenly snapped throwing him into the air. It could have been far worse, if the lad had been near the actual break point. When Bamboo breaks it sends out dozens of shards, about two feet long. Each shard is like a sword and if you are near the point of break and are hit by one of these travelling at the speed of a bullet – it is quite capable of killing you. The corporal came round as everyone rose to their feet feeling foolish and checked and double-checked safety catches were back on. Then someone came out with a smart remark and all including the injured lad laughed and everyone relaxed.

The injured lad was badly shaken and one shard had hit his finger, cutting it to the bone. He was stitched up and as soon as he was ready, they backtracked their way carefully out of the grove and back to the camp.

The third day was Fred's section's day to stay at the base camp. By this time, there were no real improvements to be added to the camp, so it was a relaxing day and Fred read his book. He did improve his sleeping place, hollowing it out, making the ground soft and then adding new leaves. He had a good comfortable night along with some hairy spiders as big as your hand, which had slipped under him to share his body warmth.

On the fourth day, they packed up and headed back to the main camp. Although the feeling was that no Commies were around, they still kept a watchful eye. As they moved out of the jungle into the plantations the local Malayans and Chinese workers greeted them as they passed, often in English. It was nice to feel so welcomed by the locals Fred noted.

As soon as they got back, after first checking weapons and ammo, they set off for a shower, a decent shave and a bite to eat. The rest of the day was left to cleaning gear and repairing or replacing anything damaged.

The next day Fred was on Company orders to give his decision on keeping his office job. Despite everyone still trying to talk him out of it, he informed them he wished to remain on jungle duty. He felt he was probably the only one looking forward to going back to the jungle. Three days later, he joined 6 Platoon B Company and his time in the Malayan jungle began. As he stated he did not realise at the time just what that would mean and what was in store for him.

The full story of Fred's jungle career is contained in his excellent book *Loyal to the End.*, This account was drawn from his first three chapters. The rest of his story is an extraordinary and detailed account of his active duties during the Malayan insurgency and one written with great humanity. He finished his book with a poem that he wrote at the end of his service, dedicated to those who served in the campaign, which he stresses was not just about fighting but about winning hearts and minds. With his kind permission we quote this below, He has also written a second book, 'National Secret Service' on a specific secret operation he was in charge of towards the end of his time in Malaya, also highly recommend. In 1959, his National Service ended. He was sent back to England and returned home to Wrea Green, to his wife Betty and civilian life.

I have been to countries that I had no wish to visit
I have conversed with people I had no wish to meet
I have done things that I had no wish to do

I have treated the old with respect
I have looked upon the children as friends

I have regarded the peasant girls as ladies
I have looked with my heart and stretched out my hand
I have known the fears of the hopeless
I have touched the despairing fingers of humanity

Freddy Hudson,
Ipoh, 1959

'Loyal to the End' by Frederick W Hudson, 2006. Published by Cremer Press.

'The Best Thing That Happened To Me'

Reuben Boyd

Service No 23582856

Reuben in Jungle Kit with F.N. rifle Jan 1959
(Note Atap wall of basha behind)

Born:	11 March 1939, Bamber Bridge
Service Dates:	1957–1960 (2 years)
Place of Enlistment:	Preston
Units	1st Battalion Loyals
Awards:	General Service Medal (Malaya)
Main Theatres:	Malaya

Reuben's call up came in late 1957 and he did 12 weeks basic training at Fulwood barracks. 'It was 'hell' but a real adventure,' he said. Before he joined up he was a Teddy boy but that soon went with the army haircut. After the haircut, it was to the Quartermaster stores for kit and uniform. The general army rule was that the soldier should fit the kit not the other way round. If the kit was a ridiculous fit then you could take it back to the Quartermaster stores but only to the Quartermaster's great displeasure. If you cap was too big you soaked it and kept soaking it until it shrunk to fit your head. The belt was the hard part, as you had to start by scrubbing off all the old blanko. Then you had to hammer the brasses flat. Finally, you got to work on making the belt presentable so the brass shone and the belt was perfectly white. The brass and the boots had to shine so NCOs could see their face it in it. Rueben and other recruits were trained by ex SAS people who instilled great fear in them but this helped them to bond together as a unit.

Soon it was the passing out parade, followed by a weekend home, before reporting to the barracks with kit bag ready for whatever the army had decided. They soon boarded a train for Stanstead Airport and then flown out to overseas posting to Malaya. They boarded a Hermes Mk 5 flown by the Lancashire Aircraft Corporation. They were off but unlike today the flight was a week's journey: via Brindisi (Italy), Ankara (Turkey), Karachi (Pakistan), Bombay and New Delhi (India) before finally arriving at Singapore. 'Despite our air sickness, it was really exciting for us 18 year olds,' Reuben added. At Singapore, they were dispatched to a nearby transit camp for acclimatisation. This involved being ordered to stay inside for a week and not to go out. From Singapore, they were sent up country into Malaya to Colombo Camp, near Ipoh in Perak State. This was a purpose built camp in the jungle, surrounded with razor wire. They still felt it was adventure. They lodged in Bashas, which were huts made from attap (dried leaves), resistant to the hardest downpour even in the Monsoon.

Now they got down to the business of jungle patrols against the communist insurgents. They were taken from the camp by helicopters – Whirlwinds and Sycamores. The latter were very unreliable with many accidents and Reuben witnessed one drop 1000 feet, both pilot and navigator being killed. The Sycamores were then withdrawn, as no one wanted to go near them.

They used Sarawak headhunters, the Iban, from Borneo as the trackers. They did use dogs but dogs got infections from thorns and thus were unreliable. The Sarawaks though proved very effective trackers and became essential to the Army. If any one of them said 'do not move', the battalion soon learnt to listen intently. Sarawak Rangers got the best the Army could provide, such as the Remington Winchester Shotgun. They were ruthless and they would decapitate communists when they came across them. Reuben had pictures of decapitated communist insurgents but the SIS (now MI6) confiscated them from Reuben before he returned to England. He also remembers that when the Sarawaks were

A Gunong

A pig bogged down

SECTION 1: ARMY

The offending Helicpoter

Python taken in village

The tiger cub

Iban – Sarawak Rangers from Borneo
Nine kills recorded on the board

Communist Prisoners

Sawarak Rangers

SECTION 1: ARMY

paid they would go and have holes cut into the enamel of their four front teeth. These would be in the shape of a diamond, heart, club and spade and they would have been fitted with a piece of enamel to the appropriate colour and every time they smiled it was 'like of pack of cards been flashed at you.'

The communist insurgents were armed with weapons and other war materiel that they had dug up from old caches ironically put there by the British Army during World War Two. Their weapons were not reliable but this was offset by their efficient and deadly tracking skills. Reuben remarked that when you captured a communist they always seemed to have a photograph of you. They took them when you passed, unknowingly, one of their positions. They also used booby traps; even rigging dead comrades with a finger placed inside the pin of the grenade, so that when you inspected the body and pulled it over – boom! So as a rule, you carefully felt underneath the body first. Reuben witnessed communists brought in for interrogation. Blindfolded, they were taken up in helicopters. Then they were slowly pushed out of the helicopter in order to make them talk. They were terrified and usually did talk, however, what they did not know was the helicopter was only 3 feet up and they were attached to it by a rope.

When out on patrol they used what they called a Pig – a 3-Bedford truck with a 1-inch armoured shell over it. 'Imagine being in that for several hours in the sun' Reuben commented. Around the camp were what were called Gunongs, small isolated mountains dotted throughout the jungle. At one, they found the remains of a Zero shot down in the last war with the dead pilot still there.

On another trip, they came to a village in a high state of excitement. This was due not to the nearby presence of communists as they first thought but to a giant python that had eaten the village pig. One lad took control, cut the python's head off and pulled the pig out. While still whole, it was dead and so the villagers had to be content in just cooking it and eating it then and there. They gave the lad the snakeskin. On one patrol, they came across an orphaned tiger cub and brought it in. It was later sent to Bellevue zoo.

They worked with a number of other units especially the 2/6 Queens Own Ghurkha Rifles. Reuben had the chance to witness the Ghurkha Dashera Ceremony. This was an annual ceremony and consisted of cutting the heads off various animals. This had to be done in one single strike otherwise; it brought bad luck to the unit. The Ghurkha chosen had to practice this one crucial act all year. As soon as the heads were cut off, they were placed in front of Ghurkha's guns and rifles to bring good fortune to the regiment for another year.

A group of American soldiers arrived with an arrogant attitude towards the jungle. They agreed to go on a forced march with a British patrol led by SAS

*Ghurka Dashera ceremony
(pictures from
Reuben Boyd)*

Odeon Cinema at Iboh

officers. Reuben did not go on this patrol but after two weeks in the jungle, the Americans were desperate to leave while the British were still fine. The Americans were withdrawn.

There were also Australians at Ipoh. The rubber plantation surrounding the camp was divided into black and white areas. The black areas had a curfew and anyone caught in them after dark would be shot on sight. A young rubber plantation worker, a girl of no more than 18 years old, wandered by accident in to such a black area. The Aussies, who were 'nervous and trigger-happy', machine gunned her to death. After that, the Loyals did not much want anything to do with Aussies. There had been no mistaking who she was and they felt the response was over the top.

Reuben described what it is like when you got back off patrol. You are bearded and covered in sores and bites. The leeches were the worse. They could get through the lace eyelets of your Robin Hoods (Green boots). You had to take your boots off very carefully. You used a lit cigarette to get the leeches off and then rubbed salt into the wound. They still left scars. As soon as you were shaved and cleaned up, you were off up to Ipoh to wind down.

Reuben's favourite place in Ipoh was the 'Federal Muslim Restaurant' and here he had his first curry. He got the curry sauce and chicken separately. Unaware of the true nature of the sauce, he took a big spoon of it, thinking it was like soup. He was soon in the kitchen with his mouth under the tap. He did remember with affection the local Tiger beer.

The town was under curfew except to British troops. Much of the town was poor, made of wood and attap but it did have one cinema. There was also a NAAFI run by a woman in her forties. Despite her age, she was feted by the young troops; and so many wanted to go out with her, that she kept a book. The reason for the interest in her may be due to the fact that among the local young women VD (Venereal Disease) was rife. The locals were poor and to make money offered girls as young as 12–13 years old in the local brothels, however to go there was lethal. This was the land of the 'virgin soldiers'.

Reuben was appointed to the town patrol with Sergeant O'Shea from Southern Ireland. O'Shea hated the English. He was 6ft 6in, a bully and was out to get anyone who was English. Reuben recalls one lad, Spud Murphy who despite the name was English and had got on the wrong side of O'Shea. Spud was one of those lads who always had a smile and O'Shea took exception to this. He made him, as a punishment, dig holes in the heat of the day with no water and, he made Spud refill and dig them again if they were not a perfect square.

On one night out, they met up with some New Zealanders strong handsome Maori lads. A Loyals lad, called Power from Liverpool, for no real reason, stuck a broken bottle in the face of one of these New Zealanders. He was arrested and got life for it, but even so the Loyals were strongly advised not to go downtown until the New Zealanders had moved on.

Reuben admitted that the British soldiers did treat the locals badly. They took an arrogant attitude towards them on the grounds they were there to protect them. He remembers one incident, where he and a friend came out of a bar very drunk and took a trishaw each and started a trishaw race. (A trishaw is three-wheeled rickshaw.) They decided to race them up to the camp and they cajoled and whipped the drivers. Reuben's trishaw won. His friend's response, despite the desperate pleas of its owner, was to throw his trishaw into a nearby pool

Soon after arriving at Colombo Camp, Reuben joined the MT and took his test. He learned in a Land Rover Mark 1. The hardest part was learning to drive at night. He remembers being taken to a local rubber plantation on one such night to practice. The trees are in straight lines but the gap between them is only just wide enough for a Landrover to get through. There was barely any margin for error. His instructor told him to switch his lights off and drive through. Reuben said he was terrified, it was pitch black and he had to drive a mile this way. His only consoling thought was if he died so would his sergeant.

Passing, Reuben was appointed driver to the MTO (Motor transport officer). This was Lieutenant (Quarter-Master) Matthieson, a large fat man, with ginger

Another view of Iboh, showing the trishaws

hair, with the exception of his yellowing moustache, yellowing from smoking. He was a good man and Reuben, as his driver, did not now need to go jungle bashing. MTO officers do not go into forward positions and danger, although Reuben occasionally still had to do some jungle patrols.

After six months, Reuben asked for a posting to Kuala Lumpur with the RAF. He had heard that the RAF had a far easier time than the army and much to his surprise, his MTO agreed.

He left Ipoh and took the train to Kuala Lumpur. It was a 3-day journey and he noted that engine pulling the train was an English Electric 'Deltic' Diesel made in Preston. The coach he was in was packed full of people, chickens and goats, so he did not sleep for the three days. On arriving at Kuala Lumpur, he found, proper barracks, better food and yes, the RAF did have it better. He also had a boy assistant called Mohammed who insisted on doing everything for him. Reuben struggled to stop him from doing so but these were very poor people and as Reuben explained, they wanted to try to do as much as they could just to please.

He got a chance at Kuala Lumpur to witness the arrival of the first jet flight to Malaya – a BOAC Comet. It had taken 18¾ hours, which was an improvement over the week flight to Singapore that the Loyals had made in old piston engine aircraft.

NAAFI Colombo Camp Iboh Reuben 2ⁿᵈ Right (Front)

Reuben now drove a Land rover, registration 95BF26, which he kept immaculately clean. This was thanks to the Ghurkhas who had set the example for all to follow by keeping their trucks immaculate. He did have one scary moment when he came off the road into a paddy field. It was in a black area with the night curfew fast approaching. He was thus relieved when the REME turned up to get him out.

He was also the driver to three officers including an Australian Major with a quick temper. On one occasion, he was in hurry to pick them up and on arrival at the camp gate; he honked his horn to try to speed up the opening of the gate. The RAF Military Police sergeant came out and made him wait, pointing out to him that he, the sergeant, was in charge and Reuben better had not to forget it. He was thus late to pick up the officers. The Australian Major was furious and when he discovered the cause, he had Reuben stop at the gate, while he got out and told the sergeant in' no uncertain terms' clearly who was in charge. The sergeant never bothered Reuben again after that.

On leave, Reuben managed to visit Penang Island for a week. He described it as stunningly beautiful. He also got a chance to visit the famous Batu caves at Kuala Lumpur. In the pitch black of these caves, there was a large lagoon with eyeless fish. In one huge cavern, there was a Chinese Temple.

When the emergency in Malaya was over the Loyals packed up and were ordered back to the UK. They boarded the troopship 'TT Nevassa' at Penang and after 31 days reached at Southampton. They then got a month's leave before being sent to Germany for six months. They took the train to Dover via London, before boarding the ferry for the Hook of Holland. From there they went on to Wuppertal. While in Germany, Reuben was the driver to the battalion's second in command. Travelling around Reuben was amazed at how advanced Germany was, he did not realise that they had autobahns (motorways), overhead railways etc. He also had a chance to go and see Belsen Concentration camp, which deeply moved him. On 21st March 1960, he was demobbed and returned to Preston.

He thoroughly enjoyed the experience. He felt it made him and he added 'was the best thing that happened to me'. Before he joined up he was like many young men, bored, drifting and heading for trouble. From the army he got sense of community. He appreciated life more and gained a proper sense of self-discipline. Reuben has, on a number of occasions risked his own life to rescue people on the motorway, for which on one occasion was he awarded a humanitarian medal.

Learning a trade as a driver benefited Reuben as he was able to work as a driver on leaving the army, first for British Road Services, then for different Bus firms, as well as chauffeuring Wedding cars. At the time of the interview Reuben worked for British Aerospace and drives part time for the bus company John Fishwick and Sons of Leyland. He also has a large collection of photographs showing the history of Loyals 1957–60 – which is second to none.

The first jet to land at Kula Lumpur. Photo taken by Reuben on its arrival

His boy assistant Mohammad

Reuben with his truck

In 2008, Rueben was awarded a new medal for those involved in Malayan Emergency – the Pingat Jasa Malaysia. The citation states,

> This medal is awarded to the Peacekeeping groups amongst the communion countries for distinguished service, gallantry sacrifice of loyalty in upholding the peninsular of Malaysia, or Malaysia sovereignty during the period of Emergency and Confrontation.

Cook in a Crisis

Chris Hill

Service No. 23002524

Born:	11 January 1933, Patterdale Farm, Caton
Service Dates:	Feb 1954–Dec 1956
Place of Enlistment:	Aldershot
Units:	Catering Corps
Main Theatres:	Egypt (Canal Zone) – Suez Crisis

Chris was born on Patterdale Farm, Caton, in 1933 and got his call up for National Service in 1954. He was allocated to the Catering Corps because of varicose veins! His initial two-week training was at the Ramillies Barracks and consisted of constant parades and drill work. As there was 4ft of snow on the ground at the time, he had to regularly change his kit as a result. He, like the others, struggled though to find the time to take their boots off. 'It was pretty wet inside those trousers,' Chris emphasized.

Total attention was demanded when on drill parade and Chris remembers that while on drill parade he just glanced up at an aeroplane passing overhead. Spotted by the Drill Sergeant, Chris was made to run round the parade, shouting, 'I am an aeroplane'.

One morning Chris reported sick with in growing toenails, but he discovered if you were sick all your possessions went into storage in case you did not come back. Chris did not like this and decided not to go sick again. After these initial two weeks, Chris was sent to Whittington Barracks, Lichfield, in Staffordshire, for three months basic training, Chris found it cold and inhospitable place, with cold draughty barracks. They dare not use the stove, as it had to be 'bulled up' for inspection each morning. They had only open troughs for washing and this was outside where the ground was still covered in snow. 'Just you try shaving in cold freezing weather', commented Chris.

As well as the obvious training in catering, he received instruction in the use of a Sten gun for self-defence. Chris was in the running team and this got him special privileges such as: special meal times, extra weekend home leave and no ground duties.

At the time many recruits were sent abroad to Korea or Egypt. Chris discovered though that he was going to Trieste, Italy. They sent him back to Aldershot to await travel information. He was to take a train to London, a boat to the Hook of Holland and then a train down the Rhine Valley to Villach, Austria. The journey from there was by bus with a trailer to Trieste.

He was stationed with the 2nd Battalion Lancashire Fusiliers at an old Italian barracks, known as the 'Rossetti Barracks'. After two months, the battalion was ordered back to England to be disbanded.

Chris's next posting was with the REME at Donnington, Staffordshire, to work in the officer's mess. After three months, he was informed that a fellow runner, a Captain Danten of the South Staffordshire Regiment wanted Chris back in Lichfield, with the South Staffs, as one of their runners. So it was Chris now joined the Sergeant's mess of the South Staffordshire, in Lichfield, running for the regiment. Chris enjoyed his time there, although he added on the down side the IRA was active at this time and this meant extra guard duties.

In February 1956, he left and joined the reserve, but just after getting married in August he was recalled to the colours because of the Suez crisis. He already had the necessary travel papers so collecting his pay at the post office; he set off for Longmoor, a large isolated camp in Hampshire. What struck Chris on his arrival was that all the trucks and tanks had already been painted sand colour indicating the invasion must have been planned months before. He was now part of the Liverpool Port Regiment. They remained at Longmoor until late October. Following a final weekend break at home, they then set sail from Southampton bound for Valetta, Malta. On their arrival, they were not allowed to leave the troopship. They heard that British aircraft had already started to bomb Egyptian airbases and other strategic targets.

When the troopships arrived in Egyptian waters, the sight was unbelievable. The sea was full of hundreds of boats waiting to unload men and vehicles. The French were also there. About mid morning, they were summoned on deck ready to disembark into landing craft. While waiting he stood his rifle and bandolier of ammunition on a gun site, only to discover when it was time to go that the bandolier had 'walked'. This was serious, as all ammunition has to be accounted for and instead of simply lifting one from someone else, he made the cardinal mistake of asking anyone if they had seen it. Thus, the whole group knew he was missing a bandolier. Panic-stricken he went to RSM and told him about the missing bandolier. The RSM replied that he would be standing at the top of the gangplank on disembarkation and Chris had better have one. If not he would face an automatic court martial? Chris then sent off to the other end of the ship to locate one. He found one but felt bad about doing the 'dirty deed' of taking it, but he did not want to end up in Cyprus on a court marital charge. The RSM at the gangplank did not ask questions, just nodded and Chris got down into the landing craft. They then set of for the short journey to the shore.

Port Said had been heavily bombed and the port was largely deserted. Chris with others were billeted in a large deserted private house, with a garden. Sleeping arrangements were the floor, or what you could lay your hands on. Your rifle was your bedmate. After a night on the floor, it was a case of rolling around to loosen up the bones. Chris's duties were either cooking on G 10 equipment in the garden, or down at the docks working in a small galley, making meals for the stevedores unloading the ships. This lasted three weeks until Chris got diarrhoea and thus didn't cook for a week. By this time, they were now in tents in the garden. They were issued with 50 cigarettes and beer rations. On one occasion, some of those who did not drink gave their beer to a Scotsman, who then got very drunk and started to brandish a loaded rifle. 'It was quite hairy at the time, but we eventually got him calmed down and disarmed,' Chris commented

For the next three months, catering responsibilities filled his time except for occasional swimming trips. Eventually an agreement with the USA ended the operation and in December 1956, they were on their way home. Chris embarked on *HMS Theseus*, an aircraft carrier. On the voyage back, the swell

At Port Said

was so bad in the Bay of Biscay that the deck was almost level with the sea – it was not pleasant. At Southampton, they entered port with the sailors manning the rails, flags flying from bow to stern and all sirens blasting. It was Christmas Eve and thus Chris was back in time to celebrate Christmas with his new wife Eileen. 'The whole trip was an experience' he added, 'but not one to be repeated!'

Grenadier Guards

The Grenadier Guards were founded in 1656 as Lord Wentworth's Regiment at Bruges (Belgium). They were part of King Charles II's bodyguard and hold the title as the most senior infantry regiment in the British Army. Later, as the 1st regiment of Foot they earned by Royal Proclamation the title of the Grenadier Guards following their part in the defeat of the French Imperial Grenadiers at Waterloo. For their service during the Great War, Guardsman replaced the rank of Private on the orders of the King. During its long history it has, won 79 battle honours with thirteen Guardsmen awarded the VC. The Colonel in chief is always the reigning sovereign.

In the following pages are the accounts of three Grenadier Guards, Jack Phillips (1946), George White (1953–57) and John Spooner (1986–91). We have grouped these accounts as it gives a perspective of this regiment's life over 45 years. Jack was a volunteer and involved in the Palestine police action, where injuries sustained in action shortened his career. George was a National Serviceman

Guardsman John Spooner

who joined the Guards and served in the Canal Zone. John volunteered in 1987 and served in Northern Ireland, as well as being in Kenya, Canada and Belize for training. To his disgust, he was in South Georgia when the First Gulf War broke out and so missed the action. His expression of his disgust reveals the real sense of professionalism that all three reveal in their accounts. It was obvious in talking to all three that to be a Guardsman meant a great deal. They all talk of the very hard training that formed them into Guardsmen alongside the strong comradeship that it brings. George reveals also what being an ex-Guard means after you leave the service.

'Not So Armless Guardsman'

Jack Phillips

Service No 2628995

Born:	February 1929
Service Dates:	1946
Place of Enlistment:	Preston
Units:	Grenadier Guards 1st Battalion. 4th Company
Awards:	Defence Medal, Victory Medal and Palestine Medal and a medal especially presented by Nijmegen to Grenadier Guards.
Main Theatres:	Palestine

It had always been Jack's intention to join the Army. He had lost a brother in the war, Sergeant Douglas Phillips. Douglas had joined the Royal Signals and was later attached to the SOE (Special Operations Europe). As a SOE operative, Douglas was dropped into Greece in 1942 to destroy Gorgopotamos Bridge. This was the main German supply route to North Africa and it was a matter of great strategic importance that supplies were disrupted for several weeks before El Alamein. Greek roads were notoriously bad, so the Germans always transported their supplies by rail. The Gorgopotamos Rail Bridge, a curved structure, was chosen as the most difficult to repair. In fact, it took six months for the bridge to be repaired after its destruction, by which time the North African campaign was over. This event is still commemorated in Greece. Douglas then linked up with Greek resistance and he was later killed on 24th May 1944 while attempting to blow up another bridge. Jack had a second brother, Eric, who served with the South Lancs. in the D-Day landings. There is a photo of Eric on the D-Day beach, which was used by the Sun Newspaper for its front-page celebration of D-Day landings, 2004 (7th June).

Jack tried to join up when he was 15. At the recruiting office, he was not sure what to join and just pointed to a poster of the colourful Gordon Highlanders and asked to join them. His National Insurance card though gave his age away. Thus, it was not until 1946, when he was 17, that he was finally able to sign up at Preston and this time to join the Guards.

Basic Training was very tough and discipline was very hard, but without the need of obscene language. Defaulters were made to run around the parade ground until they physically dropped. Overall Jack felt that although it was very tough, when he looked back, he felt it 'made you' and would not have it any other way.

Jack remembers the CO, Major Bowes Lyon – 'a great bloke', Jack noted and added, 'He was a great help in getting me compassionate leave when my father was ill.' After 16 weeks basic training at Caterham they were moved to a Training Battalion at Pirbright, Surrey. He was promoted to Lance Corporal and in May 1947, joined the 1st Battalion at Windsor for Guard duty at the Castle. As an NCO, his job, six hours on, six hours off was with posting new sentries every two hours. In addition, Jack had to be ready at all times to accompany the Captain of the Guard for the inspection of the sentries. Jack really liked his time at Windsor and saw King, George VI on a number of occasions. He remembers though that he once came up to the gate and realized he had forgotten the key. He asked an 'old hand' what he should do. He replied, 'Check the King is not looking out and just jump the Gate.' He looked and then jumped the Gate. He discovered later that this was quite common occurrence.

In November, their battalion was sent to Palestine to relieve the 3rd Battalion. Jack was in the 4th Company, which formed the advance party to start the changeover. This always took time, as the advance party has to acquire the local knowledge and procedures from the existing battalion before its own battalion arrived. The battalion's role was mainly security such as manning roadblocks and escorting illegal Jews to ships. Jack said they got on really well with the local Arabs but had to be aware of the serious threat from local Jewish terrorist attacks. The battalion was based at Netanyu and shortly after they arrived, Jack was involved in a firefight – an action that would lead to ending of Jack's army career.

A fellow Guardsman Frank Sergeant's wrote the following account of the action.

> At Netanyu, we had a Sandbagged Bren gun position guarding the camp's main entrance. Covering the rear was a watchtower, another Bren and a searchlight, which took three minutes to warm up. One night the Arabs attacked through the Orange groves to the rear. The searchlight did not work and the Bren jammed. They got into the Guardroom, just as Corporal Phillips was about to change sentries. After a brief exchange of fire, he was hit in the shoulder and later lost his arm through gangrene. The Arabs got away. (*Once a Grenadier*, by Oliver Lindsay, 1996)

Jack feels it was more likely they were Jewish terrorists after weapons rather than Arabs. In addition, Jack did not lose his arm, as Frank suggests. He was bandaged up by a friend, who had just done a stretcher-bearers course and then sent onto the military hospital. As the Palestine Mandate ended in May 1948, he was evacuated on a hospital boat from Haifa to Tel El Kebir in Egypt, while the rest of the battalion was sent to Tripoli.

Although not yet fully fit, Jack was discharged from hospital and moved to a Transit Camp at Port Said. From there, he was sent on to join up with his battalion at Tripoli. As he was not fit, he did light duties. His arm had been saved by an operation to transfer flesh from the waist to the shoulder. This had gone wrong and the wound kept going rotten. He was now going back and forth to Hospital for treatment and in the end, it was decided to repatriate him. He was sent first to a Hospital in Malta, before being returned to England and Netley Hospital. From Netley (South England) he was sent to the Military Hospital at Chester. While on his way from Netley Hospital to the local railway station Jack meet, either a Scot in the Irish Guards or Irishman in the Scots Guard, who was in need of help. Therefore, Jack gave him his (healthy) helping hand. While doing so, a young lady passed by on her bike. She stopped and picked up Jack's kitbag and while Jack helped his fellow Guardsman, she carried the bag for Jack to the station and left before Jack could thank her. He has always remembered vividly the young lady and her kindness.

At Chester, to Jack's disappointment, they decided to discharge him from the army. Jack recalls that despite his plea that he still could do a reasonable present arms, it fell on deaf ears. His final order was 'Turn to your right, but

'Where is the Grenadier?' Queen (Colonel in Chief) greets Jack at
Royal Garden Party

don't salute, your arm might fall off'. Thus ended what Jack had hoped would be a career in the Guards, it had not worked out. It was now 1950 and Jack came home, met and married his wife and had four children and nine grandchildren. He worked at a local Ironworks in Silloth, but when the new Prison opened, he joined up as a Prison Officer. He said many of the officers were ex-serviceman and he thoroughly enjoyed the work until he retired. He did not forget the Guards. He joined the Grenadier Guards Association and after 12 years concentrating on bringing up his family, he turned to becoming fully involved in the Association. 'It is less an association,' Jack stated, 'more a 'family'.' Meetings were held every month and it had that atmosphere of a family get together. Each branch has a welfare officer and Jack stressed it is hard to put into words the sense of comradeship one has, first through the regiment and then in the association. Even if you served with your comrades a long time ago, the intensity of comradeship never leaves you – you 'feel for another' and a sense of comradeship that goes all the way to the top to the Colonel in chief herself. Jack remembers at a Royal Garden Party, the Duke of Edinburgh spotted Jack's Association badge and tie. He informed the Queen, 'there is a Grenadier here.' Her Majesty immediately came over with outstretched hand asking 'where is the Grenadier, where is the Grenadier?'

One of most important events for Association and Guards as a whole is the Black Sunday Remembrance. Black Sunday is when a V1 flying bomb hit the Guards Chapel, Wellington Barracks on June 18th 1944. 119 people were killed, 102 were seriously injured and a further 39 received minor injuries. A survivor recalled, 'One moment I was singing the 'Te Deum' and the next I lay in dust and blackness, aware of one thing only – that I had to go on breathing... my eyes rested with horror on a blood-stained body... of a young soldier whose eyes stared unseeingly at the sky.'

The Guards remember this event every year with a service at the Chapel and march with the band to the Memorial on Horse Guards Parade. An Irish Guardsman pulled an ATS woman, Jane Knight, out of the ruins of the chapel that day. Ever since, she always follows the Guards on their march. At time of the interview Jack was involved in work with the local Weal Museum. This museum has exhibits on local industry, the RAF and a 'Guards Room', to celebrate the Guard regiments.

'It Is Lot Easier To Get In Than Out'

George White

Guardsman
Service No 22545993

Born: 25th January 1936
Service Dates: 15th September 1953–late 1956 /early 1957
Place of Enlistment: Carlisle
Units: 2nd Battalion Grenadier Guards
Awards: General Service Medal
Main Theatres: Canal Zone

On joining the Grenadier Guards in September 1953 for his National Service, George was sent to the Guards Depot, Caterham for 3 months basic training. 'Not easy', he said, 'I had two 'left legs'.' Just before Christmas, George was sent on to Pirbright (near Brookwood) for three months advanced training. This was tough and there were a number of attempted suicides although mainly out of a fear of going overseas. He remembered that at 11.15pm he was laying on his bunk when he heard a bang – a fellow in a nearby bunk had shot himself in the leg so he would not go overseas.

After Pirbright, George moved to Pickering, Yorkshire, for live firing and the 'final toughening up before returning to Pirbright to be issued with K.D. (Khaki Drill), tropical kit and injections in readiness for overseas service.

They boarded the troop train at Brookwood and headed for Liverpool, where they embarked on the MV Cheshire bound for Port Said. After not a good passage, their arrival at Port Said was greeted by no food! The 2nd battalion was ordered to send out its wagons to locate the food, under armed escort, armed with Sten guns but with just four magazines only! George and his fellow recruits sent with the wagons had not yet been issued with ammo for their arms; therefore, they were told that if attacked they had to get out, lie down and leave it to the other escorts.

After their arrival at Port Said, the battalion was driven to St Pierre Barracks, Fayid, to begin their week's familiarization with the climate. The accommodation was tents and it was hard to sleep in them due to the heat. The canteen was just four tents put together. What stuck in George's mind were the lunches, rehydrated kippers, peas and potatoes. The latter if not rehydrated properly could break the plate as it was slopped on.

Duties consisted of night patrols, roadside patrols and 'pachyderm patrols' – the latter were sweeps for terrorists. One of their guard duties was the Abu Sultan ammunition dump. After been dropped off by a Bren carrier, they swept the ground as they went in. This was in order that 'foreign' footprints could be seen the following morning.

Returning from one such guard duty the guardsmen started passing out. Panic swept the camp with a fear that a terrorist had poisoned the water supply. Actually, it turned out to be the cook. He had cut his finger in making up the milk and subsequently poisoned them all. George was in hospital for ten days, constantly being sick and on the runs at the same time. On arrival at hospital and getting into bed, the Nurse told him to immediately get out and take a shower!

On his return from Hospital, he found that the battalion had moved to Ordnance Base Depot (half an hour from the barracks). They now were working alongside the Mauritian Pioneer corps. They got friendly and one day asked them to join them for tea. Rations were tea and two slices of bread (which George adds was more like half a loaf) but this was still better than what the Mauritians got, which was only a handful of peanuts! The Mauritians made the tea, while George and his companions shared out their rations with them.

At the Sea view Holiday Camp 11th July 1955 Aubrey Eales (Left) Co or Major Ways Batman (centre) and George White (right)

Life was still guard duty and patrols but they did build a rifle range just outside the barracks. With two thirds of it finished, they had a NAAFI break. When they got back, all the sandbags had gone. Therefore, they got more and at the next break left Tom Walker with a Bren gun to watch over it. As they had their break, they heard firing and when they got back, Tom had the thief with his hands up.

One did not hear much of what was going on elsewhere, George stressed. He does remember a support company sent to Petra (Jordon), but the wagon turned over and six men were killed. They held a 'Drumhead Service' on the rifle range for these men. (A drumhead service is when all drums are marched up, stacked and the service is held around them.) Even so, George added, nothing was seen or heard officially about this incident.

George heard that the job of battalion silverman was available and applied for it. The main responsibility was simply keeping the battalion silver clean. He then heard that the Captain needed a batman so he went for this job instead and was successful. He moved, as new batman, to Port Said. Hostilities had now been declared over (October 1954). This meant coming off 'active service' on to 'general service' – which meant losing your overseas allowance – a real cut in pay.

At Port Said, they moved from the Golf Course camp across the water to 156 Transit Camp, Port Fouad. Most batmen were here as it was close to officer families, but later George moved into the captain's family flat. A batman became a general housekeeper but was fed well, looked after and allowed to use the Seaview Holiday camp, for swimming and drinking. George was proud of his work as batman, his officer, Captain Anderson, was always immaculately turned out.

After a year, it was time to return to England. The battalion embarked on the troopship Devonshire and picked up the Horse Guard detachment at Famagusta. The 2nd Battalion would be the last full battalion to leave the Canal Zone. They arrived back at Liverpool and while the battalion went onto Chelsea, George got leave. After his leave, he rejoined the battalion at Pickering and continued as Captain Anderson's batman. As batman, one tried to keep a low profile from the rest of the army. One day though he did have to come to the depot with the Captain. As soon as he entered the Duty Sergeant seized him, with the words, 'we have got you" George was overdue for many medicals and the sergeant had arranged them to be all done that day.

Demobilization now beckoned and George was definitely feeling demob happy. While watching the trooping of the colour at Pickering from a window and thinking of his future after the army, he was approached by a Brigadier who told him he would write to his officer, offering George the job of handyman and driver on his demobilization. George was immediately warned by others to avoid such offers; it was just an opportunity for cheap labour. Therefore, George decided to do a police course but before he could do so, he came down with laryngitis and was dispatched to hospital. There, they asked him if he would like to be a 'guinea pig' – no way, he wanted nothing to get in the way of his demob. On returning from the hospital, he was surprised to be immediately arrested by the Sergeant Major (Irish Guards) for going AWOL. Brought before the CO, he showed him his discharge papers from Catterick infirmary and thus escaped an injustice and the threat to his demob day – just two weeks away.

The CO's (Major Graham) batman, Sandy invited George out for a night out to celebrate their imminent demob. A Lieutenant Cobbles joined them and they had a great evening out.

Next morning Sandy and George were again arrested by the Sergeant Major with the words 'got you now!' They were charged with smashing windows of the sergeant and officer's messes and shouting and disturbing the peace, with the Sergeant Major acting as the witness. They denied it and it was referred for further investigation.

The next day they were brought before the CO, where he informed them that a brother officer had admitted to it. This was Lt Cobbles, who after they had left him at the end of evening, had gone on a rampage around the camp. The case was thus dismissed, but the Sergeant Major was called in for a telling off in no uncertain terms. He could have ruined these lads' lives if the charge had stuck.

So despite these two 'hiccups', demobilization day had finally come and George headed down to the station at Scarborough, only to be stopped by the duty sergeant major and told to report back to barracks. 'What now?' George

George (now oil drilling engineer) in the Libyan Desert, with a Boyes Anti-tank gun found left over from the war

thought. On getting back, the whole battalion was marched up before the CO to hear the Queen's Proclamation declaring a state of emergency (Suez Crisis), there was to be no demob.

It would be another 101 days before finally at Aldershot he got his demob suit, shoes, collar and tie, socks and topcoat. He almost thought he would never get out, but he was demobbed at last.

George found being ex-Army and in particular ex-Guards opened doors for him in terms of work. He joined an oil company, first as an explosives expert in oil prospecting and then as he leant the trade he became a drilling engineer. He worked in Libya for 17 years until the arrival of Gaddafi and then in Sudan for eight years. He admits he saw more action here than in National service. One of the worst moments for him was when terrorists kidnapped one of his European workers. Through tense negotiations, the worker was finally released. It could be scary in this work, George stressed, but his motto through these years was 'One may be prepared to die for one's country but not for one's company.'

A Natural but a Hard Choice

John Spooner

Corporal Guardsman
Service Number 24783047

Born:	13th December 1967
Service Dates:	February 1986–September 1991
Place of Enlistment:	Manchester
Units	2nd Battalion Grenadier Guards
Awards:	Campaign Service Medal, clasp Northern Ireland Guards Depot – best shot medal
Main Theatres:	Northern Ireland, Kenya, Belize, Canada, South Georgia

John is six foot five inches tall so when he joined the army he was a natural choice for the guards. One had to go through six hard months of basic training before getting into a battalion. His uncle Eric who had been in the Korean War helped him. *"Take each day at a time"*, he told John, *"Do not think of the long term and just try to understand the logic of whatever was happening."* This helped John through what was very severe basic training. John said that recruits were gradually broken down by sleep deprivation and the constant demands made on them. They were constantly nodding off when trying to clean their kit. They would be woken in the middle of the night, the barrack room trashed by a NCO and they would have to sort it out straight away. They could be hit in the forehead, which drove the pins in their caps into the flesh, or alternatively hit on the head while wearing a helmet, which equally caused bleeding. If a recruit failed tests on the assault course, he could then be 'back squadded'. This meant he faced an extra month of training. Harassment by NCOs was

John with his GMPG in Northern Ireland

constant and on one occasion while they were cleaning kit a corporal came in and challenged any member of the squad to a fight. Eventually a 7ft 4in recruit accepted the challenge, knocked the corporal out and threw him out of the barrack room. This constant pressure proved too much for most of the men and many recruits dropped out or were rejected on medical grounds. Of John's group of 74, three committed suicide and only six passed out.

John's first posting was to Northern Ireland at the height of the troubles. He was armed with a GPMG (General Purpose Machine Gun) and patrolled the streets. They also did 'lay ups' which is where they would bring in the SAS to do a close assault. John's company also did attacks and he described an incident when they were called to an isolated farm where armed terrorists were supposed to be dealing in drugs. The area was surrounded at night and an attack plan was developed. John and his mate Rob were to go to the back, wait for a green signal flare, knock down the door and prepare to kill any combatants. John said that the GPMG took the standard 7.62mm bullet but he instead filled a 200 round belt with alternate tracer and armour piercing rounds. The latter had a range of three miles and could travel clean through a house. With the high rate of fire, they could literally cut a man in half. While waiting for the signal Rob, who was an atheist, started asking John who is a catholic, if

John (right) and his mate Rob 1987

there might be an afterlife. He replied that they might be soon finding out! When the signal light went off John said he had an almost mystical experience. His senses were so heightened that his vision became so acute that it seemed to him as if was daylight. When the door went down everything seemed to be in slow motion and he seemed to have plenty of time to sweep the interior and watch other members of the squad coming in through other doors and windows. The only occupant was an old farmer with a pipe in his hand looking at them with wide-eyed astonishment. This had obviously been a false report, but John said that the IRA often did it this way as a means of testing the readiness of the British troops and in the hope that they might kill an innocent civilian, sparking increased anti British feeling.

John said that other units such as the paras and marines were less careful. The Guards, if they came under fire in a built up area, would search it house by house. The Marines and Paras, he said, would simply respond with overwhelming fire, which might well kill innocent civilians. Despite the danger and tension, the army could still demonstrate a sense of humour. On Christmas Eve, before going on patrol John's NCO told them to get candles, mats and hymn books. Then they went to a well-known IRA man's house. His mother opened the door and gave them a torrent of abuse. She then went and got her son. When he got to the front door, he was greeted by a 'brick' of seven soldiers holding candles and kneeling down singing 'We wish you a merry Christmas'.

John's company commander was Lord Valentine Cecil the third, who John added, was incredibly rich and claimed that the army was just a hobby and a lovely game to play! He was quite a character and always carried a swordstick. Lord Cecil would frequently leave Ireland for England by private jet, to get back there in time for tea and cakes. He did though help John with his dyslexia through a school he owned.

In early 1989, the battalion was sent to Kenya to take part in what was billed as the biggest live exercise since World War Two. One of his first impressions was of the Masai whose land was to be obliterated. The Masai

G Company North Ireland

looked on with disgust. John had every sympathy for them. The exercise was a brigade level attack. As they advanced, John could see long lines of troops to the right and left. The attack was supported by mortars and artillery operated by a New Zealand regiment. The burst radius of the shells was 250 metres and the infantry was within 300 metres of the explosions. Officers were constantly talking on their radios giving the distances that they had covered, at the regulation 22in pace, so that the barrage could be gradually lifted and moved forward. Even so, John could feel the heat of the blasts as they were showered with dust and stones. Dummy enemy trenches were taken by using close range small arms fire and grenades. John was armed with a Karl Gustav rocket launcher and was told to fire at a trench 200 metres away. The Karl Gustav was a powerful weapon, difficult and dangerous to use. His number two had to arm the rocket, load it and check that no one was within 40 metres behind as they could be burned. He then grabbed John round the waist so that he could resist the recoil and shout 'clear'. John would shout 'stand back' and 'firing now' at which, every one nearby would cover their ears and open their mouths. Failing to do so could result in severe injuries to the eyes and nose because of the suction effect of the blast. As they watched the rocket spiralling towards the target, they were horrified to see a section attacking the trench from the flank. Fortunately, it quickly dived for cover. The NCO commanding it was furious and pointed an accusing finger at John to which he responded by putting two fingers on his left shoulder suggesting an officer's pips and that he had been following orders. Later on, while John was carrying the medical bag he was called to a genuine casualty. An NCO had thrown a L2 grenade but it had hit a bush, bounced back and exploded nearby. His chest had been ripped open by some of the 7000 ball bearings. A spray of blood came out of his chest when he breathed, but John was able to stop the flow of blood and aid his breathing until a helicopter arrived, he survived. Even after training had been completed, NCOs could still play the martinet, but in so doing, they ran the risk in action of being killed by 'friendly fire'. John describes a unit that waited for a sergeant to be out in front of them. Then they each fired a full clip of blanks in his direction. He took the hint and transferred out!

While in Africa, John's squad camped within yards of a hillock occupied by a tribe of baboons. These particularly strong and aggressive creatures are more than prepared to protect their territory. One night the squad decided to have a laugh and it was agreed that the man who could get nearest to the top of the hillock would win a case of beer. Each soldier in turn put on a flak jacket and helmet and ran forward to be greeted by a hail of accurately thrown rocks. When he had received as much punishment as he could take, he planted his stake to mark his advance and withdrew. In each interval, the baboons came forward to collect thrown rocks and returned to the top of the hill to wait the next attack. Not just human troops can set up a well-organized defence.

After Kenya, John was on exercise in Canada. The area over which they were to operate was declared clear by the marshal of the range. Then a previously unexploded shell blew up two soldiers while digging a trench in the area. One of them was literally blown to pieces, while the other lost both legs. Remarkably, he returned to duty and John saw him months later at a depot completing the basic fitness test, a one and a half mile run in ten and a half minutes on his artificial legs.

On completing two years service John had the option of signing for extra time or for him to go on open engagement. John chose the latter, which meant he would be on less money but could leave when he wanted. John decided to join the reconnaissance team, which meant that he had to do the Basic fitness test in eight minutes in full kit. It also meant a lot more training in map reading, shooting, use of enemy weapons and silencers. He said that he was also removed from the electoral register, so if he was captured or killed on covert operations, he would officially not exist. He was then sent to Belize where the team operated in four man or two man units. They exercised with the US marines, with whom John was not impressed. The Guards did not wear waterproofs because they made a noise. They moved everywhere slowly

John Spooner – Ceremonial duties

and without speaking, while the marines on the other hand chatted and allowed equipment to clash. Consequently, in the exercises against one another the Guards found it easy to outmanoeuvre them, ambush them and to lead them into booby traps. He said that the marines were all 'gung ho' but this did not extend to being under fire.

The jobs undertaken were mainly reconnoitring drug-making factories in the jungle defended by armed gangsters. They would record movements and then bring in an air strike or a ground attack on the factories. The camouflage that they used was so good that John reckoned he could not be seen if he kept still. If the enemy were close by he would also look down so the glint in his eyes could not be seen.

The US marines, John remembers were once spotted and fired upon. The last John saw of them 'was them running wide eyed through the Guards position to the rear.'

Ceremonial duties were never a priority for John but he took part in the Trooping of the colour and sentry duties in 1988, 1989 and 1990. In 1988 he was a 'guttersnipe', that is he just guarded the route to Whitehall but in the 1989 and 1990 Trooping of the Colour he was part of the trooping itself. He was the company right marker. He added that there were coin size studs in the parade ground and each person had to hit their own exactly to join up properly. John also explained 'the phenomenon of the fainting guardsmen'. The general assumption is that it is a result of the thick heavy uniform and the hot weather. However, John said this was not the case. It was the tradition to have a drink on the previous night. The NCO's investigated any Guardsmen who subsequently passed out, would enquire if they had been drinking the night before and more significantly if they had any breakfast that morning. Failure to do the latter was the real cause for the faint and in that case, the Guardsman was duly fined £200.

As a sentry at Clarence House, he was stationed in a sentry box in the bright summer sun. A little while into his 'stag' and as the sweat poured down, he felt

Operation Mulberry Tree
8 - 22 AUG 1998

A 1-148 INS(M)

To all who shall see these presents, greeting:

This is to certify that the commander has authorized this

4BN QLR

Certificate of Excellence

to

FUS JOHN H. SPOONER

From the Joint American-British Task Force Command, in recognition for:

During the Iron Soldier Competition on 11 - 13 August 1998 FUS John H. Spooner on numerous occasions took it upon himself to ensure the safety and welfare of the soldiers participating at his station. Through his efforts numerous weather related injuries were avoided. Your actions were a sterling example for all to follow. FUS Spooner's actions during the competition have gained the respect and admiration of all the soldiers who participated in the event.

Given under my hand this 22nd day of August 1998.

1LT DAVID S. BAIRD
AMERICAN COMMANDER

Lt Col MJ SHEARMAN
BRITISH COMMANDER

Certificate of excellence

a tug on his sleeve. It was the Queen mother and the following conversation took place.

'My dear, go and stand in the shade',
'I can't do that the sergeant would go mad',
'You are guarding me and I am telling you to stand in the shade!'

John did and as John had anticipated the duty sergeant arrived and played hell. His explanation about the Queen Mother was seen as just insubordination and this compounded his guilt. Eventually however, the sergeant agreed to phone a lady in waiting to clear up the matter and John was vindicated.

One night John was on 'stag' in the gardens of Windsor Castle, in the middle of the night he heard a rustling near the outer wall and therefore moved to head off the intruders. He waited for them to approach and shone a bright torch into their faces. To his horror he found it was the Queen and a butler walking the dogs. He stammered an apology to which the Queen replied that he was just doing his job. The butler 'looked daggers' however. John expected trouble on his return to the guardroom. He was summoned to see the guard commander. He said he had received a telephone call and John had received a 'Queen's credit' which gave him a weekends leave.

In 1991 as the Gulf War, started John to his disgust found himself not in the Gulf but with the Reconnaissance Unit in South Georgia. As John put it, 'it is like going to college for years to become a bricklayer and then not being allowed to build a house.' Therefore, he decided to terminate his time in the army. His sergeant hit him when he told him and was later in tears as he was losing one of his best men.

After his discharge from Caterham barracks in September 1991, he joined the Fusilier Regiment (TA) in Manchester. During his time with them, he had the novel experience of training with US soldiers on Dartmoor. The weather was poor but as far as John was concerned, no worse than one could reasonably expect. There were also girls doing their Duke of Edinburgh's Award. The US soldiers though were becoming more demoralized. Therefore, John demonstrated his disdain for the weather by taking his clothes off for a while, but looking at the US troops, he concluded that he had to get them into cover and off the moor. For these services, he was stunned to receive two certificates of merit from the US Army.

Other Aspects of Post-War Army Life

This section begins with Alfred Wyatt's experiences. For his National Service Alfred joined the Parachute Regiment renowned for its hard physical and mental training. He thought they would be good as there would not be much marching as they were flown and in addition were paid more. On former he was to be disillusioned. He found the harshest training and selection process of any British Army regiment, which has led to Parachute regiment being one of the elite units of the Army. Its role is to operate behind enemy lines with minimal support and in outnumbered situations.

Following his time in the Paras, Alfred joined the Territorials – the part-time army. It forms one quarter of the army and consists of civilians who for a few weeks a year train to form an army reserve. The original Territorial Army was created in 1908, combining a civilian administered 'Volunteer Force' with the local Militia and Yeomanry forces. The force then had a strength of over 250,000 and was for home defence not for overseas service. The Great War (1914–18) altered that condition and TA regiments came into their own as good as regular units. Following the war, the Territorial Force was renamed the Territorial Army and reduced much in size, until the Second World War. During the war, it expanded from 130,000 to over 400,000 men serving as frontline troops all over the world.

After the war, the TA was maintained as the home defence force of considerable size but with the reduction of Army in 1967 the TA was reorganised into the smaller TAVR (Territorial and Army Volunteer Reserve) and sadly for its members, the old Regimental and divisional structures of the TA were abolished. In 1979, the title Territorial Army was restored and its regimental system slowly put back into place. With the smallness of the Regular Army and the high demands on its role in first decade of the 21st Century, the TA forces now find themselves regularly used for active service alongside the regulars in such wars as the Gulf Wars and other overseas police duties. The only rule for a TA solider is that he or she may not be used for more than 12 months active service in any three-year period.

The second account is of one TA solider, Tom Martindale, who gives an account of TA life in the early sixties. He reveals the great humour and fun of TA life. His account of Burial of Corporal Jones's Turd, must rate as one of the funniest stories of Army life recounted in this book. Tom's account also gives us an insight into the musical side of military life as he recalls his time as a member of the Corps of Drums.

The tradition of using 'fife and drum' to set marching pace as well as boost morale for British infantry regiments dates back to the 16th century, (see also Len Henson earlier account as a piper in Highland Regiment). By 1900, there was a fife and drum band with every infantry battalion but with cuts in the army after the 1960s, their numbers were reduced and bandsmen today need to double up as regular soldiers.

The final account is one of only three officers, who wished to tell their story Major (Regular) and Lt Colonel (TA) Mark Lodge. He gives an insight to officer training, in particular the humour that underlines much of British Army life and forms the solid core of comradeship that holds units together in action. It is obvious from all of these accounts that humour in the role of pranks is as important in army training as fitness and arms drill etc. Mark finally saw service as a TA officer in Iraq, doing a tour of duty in 2008.

Better Than Marching

Alfred George Wyatt (Lubeck 1948)

Private
Kings Own Royal Regiment/Parachute Regiment
Colour Sergeant, King's Own (TA) Lancaster

Born:	18th August 1929, Kendal
Service Dates:	September 1947–1949, 1949–1984(TA)
Place of Enlistment:	Bowerham Barracks, Lancaster
Units:	Kings Own Royal Regiment/Parachute Regiment and King's Own (TA)
Awards:	Territorial medal with two long service clasps
Main Theatres:	Germany, UK

Alfred was called up to do his National Service in September 1947 joining the Kings Own Royal Regiment. He was initially sent to Bowerham Barracks, Lancaster, before being sent up to No.1 Infantry Training Centre at Hadrian's Camp near Carlisle. He completed his basic training but because he had volunteered for the Parachute Regiment, he had to wait another couple of weeks

George top left

for the next intake for that regiment.

The reason he volunteered for the Paras he explained was that he thought 'he would not have to march as much because they fly everywhere.' In addition, their pay was considerably higher with the prospect of receiving an extra 2*s*. 6*d*. per day on top of the basic pay of £1 7*s*. 6*d*. per week.

He joined 23 squad made up of 50 volunteers from various infantry regiments and began training at Aldershot. He said the barracks were vast Victorian buildings with very little heating, few washing facilities and no sheets. On the first parade, the NCO told him to remove the marksman badges he had gained at Carlisle, as he had not qualified for them in this regiment. Alfred said that the food was atrocious and sparse and, despite the winter of 1947–48 being one of the worst on record, they only got one bucket of coal per day for their hut!

Training consisted of assault courses, weapon handling and drill. For the latter the only words of command were 'Right Marker' and then all evolutions were carried out to the drum. Recruits were gradually weeded out and 'returned to unit' (R.T.U). This could be for instance for not being sufficiently aggressive in the 'milling'; that is where they were lined up and had to punch each other to the ground. On one inspection in the barracks, one of Alfred's squad was considered to have grubby feet and was given the option of being R.T.U. or receiving the R.S.M.'s punishment. He chose the latter. The next day the squad formed three sides of a square with the defaulter, naked facing them. He was then doused with cold water and then scrubbed with floor brushes until he was raw. He was still R.T.U.!

Albert was put on a charge of extreme idleness on parade for not lifting his foot the regulation 12 inches and as a result received 14 days extra drill. All recruits had to see a psychiatrist where they did an inkblot test and wrote a story. From these the Psychiatrist concluded whether or not the recruit would 'jump'

SECTION 1: ARMY

and if not, he was immediately RTU. Having survived all this, Alfred went to Upper Heyford in Oxfordshire for his actual parachute training, which he enjoyed. Most of the NCOs at the time were veterans of World War Two and had been at either D-Day or Arnhem.

He had to jump twice from a balloon and then from a Dakota aircraft. A 'stick' of 16 men could be out in 10 to 15 seconds. The normal dropping height was 800 feet but this could be modified to 500 in action, where the increase in injuries due to the lower height it was argued would be compensated by a decrease of injuries from ground fire.

Wyatt (left) training near Thetford.

Care had to be taken on exiting the aircraft as your lines could become entangled. If this happened, you had to twist yourself rapidly round to untangle them. Alfred asked a sergeant what he should do if he could not untangle the lines; the reply was, 'Cross your feet so it will be easier to unscrew you out of the ground!' On one occasion, Alfred had a 'lazy chute,' that is one where the canopy does not deploy properly but he did not notice.

After getting his wings, he joined the 19th Independent Parachute Brigade at Lubeck West Germany, which then went to Nuremberg to train jointly with the American 1st Division in assault river crossings using boats. The Americans treated them very well but they had to stay in tents and eat compo rations rather than avail themselves of the luxuries of U.S. Army life.

During a period of leave at Bad Hartzburg he was arrested by Military Police for being improperly dressed – he was not wearing his beret. His CO Lt Col Cubbin dismissed the case however when Alfred persuaded him that it was local custom of the area not to wear headgear.

At the end of 1949, Alfred decided to leave because the regiment was returning to Aldershot.

His military career did not finish however as, like his father, uncle and cousin before him, he joined the King's Own (TA) in Lancaster which was later termed the Lancastrian Volunteers. The CO was Major Long, who had been in Italy in 9 Commando winning the Military Cross. The sergeant had been in the SAS. Alfred himself became Colour-Sergeant and led the shooting team to a number of victories using a SLR, (Self Loading Rifle). He later took charge of stores and supplies as the Quarter Master Sergeant.

As well as military manoeuvres in different parts of the country, they also had to train for the possibility of taking over from, or supplementing civil authorities in the event of a nuclear attack. Informed that if a warning were received the TA personnel would be moved to Scotland, presumably a nuclear attack was expected to exclude Scotland. From here they were to move down through England from North to South. They were to save whom they could and shoot anybody very badly injured.

In 1984, at the age of 55 Alfred received a letter saying that his services were no longer required. He was, understandably, insulted by this curt dismissal of his many years of loyal service and protested. He then received another letter correcting it to 'discharged having reached the upper age limit.'

Major Long

SECTION 1: ARMY

A TA Drummer

Tom Martindale

Service No 23081197

Born:	November 1936 Lancaster
Service Dates:	1954–6, 1958–77
Place of Enlistment:	Honiton Devon
Units:	REME (NS); Corps of Drums Battalion Kings Own Territorial
Awards:	TA and Volunteers Medal
Main Theatres:	UK

Tom did his National Service from 1954–6 joining up at Honiton Devon. He trained to be driver and learnt to drive at Barton Stacey, Winchester. Civilians trained them during the day and NCOs during the night. Afterwards he was posted to Arborfield, Reading – the garrison town for the REME. He joined the No. 3 Training Battalion – Communications and Telephone. He was to be a driver but there was no job for him there so he joined the regimental police instead. On leaving National Service, Tom decided to join the TA, the Kings Own 4/5th Battalion. As one of the first to do so that year, he got a £120 bounty

We asked him what it was like in the TA. 'Ah', he replied, 'People did not always take it as seriously as they should. You do drill once a month and each year do a fortnight camp, but while you are doing TA duties, you are in effect Army personnel.' He remembers, for example, one chap just going home during a camp. He soon found himself arrested by the Military Police and doing 28 days detention for going AWOL. For the fortnight camp, you got paid two weeks wages plus bounty. Tom tried to time his camp with his fortnight holiday. Leaving his wife with relatives nearby for her holiday, he would thus, get both his army pay and his holiday pay from work. Otherwise you got only army pay. One year, when he was unemployed, Captain Davies asked him to be his driver for a year. The Captain regarded Tom as one of his best ever drivers and asked him to do seven camps that year, which meant that Tom could draw extra army pay on top of his dole – a real help.

On joining the TA, a friend, a Lance Corporal Joe wanted Tom to join him in the regiment's Corps of Drums. Tom started on the kettledrums and then moved on to flutes. Like many in the corps he could not read music and like everyone else had to 'fluke it.' However, Tom did not like 'busking it,' so he transferred to the tenor drums. This is less about hitting the drum as the ability to do lots of hand movements. In fact, you often did not even touch the drums at all. Tom worked at these hand movements but struggled with the 'cartwheel'. This is to twirl the sticks horizontally around each time and bring them to the perfect horizontal. Struggling with the manoeuvre Tom noticed one day a young boy playing with a yo yo. He asked the lad how he did it so well and was shown the elastic which boy used around his wrist to help. Tom took the idea for himself attaching the elastic to his wrists and the sticks. It worked like a dream. The Drum Major was so impressed he placed Tom to the front of 'A formation' of the tenor drummers, allowing him to do the cartwheel movement for seven and half minutes.

In 1961, they won the NW command Brigade competition. In 1962, they were presented with new drums, supplied by the Lancaster and Morecambe council, Storeys, Lansing and other Lancaster companies, as well as the Fleetwood Kings Own club. Their greatest honour was to Beat the Retreat in Horse Guards Parade that year, as well as the trooping of the colour in Lancaster. It was first time the TA had trooped the colours in Lancaster for forty years. They marched through the town and down to Giant Axe Field (now Lancaster's football ground).

To join the corps you needed to be able to do five instrumental chores, namely:
- Write a piece of music
- Play a piece of music
- Blow a bugle
- Train as Drum Major
- Take on one of the roles of a drum major such as leading a band.

Actually, Tom did not do any of these when he joined as they were short of volunteers for the corps. Tom told us the Corps of Drums were known as the 'bullshitters' by other units – as they did not do real soldiering at camp, they concentrated on cleaning kit and parade. The corps had to be immaculately turned out and they also formed the Colonel's bodyguard. They regarded themselves as the cream of the battalion and many were jealous of the privileges they got as a result.

Tom now mentioned one camp he attended back in 1959/60 at Pennybridge near Beacon. As camps were not near 'civilization' , it was often a case of making up one's own entertainment.

View of Pennybridge Camp

They began the camp by trying to capture a sheep, put it in Wellingtons and place it in the Colonel's tent – but the sheep eluded them. Instead, that year's camp entertainment came from one of basic functions of humanity. If you wished to go to the toilet, you took a spade from the end tent and set out into the woods and then buried your 'business.' One lazy minded corporal, Corporal Jones, while taking the spade, could not be bothered to dig a hole and bury it. Unknown to him he had been followed by the sergeant who suspected he might do this. After the corporal had done his 'business' and left, the sergeant picked up the offending unburied turd with a piece of card and brought it to the Drum Major to decide what should be done. They decided to give it a burial with full military honours. The Padre was roped into the plan and a proper box was made. Pallbearers, drummers and riflemen (the latter to fire the salute over the grave) were selected. The burial was chosen for Saturday morning and everyone turned out in Number 1 uniform for it. They had forgotten that Saturday morning was the time the colonel made his inspection. Therefore, at Hut 29 where the burial was taking place, the colonel duly turned up and was puzzled at the activity. Therefore, he sent his adjutant to ask the padre what was going on. The padre replied it was the burial of an 'unknown soldier'. In response, the colonel brought his officers over and they all stood there while the shots were fired over the grave and saluted the coffin, containing Corporal Jones' turd, as it was lowered into the ground.

Later on Colonel Gibson found out the truth in the mess. He laughed and said he would put it down to experience. He added that if had been wartime it would have been a good morale booster. Tom said he was a very good chap like that.

This was not end of the story. After the burial, the corps put a notice up in the Guardroom, which read that any troops occupying hut 29 were to put a white cross and cap badge on the grave of the 'unknown soldier. Tom told us he went back to that camp in 1987, curious to know what had happened. He found by hut 29 absolutely loads of white crosses with their accompanying cap badges. This was what camp life was like he stressed making your own entertainment. After all, he added, you only got paid 28 shillings, 14 of which you had to send home and the rest after you spent out on cleaning materials left you with very little even for the local NAAFI.

The Kings Owns was later dissolved and it became the 1st Battalion Lancastrians with the HQ at Warrington. Lancaster was the base for E company. Tom was now in a group known as CONRADS; it consisted of one captain, two junior officers, one colour sergeant, one sergeant, one corporal, one lance corporal (which was Tom) and two privates. They would go to the drill hall to receive one day's pay for the year. Their role was to take over the drill hall if the local TA was called up as for example in the Iraq war. Tom is now retired and is the secretary of Morecambe Militaria Society and a keen collector.

Duke of Wellington's Own

Mark Andrew Lodge JP

Major (regular) Lt Colonel (TA)

Born:	13th March 1962, York
Service Dates:	January 1984–June 2006.
Units	Duke of Wellingtons, Kings Own Border, East and West Riding Regiment
Awards:	GSM (General Service Medal) Northern Ireland, UN Balkan Medal, NATO Balkan Medal, VRSM (Volunteer Reserve Service Medal) Queen's Golden Jubilee Medal
Main Theatres:	Gibraltar, Belize, Northern Ireland, Canada, Falklands, Zimbabwe, Bosnia

Mark grew up with an interest in the services as his father was in the RAF and his grandfather had served with the Duke of Wellington's Regiment in the First World War. Mark's first love however was for the navy and he joined the Royal Navy unit at Lancaster University. His first trip to sea on a minesweeper however convinced him that his stomach needed to be land based, thus he joined the army.

In January 1984, he went to Sandhurst for six months as a graduate officer at Victory College. On passing out he joined the general list as he wanted to wait for a vacancy in a Yorkshire Regiment. A few months later, he was on his way to join the Duke of Wellington Regiment (DWR) at Gibraltar.

On landing at the airport, he was immediately put under arrest by the Royal Military Police for drug smuggling. Surprised, he was interrogated, finger printed and arraigned before the adjutant who unusually had a very broad accent. After a while though, everyone broke down laughing – it was his introduction to army life.

Attending his first mess proved a very strange experience. He and the other newcomers were plied with copious amounts of whisky and listened with alarm to fellow officers talking disparagingly about the CO. Then, in the middle of the meal, someone came in with a vacuum cleaner only to be immediately ejected from the room. Screams followed, suggesting he was being thoroughly beaten up. It all proved to be a further introduction to the DWR. The mess staff had been impersonating officers and vice versa. Humour and pranks is part of an officer's life as it forms part of the bonding process.

The DWR had for some time been one of the best rugby-playing clubs in the army and Mark spent a lot of his time playing for them against local Spanish teams. Rugby he added again helped to promote bonds, this time between officers and other ranks.

In 1986, the battalion moved to Belize because of the threat from neighbouring Guatemala. Mark was with C Company and HQ at Holdstaff camp next to the main airport. This gave him the opportunity to exercise his platoon in the jungle for two to three week stretches. Taken in by helicopter, they had still to carry all other equipment and food. He received training from the SAS in explosives and navigation who told him 'Don't fight the jungle'. At night, unusual jungle sounds could cause problems. Mark had his platoon stood-to all night, the screeching din from howler monkeys had been mistaken for an attack. They practiced ambushes and fighting retreats in preparation for an invasion that never came.

In 1987, Mark was back in England undertaking a platoon commander's course where he was taught tactics, skill at arms and how to run a firing range. Later in the year, he rejoined the battalion for its tour of duty in Northern Ireland. He was now a captain in command of the mortar platoon, which consisted mainly of 'old sweats'. They were used to reinforce other units as necessary and to protect ballot stations in East Tyrone. They later took part in Operation Ballet that involved living in trenches for a month on the South Armagh border, in order to protect the engineers renovating the lookout towers as well as to undertake road checks. Mark said that it gave him some idea of what his grandfather experienced on the Western front.

In 1988, at the end of his three years enlisted service Mark left the army. He quickly came to miss army life and rejoined, again in command of the mortar platoon in DWR. They went on exercise to Canada and formed part of a reinforced company in the Falklands. As well as patrols and guard duty, he had the chance of experimenting with mortar tactics. One was using illuminating shells, up to the maximum range of 5060 feet, in order to mark targets for the naval artillery. In his spare time, he had trips to the battlefields and stayed with a local family. The army mess entertained many visitors, usually naval. One submarine officer group amused them by getting drunk, hanging from the ceiling and urinating into the lampshades.

After helping with an Operation Raleigh expedition in Zimbabwe, he was selected by his CO to become an instructor at Sandhurst. Part of the training was to deal with riots in Northern Ireland. Scenarios were made as realistic as possible and Mark revved up his side, to such a degree that the army gave the 'rioters' a hard time. He was arraigned before the CO and advised to curb his enthusiasm! Part of his responsibility at Sandhurst was security and therefore when an unidentified case was spotted in the mess he initiated the security drill. The entrance gates were closed, no one was allowed to enter or leave. Traffic on the A11 was stopped causing major tailbacks and the bomb disposal squad was called. They used a robot vehicle, which smashed in the mess room doors and carried out a controlled explosion of the case. The case was found to be harmless. The owner eventually arrived from the rugby field wondering what was going on and he was presented with a bill for the mess door repairs. The next day Mark came in to breakfast and found everyone was wearing steel helmets!

Mark re-joined the DWR as acting CO of C Company. To be promoted to the post of major he needed to go to Camberley to undertake a Staff course. He passed the exams but he was not accepted. He continued with exercises in Norway and Kenya and then was given a staff officers job in the Combat Service Support Group (CSSG). In this role, he went to Bosnia, to Split and Ploce with the UN and later NATO. The latter he found much more efficient, up tempo and decisive. His task was to oversee supply and check the security of bases. At the end of a six months tour in 1996, he decided to leave, as he was now married. He finished his regular army training as a Training Major with the Kings Own Royal Border in Lancaster. He remained in the TA, moving to Yorkshire where part of his duties was to recruit ethnic minorities. He noted that just before the 9/11 attacks they had been an influx of Muslims. The recruits learned about the use of firearms and then left. Mark continued to command the East and West Riding TA Regiment until 2006 during which time he had several trips to Iraq where parts of the battalion were being used to guard convoys and HQ's.

Section Two

Naval Life

Life in the Navy

Action in the army is often the combat of individuals, but in the Navy, it is action between ships. A ship is like a living being whose crew form its different cells and the vast majority of them are below decks and never see the action or the enemy. This is demonstrated in our first account, from Frank Lampson. Although the ships he served in during the war saw much action, he himself only got see the enemy once in 1944, when by chance he was on deck when a Zero flew over. Following the war, he served on the aircraft carrier *HMS Triumph* and he reveals the dangers that pilots faced in carrier service at the time.

In addition, the Navy is not just about fighting ships and their crew, many men serve in the support ships. There are few more important support ships than the minesweepers. Bill Lyons served on *HMS Persian,* (an Algerine Class Fleet Minesweeper) in the East Indies Fleet, 1944–5. The East Indies Fleet, along with its sister fleet the British Pacific Fleet are known as the 'Forgotten Fleets' In the words of the Rt. Hon. Lord Callaghan of Cardiff, their history has 'remained sadly under-recorded and unrecognised for too many years.' The East Indies Fleet was established in November 1944 and we have two accounts to add to EIF'S history. Bill Lyons in *HMS Persian* served as part of 6th Minesweeper Fleet April 1945 and Ken Webster who served as a pilot flying Grumman Avengers from the aircraft carrier *HMS Illustrious.*

From the post war experiences, we have two submariners' accounts. The first is Thomas Holden who served on *HMS Andrew,* when she became the first British submarine to across the whole Atlantic underwater. Like Frank, he also served on the carrier *HMS Triumph* and records the many accidents the carrier pilots had just after the war.

The second submariner is Jim Stokes. Jim like Thomas began on surface ships, serving on *HMS Palliser* and took part in the first of the Icelandic Cod Wars in the early sixties. He then transferred to submarines serving both in a conventional submarine and in a SSBN – a nuclear powered Polaris armed submarine. He reveals very different accounts of the life on both types of submarines.

Robert Dix and Don Potter were both National Servicemen who got into the Navy. Don stressed that the Navy was the hardest service for national servicemen to join. Before his national service, Don was in RNVR (Royal Naval Volunteer Reserve) and was anxious to tell the story from his time in the RNVR of *HMS Maidstone* and the wreck of submarine *HMS Sidon*. For his national service, Don was a 'writer' at Portsmouth dockyards. A 'writer' is a naval clerk, as not all who serve in the Navy are on ships. His account reveals the truth that as one ex sailor told us, the radio comedy the 'Navy Lark' is really close to the truth of naval life in the sixties.

Roger's account covers his time working in stores at a Royal Naval Air Station, *HMS Nuthatch* and again reminds us that a lot of naval service was not on ships. For national service, Roger explained, they had no chance being on a ship; it was simply not an option for them. Roger for example was keen to serve on a carrier but was told that this would only happen if he signed on after finishing his National Service as a naval volunteer.

Naval life can be on the sea, under the sea, above the sea and on shore, but it also can be the life of a 'fighting soldier' – the Royal Marines. Originally, ships carried marines to ensure ship security, but during World War Two, they developed into an amphibious commando force. Today they form the elite commando units of a Rapid Deployment Force and are the UK specialists in mountain warfare. Royal marine, Jack Fletcher recounts his time first during the Malaya Emergency and later in the Canal Zone; a story which adds to accounts in the Army Life Section of the military experiences in Malaya and the Canal Zone.

Our final account in this section is from a sailor but not in the Royal Navy, he served in the Merchant Marine. In 20th century naval warfare, it is easy to overlook the role of the merchant marine. They were however at the frontline at the battle for Britain's survival in both world wars and took the heaviest percentage of casualties of any service in the Second World War. The British Government did overlook their role first in the opening years of the Second World War, where merchant seamen received none of the privileges that other servicemen received. We are delighted to have Jack Armstrong's account as a 'Convoy Cook,' to remind us of the great service that the merchant marine did give to winning the war. By 1943, the role of merchant service was finally officially recognised not only in giving them the privileges that the army, navy and air force servicemen enjoyed but a campaign medal was struck for them – the Atlantic Star.

Below Deck

Frank Lampson

Rank Engine room Artificer
No. CMX 56148

Born:	30th August 1922, Portsmouth
Service Dates:	January 1938–1953
Place of Enlistment:	Chatham
Units	*HMS Suffolk, HMS Triumph*
Awards:	39/45 Star, Burma Star, Pacific Clasp, Atlantic Star
Main Theatres:	Murmansk Run, Asia from 1943 – Convoy Escort.

Frank joined the Navy as an apprentice engineer artificer in 1938, initially at Portsmouth, but quickly transferred to Chatham. The coming of the war accelerated his training and he joined *HMS Suffolk* in 1941, just after the Bismarck action. *HMS Suffolk* was an old armoured Heavy Cruiser, commissioned in

HMS Suffolk in 1942

1928. She was 13,000 tons fully loaded and carried an armament of eight 8in guns in four-twin turrets, plus numerous AA guns. She had a speed in excess of 30 knots.

When Frank joined *HMS Suffolk,* she was on convoy duty on the treacherous Murmansk (Russian) route. As for most of the crew, Frank was only aware of battle when the sound of action stations came down to the interior. Frank's job as artificer in this situation was to be ready to flood the magazines and other combustible areas – something he was glad he never needed to do.

After 18 months on the Murmansk route, the *Suffolk* was sent to SE Asia, to escort convoys from Australia to Burma. Much of the war was spent on this essential routine work. On just one occasion, off the Burma coast, did Frank did see the enemy. The *Suffolk* had broken an anchor chain and Frank was on deck supervising the anchor's recovery. At that moment, a Jap plane flew overhead, although it did not attack,

This was the only time in the entire war he actually did see the enemy. Within the cocoon of the ship, as Frank pointed out, you do not see any action at all, you were just aware of it above you and you put your trust in those above deck.

After the war, he joined the newly commissioned carrier *HMS Triumph.* She was a new carrier commissioned in May 1946. She was only a little larger than the old *Suffolk* at 18,000 tons fully loaded. She made 25 knots and had twenty-four 2pdr cannon for her own air defence. She had a complement of 1300 men including aircrew and she carried 48 aircraft. Like Jim Stokes, Frank commented on the many fatalities that took place among the aircrew. After his service on the *Triumph,* Frank became shore based, working on the construction of nuclear weapons at Aldermaston. This was a topic that Frank felt he should not talk about.

'Better Than Trenches'

HMS Persian, 'The Lion of Judah'

Bill Lyon

Able Seaman, Royal Navy
P/MX727050

Born: 17ᵗʰ March 1927, Morecambe
Service Dates: 16ᵗʰ September 1943–September 1947
Place of Enlistment: Skegness
Units   *HMS Persian*
Awards: 1939/45 Star Burma and Pacific War bar, 1939/45
                         Medal, 45–57 General Service medal, Volunteer
                         Medal
Main Theatres: Burma and Malaya

Born in Morecambe, Bill was only 12 years old when the war broke out and had an early introduction to its horrors. As a telegram boy, he had to deliver the news to a Mrs. H. in Morecambe that her three sons had been killed when *HMS Hood* blew up fighting the German battleship KM Bismarck. Soon afterwards, her husband died at Heysham dock being crushed between the dock and the battleship *HMS Duke of York.*

He also had to deliver telegrams to General Montgomery and Winston Churchill who stayed at Elms Hotel, Morecambe and another personally to General James Stewart, the Hollywood actor and airman who was staying on the promenade.

In September 1943, Bill lied about his age in order to join the Navy 'I had heard about sludge and dirt of the trenches from my father in 1914. I wanted a dry bed, but didn't think of the two miles of water below me.'

He began his naval career at the shore stations, HMS *Arthur,* Skegness, HMS *Iron Duke*, North Wales and HMS *Victory*, Portsmouth. In February 1944, he was sent to Ceylon. While playing music in the NAAFI he got to meet Lady Mountbatten. She had delayed her departure in order to listen to their playing of *Scheherazade.*

Bill was assigned in 1945 to the newly arrived minesweeper, *HMS Persian* (J347) of the 6th Minesweeper Flotilla. The 6th MSF had just arrived from the UK to join the East Indies Fleet. The 6th MSF consisted of 8 Minesweepers: *HMS Gozo, Lightfoot, Melita, Postillion, Larne, Friendship* and *Persian*, led by *HMS Vestal. HMS Persian* was a new Algerine class of fleet Minesweeper, commissioned in November 1943. 110 of this class of Minesweepers were built for USN, RCN and RN. 98 served in the RN, a number on loan from US, including *HMS Persian.* She was 850 tons, with a speed of 16.5kts and armed with one 4in AA and four 20mm AA.

Bill's first action on HMS Persian was sweeping the Nicobar Islands in order to allow the approach of the main fleet led by *HMS Anson*, a King George V class battleship, which then bombarded shore installations and stores used by the Japanese submarine fleet, (Operation Collie, July 1945). It is recorded that 6th MSF cleared 167 mines to allow the fleet in.

In 1945, the Pacific fleet awaited the delivery of the landing craft used on D-Day for a similar landing operation in Malaya. However, the war in the east ended before it could be put into operation

Bill had in the meantime been sweeping of seas around Malaya. This involved a series of minesweepers equipped with paravanes, towed from wire attached to arms at the bow. The wire was held at depth by the paravanes (like a mini aircraft that flew in the water), in order to cut the anchor cables of the mines. These were then exploded by rifle or machine gun fire. An electrical device was tried at the time but was found to endanger the ship and therefore abandoned.

At the end of the war, *HMS Persian* led the way into Singapore harbour where hundreds of unarmed Japanese lined the harbour. These were the first enemy he had seen.

Bill anticipated a quick return to England but it was not to be. Churchill and Roosevelt had promised the Burmese militia that they would be allowed to have a free election after the war had finished. When it was discovered that the militia were Communists, the promise was ignored and not surprisingly, they started fighting the British. Bill said this continued until 1948 with the final granting of independence to Burma.

Therefore, while *HMS Persian* was quickly taken out of service and returned to US naval control in 1946, Bill was to remain in Burma until 1947 to help fight the communists. He left as a result of a burn caused by a soldier using a flamethrower on a Basha (hut). He was sent home via Aden, Malta and Toulon and demobilized in 1947.

However, while waiting at a railway station, a friend, who had also been demobbed, used a small white ensign as a handkerchief. The Royal Navy Police spotted this and promptly arrested him and Bill. They were subsequently called to a Court Martial. Bill therefore had the experience of being demobbed twice and despite protests, was given a second demob suit.

Illustrious Airman

Ken Webster

Wireless Operator Fleet Air Arm

Born:	6th December 1922, Bolton
Service Dates:	1943–1945
Place of Enlistment:	Bolton 1943
Awards:	1939–45 Star, Burma Star, 39–45 Medal and Defence Medal
Main Theatres:	East Indies

Ken was born and brought up in Bolton. At the outbreak of war, he was working in a reserved occupation in the family timber company. Having heard of the exploits of the Fleet Air Arm against the Bismarck and at Taranto, he was keen to join up. In this, Ken was lucky, for at the time there was an expansion of the Fleet Air Arm service and those in reserved occupations could join. Ken joined up at Bolton in early 1943.

He began his basic training at Skegness, which involved drill and fitness; he then moved onto learn to be an air gunner and W/T operator, which involved a long period of further training. This began at RNAS Worthy Down in Hampshire, where he was introduced to Lysander and Proctor Aircraft. He had to learn the intricacies of the W/T equipment, which was prone to malfunction and to use the Lewis gun, a hopelessly inaccurate but reliable weapon from World War One.

From Worthy Down, he continued his training, first at St Merryn, Cornwall and then Dunino, Fife, arriving at the latter on 17th February 1944. Ken commented on the vicissitudes of bad weather, a fact that was brought home to him when an aircraft en route from England to Dunino was lost in the fog and ended up on the Isle of Man, hundreds of miles away. By this time, Ken had flown in the legendary Swordfish and in the Albacore. On 11th July 1944, he was transferred to RNAS Inskip near Preston to join 763 Squadron equipped with Grumman Avengers.

Ken in his flying gear

It was here that he met sub lieutenant Bryne, who was to be his principal pilot for the next 18 months. While at Inskip he was introduced to the new (well new to him) Browning .5 calibre machine gun, a powerful and accurate American machine gun. He practiced live firing air to air and air to sea.

Having completed a very thorough training, Ken volunteered for overseas service. He was sent out in a convoy to Trincomalee in Ceylon, via the Cape of Good Hope. Here he joined 854 Squadron at Katukurunda. 854 Squadron was originally formed in the USA as a torpedo reconnaissance squadron armed with Grumman Avenger 2s. It took part in support of D-Day landings before being sent out to Katukurunda in September 1944, where it was re-equipped with Grumman Avenger 1s. Ken joined them as they were practising glide and low-level bombing. After the Squadron was well versed in its new role, it joined the aircraft carrier HMS *Illustrious* and Ken was soon able to put his new training into practice. On 20th December *HMS Illustrious* and her sister ship HMS *Indomitable* launched an attack on Medan airfield in Sumatra. Medan was the capital of Northern Sumatra, consisting of a significant harbour and airfield. There was no intervention from the Japanese air force, but the anti-aircraft fire was significant and Ken reported that his commander was killed on this his first mission. The mission was not as successful as anticipated, but a month later, another attack completed the task but by that time, Ken had left the squadron.

Before then the squadron was sent to the China Bay station in Ceylon for further training. Ken continued with sub lieutenant Bryne to practice exercises such as mast high bombing. Illness though prevented Ken from re-joining the *Illustrious* when it left at the end of January 1945 to join the Pacific Fleet and 854 Squadron later moved to Australia. Ken remained in Ceylon to the end of the war. A local family who involved him in the local religious festivals and celebrations befriended him.

Ken had spent two years in Fleet Air Arm and as listed in his logbook that he flew an extensive range of aircraft.

Lysander	Proctor
Shark	Swordfish
Kingfisher	Beaufighter
Avenger	Vengeance
Stinson reliant	Defiant
Seamew	Chesapeake
Blenheim	

Grumman Avenger and HMS Illustrious 1944

HMS Illustrious was built in Barrow, launched in 1939 and commissioned in May 1940. An armoured carrier, her hangars designed to withstand a 500lb bomb and 6in shells. She was 23,000 tons in size, with a speed of 30 knots. She had 36 aircraft, with 350 aircrew added to her complement of 900 men. She joined Eastern Fleet in December 1944, taking part in attacks on Medan and Palembang, before being transferred to the Pacific Fleet in January 1945. She was paid off in 1954.

Snorkelling the Atlantic

Thomas Holden

Acting Leading Seaman
Service Number C/SSX820235

Born:	1st April 1931, Carnforth
Service Dates:	17th March 1947–31st March 1956
Place of Enlistment:	HMS *Ganges*
Units	HMS Triumph, Bleasdale, Superb, Andrew and Alcide.
Awards:	1939/45 Star, France and Germany Star, Defence Medal, 1939/45 Medals
Main Theatres:	Mediterranean, American West Indies Station and Home waters

World War Two was still raging when Tom entered his teens. He was so inspired by the exploits of the Royal Navy that he wanted to join up as soon as possible. So, just before his 16th birthday, he went to *HMS Ganges* training depot in Suffolk as a Boy recruit. He stayed there for twelve months and was a member of 29 Mess (a Mess consists of fifty recruits). His first four weeks was foot drill, but then he moved onto gun drill – learning the laying, loading and firing of the 4-inch naval cannon. In addition, he learned to row, to do knot work and learn mathematics, navigation, electronics and history. He pointed out that at any one time two thousand boys would be undertaking training at the depot. His rank was Boy 2nd Class receiving two shillings per week, which rose to two shillings and six pence when promoted to Boy 1st Class.

Tom described the conditions as quite spartan. They were not allowed to have any valuables or more than two shillings and six pence in cash. Anyone who could not swim properly was simply pushed into a pool to learn and with no instruction. This was learning to swim the hard way and one recruit did drown whilst Tom was there.

Punishment or 'jankers' mainly consisted of double drill with a rifle, or being caned. HMS *Ganges* was apparently the last place in the services to abolish corporal punishment. If someone was considered 'unclean', they could be ordered to undergo a 'mess scrub'. They were hosed and scrubbed with soft brush if they were popular and with hard floor-scrubbing brushes if they were not. For being improperly dressed, they were ordered to wear a tin hat and oilcloth for a week. One of his fellow messmates called Dennis was always receiving punishment, constantly having his pay docked and often feigned fainting to avoid drill. On what turned out to be his last pay parade Dennis grabbed a handful of half-crowns and ran off. He was discharged from the Navy. Tom did not see him again until Tom was a police inspector in West Yorkshire, where Dennis was arrested for assaulting his wife.

In April 1948 Tom was sent to join the aircraft carrier HMS *Triumph*, which flew Seafires, (a naval version of the Spitfire) and Fireflys, which could be armed with rockets, bombs or a torpedo. Landing aircraft, Tom stressed was still a pretty hit and miss affair, particularly in rolling seas or at night. There were numerous crashes because of the undercarriage collapsing on a heavy landing or aircraft missing the arrester wire. In the latter case, a barrier was set up to stop such careering aircraft ploughing into other parked aircraft on the flight deck. Even so, casualties were frequent including a number of deaths. HMS *Triumph* was part of the Mediterranean fleet and operated off Palestine. In conjunction with her escorts, her role was to intercept ships carrying illegal Jewish immigrants. If caught, they were sent to a holding camp in Cyprus. When the *Triumph* was at anchor in Limassol, explosive charges were regularly dropped over the side to deter possible underwater Jewish bombers. The *Triumph* returned to the UK in April 1949 and was quickly rerouted to Korea. Tom however was kept behind to undertake a Radar Plotter RP3 course at HMS *Wildfire*.

He then went on to spend a brief period on the Hunt class destroyer *HMS Bleasdale*, undertaking anti-submarine exercises in the channel, but soon he

HMS Triumph, with Seafire crashed on aft deck

Firefly crashed into the barrier.
Damage, prop broke, 2 wheels and flaps torn away, port wing broken
Pilot: Lt McArthur

was transferred to *HMS Superb* an eight 6in gun cruiser. As he had trained as a navigator's yeoman, he was responsible for updating all the ships charts from monthly modifications sent out from the Admiralty. *Superb* was on the America and West Indies Station and in January 1951, attended the ceremonial investiture of President Vargos of Brazil in Rio de Janeiro. This formed part of a formal cruise that *HMS Superb* undertook that year right round South America.

HMS Andrew after making the first crossing of Atlantic underwater.
Tom is standing right behind the lifebuoy, 2nd right

In 1952, Tom was transferred to the submarine *HMS Andrew*, a conventional diesel powered craft with a crew of sixty, built at Barrow. She was based at North Rothesay, Isle of Bute, attached to the depot ship *HMS Mont Clair*. She was for a while lent to the Canadian Navy as a target for their anti-submarine exercises, based at Halifax, NS.

Tom described life on board as very cramped, necessitating 'hot bedding'. That was sharing a bunk with someone from the other watch, so while you were on watch he was in your bunk and vice versa. Thus the bed was always warm and hence the term. Smoking was normally not allowed, but occasionally the captain would 'pipe all round' which meant each of the crew were allowed one cigarette. Some men were so desperate that they asked to be woken up if such an opportunity arose. Oxygen was always a problem on a submarine and therefore whenever possible they surfaced to allow air through the conning tower. If submerged for any length of time they used an 'oxygen candle', which was a tube of chemicals that produced oxygen. In addition, air was pumped through a CO_2 absorption unit, to help purify it. Even so, the air could become so stagnant that a lit match would not burn and crew would become listless, lacking in concentration. This may have contributed to some of the losses of submarines that occurred in the fifties. One of *HMS Andrew's* sister ships, *HMS Affray* was lost in 1951.

In June 1953, *HMS Andrew* was equipped with a snorkel to take in fresh air. They then 'snorkelled' from Bermuda all the way to the Channel, a voyage of 15 days totally submerged. It was the first known underwater Atlantic crossing by a Royal Naval Submarine, (the first ever by a submarine was U977 in 1945). The voyage was completed the day before the Coronation of Queen Elizabeth II and the news was announced at the same time as two other great feats: Edmund Hillary and his team conquering Mount Everest – 29,000 feet above sea level and England winning the Ashes. Since the commander's name was Scott, this lead to the newspapers carrying the headlines of 'Captain Scott of the Antarctic now Captain Scott of the Atlantic'.

In 1954 Tom did an RP2 Course for Senior Radar rating and then joined *HMS Andrew*'s sister ship *HMS Alcide*. In 1956 he decided to leave the service altogether. He was now married and found the navy less than considerate in its terms of leave arrangements. Three days after being demobbed, he started police training and spent twenty-eight years in the police service, retiring as an inspector. Tom is now a member of the Submariners Association.

Daring to Revenge

Jim Stokes (on the right)

Chief Petty Officer
Marine Engineering Artificer (propulsion)
No. P/M 956466

Born:	20th November 1940, Birmingham
Service Dates:	7th May 1956 to 16th December 1970
Place of Enlistment:	HMS *Fishguard*, Torpoint, Devon
Units	HMS *Daring*, HMS *Palliser*, *HMS Ark Royal*, HMS *Otus*, HMS *Valiant*, HMS *Revenge*.
Theatres	Indian Ocean, Iceland (1st Cod War) Indonesia, Faslane

On 7th May 1956, aged 15, Jim joined the Navy as an engine room artificer apprentice. On completing his training, he joined *HMS Daring*, a post war 4.5in gun destroyer, which he described as a fast gun platform. She had a top speed of 32 knots plus and was armed with six 4.5in guns in twin turrets, five

HMS Daring

Torpedo tubes and one Anti-submarine Squid. She was described at the time as an 'ingenious and comprehensive light warship.' She was one of the post war D Class destroyers and one of the largest built by the Royal Navy at 3,600 tons, with a complement of 12 officers and 285 ratings. She had twin screws and as Jim pointed out, by putting one into reverse and the other forward, she could turn very sharply.

The *Daring* also carried five torpedoes tubes, but she practiced with dummy torpedoes, powered by diesel. When a torpedo reached the limit of its range a lever flipped up which allowed it to just float and thus be collected. On one occasion Jim remembers, the lever came up prematurely causing the torpedo to make a U-turn and head back at full power towards the ship, forcing the ship into taking frantic avoiding action.

In 1961, he joined *HMS Palliser* an anti-submarine frigate. She formed part of the First Fishery Protection Division consisting of four ships of her class: (Blackwood Class Anti-Submarine Frigates). The other three were Duncan (squadron leader) Malcolm and Russell. These were lightly armed frigates mounting just four 40mm Bofors. However, they did carry two very accurate Limbo depth charge throwers. They had a compliment of 140, (8 officers and 132 ratings) and were about 1500 tons each. Palliser was completed in 1957 and when Jim joined her, she was being dispatched to Iceland for the first Icelandic Cod War. This came about when Iceland extended her fishing limit from 4 to a 12-mile limit (The second and third Cod war were in the early seventies when Iceland extended her limit to 50 miles.) *HMS Palliser's* role in this first Cod war was to defend the British Trawlers against the Icelandic gunboats. However, according to Jim, this was a total farce. There were two

HMS Palliser

Icelandic gunboats, one at each end of Iceland. As one came out, *HMS Palliser* would set off towards it. The second one would come out behind them. Thus, *Palliser* found itself going back and forth between the two gunboats! In addition, *Palliser* like the rest of her class made only a top speed of 24 knots, she simply could not catch either gunboat.

The frigate had a very low seaboard and in heavy seas, its upper deck was often underwater. On such an occasion, a dingy broke loose and a petty officer, roped up, went up on deck to secure it. A large wave knocked him off his feet and sent him over the side. The rope initially held, but as it slid alongside of the deck, it was cut through. The *Palliser* immediately came about, which took time as she only had a single screw. As they came back, they found him floating in his life jacket and a rope was thrown out to him but by this time, he was dead from the cold and had to be abandoned.

On the way back from patrol, they were being 'followed' by a heavy sea with an inexperienced rating at the wheel. As the storm rose and the bow slid down each wave, the helmsman needed to correct constantly the line of the ship. Then he made an error that 'broached' the ship – making her turn side on to the waves. *Palliser* completely turned over on to its side before, to relief of everyone, righting herself. The corresponding footprints on the bulkhead were retained to mark this event.

A year later, in 1962, Jim joined the carrier *Ark Royal*, then in the Indian Ocean. He was one of the replacements for the 'sailors who would rather stay with the Sheilas in Australia than move around with the grey funnel line.'

The *Ark Royal* was one of the only two large carriers built for the Royal Navy, at 50,000 tons, completed in 1955. She carried then 40 aircraft and eight

Helicopters. She also had four twin 4.5in guns and eighteen 40mm Bofors for her own air defence. With her four screws, she could make 31knots Jim's job was as throttle watch keeper or 'throttle jockey'. There was one of these for each of the four engine compartments. His task was to release the steam to power the screw, a tricky operation and it had to be done in co-ordination with the boiler room and the other three compartments.

The *Ark Royal* moved to Indonesia, carrying the 899th Naval Air Squadron. This squadron founded in the Orkneys in 1942 flying Spitfires, now flew Sea Vixens and Attackers, but at the end of Jim's service on the *Ark Royal*, they were doing first sea trials of the prototype of the Harrier. The Squadron was later to form a training squadron for Sea Harriers from 1980 until it was decommissioned in May 2005.

Jim felt the aircrews were madmen considering the risks they took. They flew flights day and night, practicing landing and take offs. As they came in to land, at the last moment, they had to lift their nose to allow the arrester hook to be as low as possible and this meant that the pilot could not see the deck, which could be heaving and rolling. If his 'crochet hook' missed the 'wool' – the deck officer would immediately fire a red Vary light, which would cause the pilot to pull away and come around again. If either were too slow, the aircraft would simply drop in the sea in front of the carrier. Then the pilot would have the unenviable experience of having to sit tight in his sinking aircraft while the carrier went overhead before he could eject. Jim said that in 18 months on the carrier they lost about one aircrew a month. One occasion, an air crewman walked behind the jet, which was warming up her engines. He was simply blown away, only his hat was found. On another occasion, an aircraft dived onto a towed splash target but did not pull up afterwards. He dived straight into the sea and not even as much as an oil slick was found to show its existence. That night the aircrew got so drunk that three of them fell down an open hatch and were killed.

Jim informed us that in those days the daily tot of rum was issued as '2 to 1' for the hands and neat for senior ratings. The Bosun was responsible for the issue and it was greeted by 'The Queen, God Bless her' before being downed in one.

In 1963, Jim transferred to submarines, being sent to *HMS Dolphin* for his basic training. What he remembered most vividly about his training there was doing the 'escape' – that is passing up a 100-foot water filled tube called the 'Tower.' His first submarine was the conventional submarine *HMS Otus*. She was one of conventional Patrol submarines completed in 1953. She was 2030 tons surface or 2410 tons submerged and had a complement of 6 officers and 62 ratings. She was powered by two diesels and two electric motors giving her 12 knots on the surface and 17 knots submerged. She was armed with eight 21 in torpedo tubes.

Jim relates, that while in a Scottish loch, he and his chief stoker went on shore to celebrate their birthdays and came back much worse for wear. *Otus* then went into the Irish Sea, which was very choppy and uncomfortable, so the *Otus's* captain, Lt Commander King, got permission from the Admiralty to submerge. The Chief Stoker's job was to top set the boat's trim to ensure that the rate of descent would be gradual. However, a little worse for wear, he made mistakes setting the trim so that the boat was far too heavy forward. When the boat dived, it went down very fast and control was only re-established just a few feet above the stated sea depth.

On a typical six week tour there was very little freshwater available and the crew simply did without washing. However, Jim was asked to look into the malfunctioning evaporator that produced pure water. This was in a very inaccessible part of the submarine, which was extremely filthy with oil. After making some repairs, Jim decided that he needed to have a wash and had to pass through the conning lower area to do so. Here Captain King was looking through the periscope. He looked up and commented laconically, 'Washing Stokes?' A week later, Jim had to do the whole thing again and this time Captain King's commented 'Not again Stokes!' Jim said that he concluded that he was meant to think that washing twice in a fortnight might endanger the whole 6-week tour.

In 1966 Jim transferred to a land based nuclear submarine course before joining the new nuclear powered hunter-killer submarine *HMS Valiant*, just then completing (1967). This was a much larger submarine, 3,500 tons on surface, 4,500 tons submerged. Though armed with six 21 in torpedoes, two less than on the Otus, she could, with her nuclear engines do 30 knots. She had a complement though of just 103 men. After a short time with *HMS Valiant* Jim was transferred to the new nuclear powered Ballistic Missile submarine SSBN *HMS Revenge*, completed in 1969. She was the last of the four Resolution class of Polaris SSBN's. She took her first operational patrol in June 1970. She was 8,500 tons and had a compliment of 13 officers and 128 ratings in two crews, each crew swapping over after each patrol. She was slower than the Valiant class with a surface speed of 20 knots, (25 submerged). She carried six 21in torpedoes forward in the bow but the crucial part was that she carried 16 A3 SLBM Polaris ballistic missiles. They had a range of 2,500 miles and were able to land within 400 feet of their target. She was based as all the SSBN are at Faslane, Scotland.

HMS Revenge (photograph courtesy of Jim Stokes)

When it put to sea, (and Jim deliberately referred to it not her) and dived they went into silent running with the minimum of talking and moving. This was in order to make the tracking by the Soviet submarines more difficult. From then on, none of the crew knew where they were and no signals were sent. Every week there would be an 'Action Station Missiles' announced by a klaxon. The submarine went to 120 feet and they readied the first missile for firing. At no point was the crew informed whether it was just an exercise or for real. Jim pointed out this was very stressful for the crew not knowing, particularly that since leaving Faslane, they had no contact with outside world. It took 16 minutes to get the first missile away and they all knew that if it came to the crunch the first missile would be their death warrant, as they certainly be destroyed before they got them all away.

On board they made their own air by electrolysis of water, which left spare hydrogen. This needed to be released at least 400 feet below the surface any shallower and the bubbles would be detected by satellite. The submarine on no occasion was allowed to surface. Jim relates that there was one time that *Revenge* had to surface. As part of an exercise, a rating was passed up to the surface on a line, but then he suddenly disappeared from the line and the captain of the *Revenge* felt he had no option to surface to find him. Having located the rating and having submerged again, a furious captain called the rating to him to explain why he let go of the line. 'Well', the rating replied, 'I cannot swim at fxxxg six knots'. The submarine had overlooked the need to reduce speed to allow for the exercise.

Life on board an SSBN was not easy. Many weeks isolated from the 'real world' and the stress of missile and torpedo drills (an SSBN patrol is always on a 'war' footing) did not make these happy ships (hence it not her). With the added pressure of a young family on shore led, Jim to decide that enough was enough and he left the service.

Hanging About in the Navy

Roger Dix

Seaman
Service Number DMX 859480

Born:	23rd May 1930
Service Dates:	20th September 1948 to 7th May 1950
Place of Enlistment:	Birmingham
Units	*HMS Nuthatch*, RNAS
Main Theatres:	UK

Roger was working in Birmingham when he was called up for National Service. A friend recommended he try for the Navy due to Roger's experience in supplies. To get into the Navy though one had to pass both a medical and an intelligence test. Roger was successful and in September 1948, he was off to *HMS Royal Arthur*, (Corsham, Wiltshire) for his basic training. He noted that Prince Phillip had been there a year before.

Roger did not like basic training as it did 'not suit his 'natural abilities'' Then on the 1st November 1948, he was sent to *HMS Ceres*, (Royal Naval Supply School) Wetherby Yorkshire. *HMS Ceres* was the base for 'trade training' in the Navy: stores division men, writers and cooks. While training, Roger put in specifically for the Royal Naval Air Service (RNAS). A colleague told him it was more interesting than dealing with basic naval stores. Thus on 17th January 1949, Roger found himself heading to *HMS Nuthatch*, the RNAS station at Anthorn on the North Cumbrian coast. *HMS Nuthatch* began life as an Emergency Landing Ground for RAF Silloth in the war, but the site was taken over by the Royal Navy in 1942 as ARDU (Aircraft Receipt and Dispatch Unit) and was eventually closed down in March 1958.

Roger began work in the office but he was then moved to 'Dispatch'. Here he supervised civilians packing stores to be sent off. This sometimes allowed him get out of the base although only as far as Kirkbride Railhead or nearby Silloth. It was still a pleasant change and he still remembers stopping on one of these

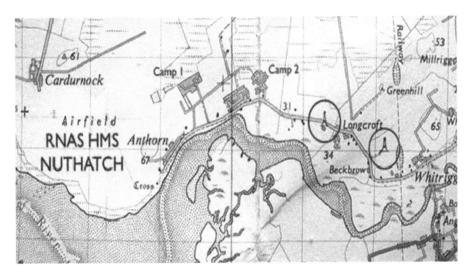

RNAS Nuthatch no long exists, but this its position located on an early OS Map

journeys just to look across the Solway – 'it was an exceptional beautiful day and a stunning view.' '

Leave was still called 'Shore leave' by the navy even though they were not on a ship. The order would come out for liberty men to 'fall in' and they would be taken by trucks to Carlisle. There, soldiers from Hadrian's camp would often join them.

The commanding officer at *HMS Nuthatch* was Captain R.P. Targett-Adams. He had a distinguished war service and. Roger found him a reasonable chap, as were all the officers. They were generally quite popular at the base.

After 6 months, Roger was moved to the Hanger Stores where he handed out basic items – such as nuts and bolts etc; but for specific items, he gave out the request forms. During his time there, he saw Seafires, Seafuries, Fireflys and the new jet fighter, the Gloster Meteor. Aircraft came in to *HMS Nuthatch* either from other air stations or from the manufacturers. In case of the latter, they came for modifications or they were fitted out with new equipment including instruments.

Towards Christmas 1949, Roger came down with Chicken pox. The medical officer ordered him home declaring it was 'better to infect a train load of civilians than a camp full of sailors.' This puzzled Roger since most of the sailors had gone home for Christmas but rumour had it that the medical officer just wanted to be alone with the chief nurse for Christmas.

At the end of March 1950, Roger was transferred to *HMS Drake* ready for demobbing. Here they mainly messed about but Roger did get involved in giving out the rum rations. In rum rations Roger explained those who did not get a rum ration were either 'UAs or Ts. Ts were the teetotallers and got a ration of lime juice instead. UAs were the underage sailors (under 21) and they got nothing. As Roger commented sadly, he was UA all through his national service.

After 18 months, Roger was finally demobbed on 7th May 1950. This was just two weeks before the Korean War broke out and if he had still been in service then it would have meant at least another six months.

He expressed two regrets concerning his National Service. First, that it prevented him from staying on longer at school, which may have given him the opportunity to go to University. Second, that there was no chance of getting onto a carrier and seeing more of the world. This was because one had to do a minimum of two years in the RNAS before one was allowed to transfer to carriers and NS was just for two years. He did consider signing on as a regular in the Navy doing the seven years (five active, two reserves) but in the end, he decided it was better to return to civilian life.

On the plus side, he did feel National Service, gave him sense of community learning how to mix with people. It also gave you a sense of responsibility and discipline. Finally it taught respect to authority although you were deterred from questioning authority, which Roger added maybe have not been such a good lesson.

Finally, we asked him what DMX on his service number meant. He explained that the D stands for Devonport and the MX for Miscellaneous Service.

Running for the Navy

Don Potter

Able Seaman
Service Number 953594

Born:	12th May 1937
Service Dates:	1955–57
Place of Enlistment:	HMS Ceres, Wetherby.
Units	Portsmouth Barracks
Main Theatres:	Portsmouth

In 1955, Don joined RNVR, in order that when it came to National Service, he could join the Royal Navy, in what his father regarded as the best service. Being in the RNVR did not involve too much work. In fact, he only got to board two ships during his time. The first was a small ship permanently docked in Liverpool. The second one though turned out to be a more tragic affair. They were sent to HMS Maidstone – a submarine depot ship, at Portland. This was in spring of 1955. They arrived at Maidstone in the afternoon and immediately went below to their hammocks. Alongside the depot, ship was the wreck of HMS Sidon. There had been an explosion in the submarine three days before and the bodies still lay inside.

The officers came down to them. They wanted volunteers to go into the submarine and clear out the bodies. They were assured they were not being ordered to. Don said it was all put very nicely and genuinely to them. Even so, Don kept his head down and did not volunteer. He was glad he did not. Those who had volunteered left immediately, 'all a bit excited and keen', but when they came back they looked very different. They looked, as Don described, like some US soldiers that he once met on a plane coming back from Vietnam. They were quiet and hardly spoke. Most did not want to talk about what they had seen or did. However, Don did get to hear what had happened.

On entering the submarine they were given sacks and told to pick up the bits and pieces of the bodies that lay around. The regulars stood back pointing out bits of bodies for them to pick up. One lad was immediately sick. One said he had to pick a head from a shelf. Don did not blame the regulars for standing back, many of the bodies were comrades, but he felt the officers were at fault for asking 17–18 year old boys to do the job and only RNVR volunteers not regulars. He had a feeling that they had been waiting for RNVR volunteers to arrive in order to do this job – but he could not be sure. He felt disgusted by the affair.

Six months later, Don enlisted into the Royal Navy for his National Service. He was not to board a ship for two years of that service. He did basic training at HMS Ceres in Yorkshire for 3 months. HMS Ceres was next to Wetherby racecourse. On one occasion the Chief took them out to the racecourse and told them to run round it. It was some run. Don was a good runner and he and a friend were soon far ahead. As they approached the finishing post, they raced for it, Don being piped at the post. Both were happy to finish and expecting to rest and wait for the rest to follow. Instead they were greeted by the Chief's words – 'round again'. So this time they decided to trot round, but only to find the Chief, who had mounted a bicycle, coming alongside them to make them race again.

At the time, there was a fear of IRA attacks and the barracks were to be under 24-hour guard. Don was partnered up with his friend Terry for the 3.00am–6.00am watch. They were given rifles (but no ammo) to defend the camp. The night was pitch black and after going round several times, Terry suggested they put their rifles down and have a smoke. Therefore, they put them behind a dorm and walked on so Terry could have a fag (cigarette) Suddenly someone shouted, 'Put your hands in the air, I have you covered'. They froze they could see nothing. Was it an IRA attack? Suddenly, from out of the pitch black, the chief emerged with one of their guns. 'I could take you to the Guardroom now,' he told them; 'you will then be facing a court martial and be thrown out of the Navy'. A disaster as Don put it, as his father would almost certainly disown and disinherit him. Then the chief added, 'You are lucky as I am the only CPO who would not do that, so don't do it again!'

After basic training they were dispatched to Portsmouth. Don remembers setting off with a friend. As the pay was five shillings a day, they felt that they could not afford a train, so they decided to hitch. A chauffer driven Rolls Royce stopped. In the back was a Lady in furs. She did not speak to them directly, but always through the chauffeur. They did a detour to Portsmouth especially for them. As they got out, the Lady asked them, via the chauffeur, if they got well paid. They replied with a laugh. She then passed via the chauffeur, what they took for a sweet, but was on closer examination turned out to be a ten shilling note.

Don now was at Pompey as a 'Writer', (a clerk). He was there for the rest of his service, (1 year 11 months altogether). An officer initially ran the office, but

Don did not see him much as he was writing a book. In fact it was the Petty Officer who ran the office. Don remembers in the pay office nearby he had a friend who was regarded as quite a 'wag'. He developed a new salute (although not for officers), which spread among the sailors, until the commanding officer got wind of it and it was stopped!

On another occasion, an Admiral rang up and his friend answered.

'Hank Jansen City Office', (Jansen being a well-known soft porno-graphic writer of the time).
'Pardon' came the reply and on receipt of same message, the Admiral now shouts
'Do you know who are speaking to?'
'No?'
'Admiral so and so'
'Oh, do you know who you are speaking to?'
'No?'
'Thank the fuck for that' and Don's friend puts the phone down.

This was not the end of it though, as a few hours later an irate Admiral arrived demanding to know to whom he had spoken to. No one including Don's friend's officer gave him away. Therefore, the Admiral says he would wait until he got the name even if it means waiting all evening. The Admiral sat down and after one and half hours, departs. He was not to be seen again.

Don volunteered to be the Drum Major. He was not very good at it but since he was the only volunteer, he got the role. Part of his difficulties as a drum major was he had problems hearing. On one occasion, at a passing out parade, they had passed the Admiral and just turned out of the parade ground, when Don then thought he heard the order left wheel, so he turned left and set off down a short road. The band on the other hand marched straight on, minus the drum major. Fortunately the Admiral or crowd did not see this debacle.

Since Don had proved a good runner at Wetherby, the Navy realized they had someone who could win races, particularly in the Interservice events. This meant he was given special privileges. For example at the Mess Hall, he could go straight to the front of the queue and was also entitled to come back for seconds. Each day there were two leaves organized. For this men seeking such leave had to spruce up and be paraded for inspection before the CPO. The CPO would then decide who got leave. However, as a runner for the Navy, Don only had to put his tracksuit on and ran out of gates to obtain his leave. Once out of barracks he could do anything for the next few hours as long as that on his return he ran back through the gates. He also got two afternoons off for training. These privileges, Don added did not make him particularly popular with the other ratings. Also as a naval athlete he could be flown anywhere in the world for important events, although this did not happen to Don. However, his application to go overseas to the Persian Gulf was turned down, as he was seen as too valuable an athlete to be let go by Pompey. Don admitted he hated running, but it did prove a good skive.

On skives, he remembered the CPO coming into the office one day and asking if anyone could play tennis. This looked a good opportunity to skive work, so Don volunteered. Only officers played tennis, but since they had not won for nearly two years and they faced a crucial needle match, they were desperate to find some good players. Don and another rating joined four officers to form a team of six. They won in straight sets and the officers were delighted. They invited them for a drink; but while helping officers win a match is one thing, other ranks and officers still cannot socialize. So having a drink meant waiting outside the officers' mess and having a drink brought out to them.

Overall Don felt National Service did him good. He made good friends with whom he still keeps in touch and it taught him to accept knocks, the unreasonable and unjust knocks service life threw at him. It also taught him how to deal with authority.

A Lancaster Royal Marine

Jack Fletcher

Royal Marines
RM 9515

Born:	29th February 1932 Lancaster
Service Dates:	25th September 1949–1st October 1972
Place of Enlistment:	Liverpool
Units	45 Commando, RMB Eastney, ITCRM, Depot RM Deal DPRORM Portsmouth
Awards:	Naval General Service Medal for Malaya, Cyprus & Suez
Main Theatres:	Malaya, Cyprus, Suez

Jack was born in Lancaster and studied at Lancaster Royal Grammar School. Here, he joined the Army Cadets and in addition excelled in sport: athletics, rugby, football and boxing.

In 1948 at the age of 16, he trained for the merchant navy subsequently joining the New Zealand Shipping Company for a 6-month voyage. On his return, he was accepted for recruitment as a naval pilot, but when they informed him that would be a six-month wait, he decided to join the Royal Marines instead.

Following his enlistment at Liverpool in September 1948, he underwent 16 months training consisting of basic training at Deal (12 weeks), infantry training at Lympstone (14 weeks), Seamanship at Portsmouth (2 weeks), Army and Navy signals (20 weeks) and finally a commando course (6 weeks).

In January of 1951, he embarked on the *SS Empire Pride* bound for Malaya. On route, secret orders revealed that the ships were to redirect to Korea to replace losses from the battle of the Imjin River. However, because he was one month short of his 19th birthday, they dropped him off in Singapore to join 45 Commando then in Malaya.

He took passage on a train to the HQ at Perak, but the train was slowed down by a block on the line and then subjected to small arms fire. Jack could not reply as he had not yet been issued with a weapon.

On his arrival, he joined B Troop of 45 Commando and was engaged in constant patrols against the Communist insurgents, (Chinese from the North or from Thailand.) He commented on the procedures adopted by the British that contrasted sharply with those of the Americans in the next two decades, particularly in Vietnam.

The insurgents forced the villages to help them. Therefore, the British combined small villages into larger ones that could be fenced and, in the

Jack Fletcher (right) April 1950, Lympstone, Devon

first instance, guarded by locally recruited police officers. It was thus easier to define the enemy as those found outside the villages. Local Iban trackers, 'head-hunters' from Borneo were used as guides in the jungle. B Troop had the biggest record of kills but it was necessary to identify the enemy against a list of 'mug shots'. So when they killed any of the enemy, they were beheaded, hands cut off and these were returned to HQ at Batu Gajah. This was stopped when a member of the signals section was photographed holding two heads and a North-East Paper obtained a copy of the photograph and published it. From then on, they were ordered to bring in the entire bodies; an extremely difficult undertaking when one had to bring them in through miles of thick jungle or waist deep in swamps.

Jack's job was as a signaller and therefore he had to carry a 40 W/T, as well as his normal pack – a total weight in excess of 60lbs. He said that the aerial brushed against the branches dislodging red ants, which dropped down the back of his neck.

Jack remembers two patrols in particular, The first was where they were ordered to support a village under attack, What had happened was that the 15 policemen defending it had been shot at, so they went to take cover away from the fire only then to find the enemy behind them waiting for them. When B Troop arrived, the distraught womenfolk greeted them. Therefore, B Troop got quickly onto the trail of the insurgents, killed three and brought their bodies back for display outside the village.

The second one was where intelligence had reported a guerrilla base on an island in the middle of a swamp. The squadron had to wade 9 miles through the swamp, with the Squadron in constant contact with an Austin spotter aircraft via Jack's W/T. Eventually Jack became a victim of heat exhaustion that became apparent to his comrades when he drew his pistol and threatened to shoot down the spotter.

During his 15 months in Malaya, he was never on leave although he was treated for appendicitis just before it ruptured. While in hospital he did feel luckier than his two neighbours. Both were from the army, one was dying from his injuries when his armoured personal Carrier was overturned and the other was fatally wounded when he fired a mortar without checking there were no branches above him.

While returning from convalescence his train was ambushed as it struggled up a steep climb. Its protection was in the hands of backline soldiers such as pay clerks and Jack said they owed their lives to the engine driver. Although hit in the back of the head he continued to drive the engine, one hand trying to stem the blood flow while the other he kept on the dead man's handle. He collapsed only when they finally reached the safety of the next station.

Jacks' signals section jeep after one ambush

In March 1952, 45 Commando was transferred to Malta from where they practiced sea landings from landing craft in Libya as well as cliff climbing in Sardinia and desert training in Libya.

In April 1953, Jack was in Egypt as part of the Suez campaign. His troop guarded the ninth B.O.D depot. One of the problems they had was that the local Arab tribesmen would attempt to steal the copper telecommunication cables, by pushing them under the perimeter fence and then dragging them out like a piece of spaghetti hitched to camels. He also patrolled the Sweet Water Canal, which was parallel to the Suez Canal. They used Jeeps with an angle iron on the front to cut wire that was positioned across the roads to decapitate the unwary. It was at this time that Jack almost killed a child. A common form of ambush was to wait in the boot of the car open it and fire, then drive away at speed. While on patrol, Jack saw a car boot open and was about to open fire on it when he saw two children peep out.

Soon after the Coronation Parade, he flew back to England. His sergeant asked him to take presents back to his family as he was going back later by sea. On arrival in England, Jack found that just after he had left the sergeant had been shot dead in a vehicle. Despite this customs still charged Jack 15 shillings tax on the presents.

From 1953–57 Jack was at Lympstone where he passed his junior and senior

A card supplied by Jack entitled 'Commando School, Bickleigh, Plymouth'

NCO courses and then his officer's course. Jack recalls that during his training a squad corporal had a novel way of demonstrating the limited effectiveness of grenades. He lay on his front with a grenade in each hand and placed them on the ground at arm's length each side of him. He then slowly withdrawing his arms and then allowed them to explode, showing dramatically that the explosion only goes up. Also during his training, Jack got to represent the Marines at National Rifle Association tournament at Bisley.

On finishing his officers course, Jack was sent to Malta to be the section commander in E troop where part of his duty was to demonstrate the new helicopter-transported 110mm anti-tank gun to NATO observers and 'bigwigs', such as Lord Mountbatten and Prince Phillip.

When the EOKA uprising broke out in Cyprus, his commando went on a four month tour there, but first they were diverted to Libya where they were used briefly to defend the palace of King Idris while it was under attack from forces under Gaddafi. In Cyprus, their base was in the Troodos Mountains and their patrols would surround a village before dawn in an attempt to capture guerrillas and search the houses for munitions. On one such occasion, while he was guard commander, they brought in a man who had reputedly murdered a local English doctor and his wife. Special Investigation Branch questioned the man, before he was taken away. Jack later discovered that the man was killed while 'attempting to escape' being hit by the full 29 rounds of a Sten gun clip.

SECTION 2: NAVY

Jack Fletcher in Tripoli

While on a patrol 6000 feet up, Jack collapsed because of an allergic reaction to the Pine Forest and as a result was repatriated and classified as unfit for active service, despite a battery of tests showing that he was fully fit.

He retrained in administration and was the first person in the Royal Marines ever to be commissioned wearing glasses. He then took on the appointments of supply officer and transport officer for 2IC HQ coy at Deal. He was then told he would never be promoted to Captain because he wore glasses! This despite that on a number of occasions in the role of duty staff officer he had been in effect the local captain. Jack, not surprising, was angry and bitter about this cavalier treatment. Thus in October 1972, he took the opportunity to take an early retirement. In 'civvy' life, he worked for British Aerospace in particular administrating the training of pilots and mechanics in both Saudi Arabia and Egypt.

Convoy Cook

Jack Armstrong

Assistant Steward,
R212617

Born:	10th May 1922, Kingston upon Hull
Service Dates:	January 1940–1946
Place of Enlistment:	Liverpool
Units	*SS Dalemoor, MV Lagarto, Moreton Bay, Corbis and others see Certificate of Discharge*
Main Theatres:	Atlantic, Africa, Indian Ocean & South Pacific
Awards	1939–45 Medal, Atlantic Star, 1939–43 Star (ribbon issued) Italy star, Pacific Star, Burma Star (pacific bar)

John was born in Kingston-upon-Hull but his parents divorced soon afterwards. He eventually found himself in the care of the Church of England Waifs and Strays Society. Youngsters at that time had very little say in what happened to them. His future was either being sent to the colonies to work, or to join the merchant navy.

He joined the merchant navy. In January 1940, at the age of 17, he joined the *SS Dalemoor* in Liverpool, as a galley boy. For the first time he had to rely on his own resources and according to Jack in twenty-four hours, he went from a boy to a man. Because of a shortage of staff, he was kept very busy. He says the food was atrocious. The food was kept cool by blocks of ice delivered to the ship, but as this did not last long, it soon went bad. Bad or not, it was cooked and eaten anyway, made into a thick stew with a huge suet crust on top. There were cockroaches everywhere and they often dropped into the cooking pots. Flour soon became infested with weevils and maggots that should have been sieved out but in practice were not and added a 'nutty' flavour to the bread.

At the Mersey bar, five other ships to form a small convoy joined the *Dalemoor*. However, even before getting out of the estuary, German aircraft attacked them damaging one of the ships. After a long crossing through very rough seas, they reached Halifax, Canada where they loaded with grain and returned to the UK. At this time, merchant vessels still came under company orders and seamen were for their time on the ship, so if a ship was sunk and the sailor was fortunate enough to survive, his pay was stopped until he joined another ship as a working crewmember.

On arrival back in the UK, Jack signed on again and the ship was sent to Wapping Basin, London to have lengths of electric cable wound around the hull a process called degaussing. This was a counter measure against magnetic mines laid by the Germans around the coast. On his next voyage, Jack's ship was part of a convoy of thirty ships and came under heavy attack by U-boats in the mid-Atlantic. Escorts were only available for the beginning and end of journeys, thus in mid-Atlantic the only protection was night and bad weather. Blackouts were strictly enforced, even so, this was difficult to maintain and in the case of a moon lit night a ship's silhouette was easily visible. One morning just as light broke and Jack was preparing breakfast, there was a sudden loud boom and he immediately dashed on deck. Across the sea, he saw just the stern of a ship sticking out of the water and in less than a minute there was no sign of it at all, just the swirl of the sea where the ship had been. A few minutes later, there was a sudden underwater explosion as the seawater hit the ships boilers. Several of the vessels were lost on that crossing.

Once back in England and after only a few days Jack signed up on his second ship *MV Largarto* of the Pacific Steam Navigation Co; this time as a mess boy for £4 7s. 6d. per month. After an uneventful, but a warm passage, to the Caribbean and South America, the *Largarto* became the Commodore ship for a convoy sailing out of Halifax. The Commodore commanded the convoy, maintaining, or trying to maintain discipline and order in the convoy and deploy any escorts. The pocket battleship *Admiral Scheer* attacked a convoy just four hours ahead of their own sinking five of the thirty-five ships. Only a suicidal attack by the sole escort, *HMS Jervis Bay* prevented further loss. Its Captain, Edward Fogarty Fagan, was awarded a posthumous VC.

It was during Jack's next period ashore that all merchant vessels came under the Ministry of Shipping. He now joined his new ship the *SS Corbis* at Manchester. This was an empty tanker and as such extremely dangerous. Large canvas sleeves were suspended from the rigging down into open manholes in the tanks, the top of the sleeves extended to form sails to catch the wind and drive air down into the tanks. This was called degassing and it was designed to drive out any volatile fumes. As a tanker, they were a prime target for any U-boat attacks and thus sailed in the middle of the convoy with other ships giving them a wide berth. Jack commented:

> I believe the only time we were really afraid was when the ship's engines broke down and the convoy just sailed on and left us. A ship without power is like a tomb. There is an unearthly silence and every hammer blow, every sound of something falling sounds like thunder... Our hearts were in our mouths knowing every sound travelled and could be picked by a U-boat. There was immense relief when the ship was under way again and belting along at maximum speed to catch up with the convoy and getting the 'welcome back' signal from the commodore.

On reaching their destination, New York, Jack and the crew had to have a 'short arm' inspection to confirm they did not have venereal disease. The only exception was an American crewmember who claimed it violated his rights. For the return Jack was part of a 100 plus convoy out of Halifax, which after a few days got the order to scatter because of the approach of an unidentified ship. Total confusion reigned, as the mystery ship turned out to be *HMS Prince of Wales* sailing through them, unannounced, carrying Winston Churchill following his meeting in Quebec.

In mid-1941, by signing the T124X articles Jack along with thousands of others were now incorporated into the Royal Navy as part of the Royal Fleet auxiliary. This was important as it gave the Merchant seaman the same rights and privileges as naval seaman. At the end of 1941, Jack sailed with the *Moreton Bay* carrying an unusual cargo – prisoners of war. These were in fact the survivors of the German battleship *KM Bismarck*. The hold had been especially prepared with metal cages for the PoWs. Jack's view of the prisoners was expressed thus

Morton Bay

Apart from the hatred of the U-boat personnel (who were alleged to machine gun survivors in life boats) there was a strong camaraderie between the seamen of the world; and the crew of the Bismarck had just been carrying out their duties for their country, the same as we were doing for ours!

The prisoners spent their time making models and one gave Jack a spitfire made of strips of wood glued and varnished. Jack now did service with the *MS Hoperidge*, which took him to the Pacific and then he joined the *SS Madras City* to North and West Africa. At Dakar on the West African coast, they had to re-coal. For this, two planks were placed from the deck to the shore and for several days natives with baskets of coal on their heads moved in a constant chanting stream until the hold was filled. From 1942 to 1944, Jack continued on trips to and from Africa. In 1944, Jack was informed, as a Veteran of Atlantic convoys that he would be issued with a 1939–43 medal and was sent the ribbon, which he proudly wore. However later entitlement to the medal was extended to such a degree that many of the 'Atlantic Veterans' felt so insulted that they refused to wear it.

After numerous trips around Africa and India in ferocious heat, Jack became very ill and spent a long period in hospital in Abadan Persia before he finally returned to England to be discharged. In total Jack made eighteen crossings of the North Atlantic during the war and twenty-six trips in the Indian Ocean and the South pacific. There are numerous references to Jack in 'Convoy' by P Kaplan and J Currie. Jack himself has written a very full autobiography and is keen that the memory of the merchant sailors, 50,000 of whom were killed in the war, is preserved for posterity.

C.R.S.102.

GENERAL REGISTER AND RECORD OFFICE
OF SHIPPING AND SEAMEN,
LLANTRISANT ROAD,
CARDIFF.

15th May, 194

DEAR SIR,

1939-43 STAR.

With reference to your recent application, I enclose herewith a supply of the ribbon of the 1939–43 Star for which you appear to be eligible.

If you hold a British Seaman's Identity Card you should take it with this form and your Discharge Book to any Superintendent of a Mercantile Marine Office, who will make the appropriate endorsement thereon. A change in your permanent address should be notified to this Office.

Yours faithfully,
W. J. KILLINGBACK,
Registrar General.

Mr J. C. Armstrong

(B59176) 252/802/W1164. 5,000. 10/44. W.L. Gp.370.

Award for 1939–43 Star

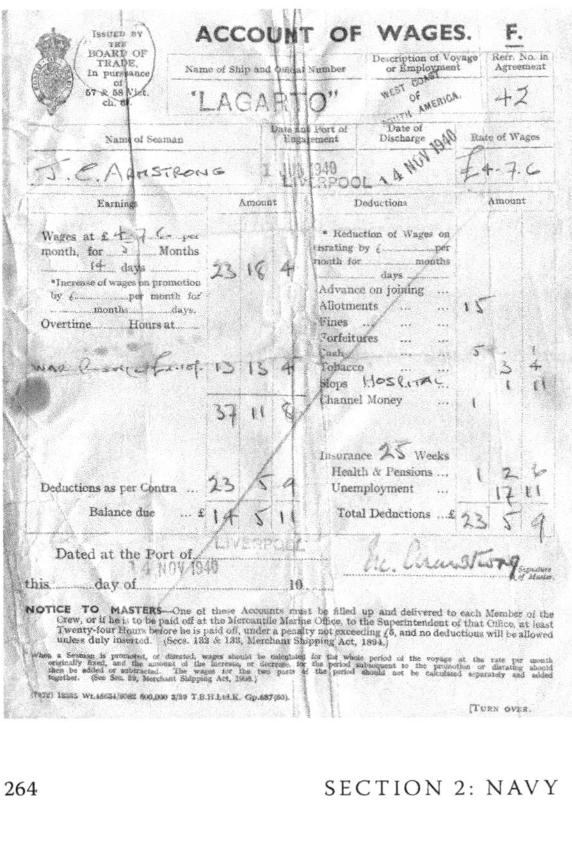

ISSUED BY THE BOARD OF TRADE, In pursuance of 57 & 58 Vict. ch. 60.

ACCOUNT OF WAGES. F.

Name of Ship and Official Number	Description of Voyage or Employment	Refr. No. in Agreement
"LAGARTO"	WEST COAST OF SOUTH AMERICA.	42

Name of Seaman	Date and Port of Engagement	Date of Discharge	Rate of Wages
J. C. ARMSTRONG	1 JUN 1940 LIVERPOOL	14 NOV 1940	£4-7-6

Earnings	Amount	Deductions	Amount
Wages at £4-7-6 per month, for 5 Months 14 days	23 18 4	* Reduction of Wages on disrating by £ per month for months days	
*Increase of wages on promotion by £ per month for months days.		Advance on joining	
Overtime Hours at		Allotments	15
		Fines	
		Forfeitures	
		Cash	5 . 1
War [illegible]	13 13 4	Tobacco	3 4
		Slops HOSPITAL	1 11
	37 11 8	Channel Money	1
		Insurance 25 Weeks	
		Health & Pensions	1 2 6
Deductions as per Contra	23 5 9	Unemployment	17 11
Balance due £	14 5 11	Total Deductions £	23 5 9

Dated at the Port of LIVERPOOL
this 14 NOV 1940 day of 19
[illegible] Signature of Master.

NOTICE TO MASTERS—One of these Accounts must be filled up and delivered to each Member of the Crew, or if he is to be paid off at the Mercantile Marine Office, to the Superintendent of that Office, at least Twenty-four Hours before he is paid off, under a penalty not exceeding £5, and no deductions will be allowed unless duly inserted. (Secs. 132 & 133, Merchant Shipping Act, 1894.)

* When a Seaman is promoted, or disrated, wages should be calculated for the whole period of the voyage at the rate per month originally fixed, and the amount of the increase, or decrease, for the period subsequent to the promotion or disrating should then be added or subtracted. The wages for the two parts of the period should not be calculated separately and added together. (See Sec. 59, Merchant Shipping Act, 1906.)

(7972) 12385 Wt.48634/8082 600,000 2/39 T.B.H.Ltd.K. Gp.687(60).

[TURN OVER.

Jack's Pay Slip , MV Lagoto, 1940

5 CERTIFICATE OF DISCHARGE 6
Or Certified Extract from List and copy of Report of Character
of Crew and Official Log Book, if desired by the Seaman.

No.	*Name of ship and official number, and tonnage.†	Date and place of Engagement.*	Discharge.	*Rating.	Description of voyage.	For ability.	For general conduct.	Signature of (1) Master and of (2) officer and official stamp.
1 3/5	Dalemoor 146548 3660 London	17.1.40 L'pool	15.3.40 Victoria Docks	M.R. Boy.	Foreign	VERY B73 GOOD	VERY B73 GOOD	
2	do	16.3.40 Victoria Docks	25.5.40 Swansea	M.R. Boy.	Foreign	VERY B72 GOOD	VERY B72 GOOD	
6	H.M.S Empire Peregrine	9.10.41 Philadel.	11.11.41 Greenock	Asst Stwd	TI2HX	VERY B116 GOOD	VERY B116 GOOD	
7	Moreton Bay 130169 London 8584	3.12.41 B'Head.	10.4.42 L'pool.	Engs Stwd.	Foreign.	VERY B72 GOOD	VERY B72 GOOD	
8	Hopebridge n.cle 165472 3132	18-7-42 m/q	4-FEB 1943 SWANSEA	M R Stwd	do	VERY B93 GOOD	VERY B93 GOOD	
9	Madras 165857 Gly	21/4/43 Msr	8-11-43 Liverpool	Msr Stwd	do	VERY B109 GOOD	VERY B109 GOOD	

R 212617

7 CERTIFICATE OF DISCHARGE 8
Or Certified Extract from List and copy of Character
of Crew and Official Log Book, if desired by the Seaman.

No.	*Name of ship and official number, and tonnage.†	Date and place of Engagement.*	Discharge.	*Rating.	Description of voyage.	For ability.	For general conduct.	Signature of (1) Master and of (2) officer and official stamp.
10	"NORRISIA" 169453 London N.T.4768	1.3.44 Glasgow	13.4.44 Liverpool	Stwd	Jap.	VERY B191 GOOD	VERY B191 GOOD	
3	"LARGATO" 137855 Glasgow N.T.3198.	1.6.40 Glasgow	14.11.40 Liverpool	Stwd's Boy.	Foreign	VERY B191 GOOD	VERY B191 GOOD	
4	"Iroquois" 124667 Belfast N.T.5283.	4.12.40 Ellesmere Port	20.6.41 Glasgow Asst Steward	Galley Boy. promoted	Foreign	VERY B191 GOOD	VERY B191 GOOD	
5	"CORBIS" 162663 London N.T.4776.	10.7.41 L'pool	8.8.41 New York	Asst. Stewd. promoted M.R. Stwd	Foreign	VERY B191 GOOD	VERY B191 GOOD	
11	Discharged from the Merchant Physically unfit for sea service				Navy Service Certificate issued			25 JAN 1946
12								Supt & N.S.

R 212617

Jack's Certificate of Discharge, page 5–8 showing vessels he served on

Section Three

Air Force Life

Training to be an RAF Pilot, Miami 1942 (Courtesy of Leslie Kemp)

SECTION 3: AIRFORCE

Life in the Air Force

Life in the air force is a marriage between aircrew and ground crew and as Lawrence Braithwaite's extensive account of life as a member of the RAF ground crew for 40 years it is not always an easy marriage. In fact, histories of the experiences of ground crew are noticeable by their scant existence. For example, from the First World War there are only two published accounts by a member of RFC ground crew. Therefore, we are delighted that in the following pages we have accounts reflecting the full range of RAF life, from ground crew to aircrew. To begin with, we have Ron Meadows story as a Spitfire Pilot operating mostly out of Malta in 1943. Alongside that, we have Fred Pickup's account as member of the ground crew in Malta at this time. He shows that it can be as hazardous working on the ground as in the air, a point made clearly by both Bill Ray and Harry Winder in their accounts as Flight Mechanics in Burma 1943–5.

To produce a pilot a great deal of training is required. Operational Training Units (OTUs) were essential in the creating top class pilots. Norman Woodford tells his time as a 'Wizard Prang' (ground crew) at an OTU and reveals there were men **and** women at OTUs who kept the aircraft airworthy for the trainee pilots. Leslie Kemp describes the extensive training that pilots had during the war, where, many like him, were sent overseas to train. His account reveals that due to a shortage of pilots in 1940–1 the subsequent major call up of young men to meet the shortage actually led to a glut of trained pilots in 1944. Then following Arnhem, where so many army pilots were lost, these 'spare' RAF pilots were transferred to the Army as Glider Pilots. Leslie gives an extensive account of the glider action he took part in, Operation Varsity – the crossing of the Rhine.

Robert Nuttall gives a full account of his life in the RAF during the Second World War as an armourer another aspect of RAF ground support. He reveals the dangers of the work particularly during his time in bomb disposal in Holland in 1945. The dream of ground crew was to finally to get to fly. Bob gained his opportunity for a short while, as a tail gunner on a raid to Cologne. He was also much to his surprise to find himself during the D-Day landings in charge of tanks! Bob's obvious leadership skills were to see him rise through the ranks to end his career as a group captain.

The Royal Observer Corps (ROC) is a civilian defence organisation founded in 1925, but during the Second World War, it was placed under RAF administration acting as the RAF's eyes. Therefore, we are delighted to have Pat Fernihough's account of her time in the ROC. The ROC's role in the war was to act as the inland aircraft tracking and reporting section of the RAF – the immediate intelligence of air home defence. Pat was a tracker in the ROC based at Lancaster, operating out of the Castle and a bank basement in Church Street. After the war, the ROC was given a new role as part of the 'United Kingdom Warning and Monitoring Organisation (UKWO) – the UK's Nuclear Attack Warning System. The UKWMOs' role was to warn the public of attack, to provide confirmation of nuclear strikes and to monitor the nuclear radioactive fallout. This information it supplied not only to the UK authorities but also to other NATO countries. It also acted, post attack, as a meteorological service. For this purpose, the UKWMO set up a chain of nuclear bombproof bunkers all over the UK operated by civilian staff of the ROC. Pat served in the Heysham Bunker. Following the Cold War, the role of UKWMO was ended and in 1995, the ROC was disbanded.

The final account is of a RAF fitter, Lawrence Braithwaite, who kindly allowed us to précis his full account of his life in the RAF from his E-booklet 'From Brigands to Vulcans' – a career spanning 40 years 1949–89. This is far as we know one of the fullest accounts of life as a fitter in RAF. On leaving the RAF, Lawrence finally came to terms with his gender dysphoria and became Lynne. As Lynne and an ex Vulcan ASC (air-service chief) she was to have the pleasure of acting as a consultant for the restoration of the last Vulcan, XH558, which flew again in October 2007. Sadly Lynne died in summer of 2008 but, rare for a RAF fitter, she was awarded a fly past at her funeral by XH558 – few ground crews are so honoured. We hope in this RAF section there is a better understanding that since its conception in 1914, the success of the Royal Flying Corps, later the Royal Air Force, has been due to a sound marriage of the skills of its aircrew AND ground technicians.

Spitfire Pilot

Ron Meadows

Flight Lieutenant
No.170635

Born:	4th December 1920, Lancaster
Service Dates:	November 1940–May 1946
Place of Enlistment:	Padgate
Units	57 OTU, 249 Squadron, 130 Squadron, 3rd Ferry Unit – 216 Group, 78 Squadron
Awards:	Aircrew Europe Star (France/Germany), Italy Star, Africa Star, War Medal (N Africa Clasp), 1939–45 Medal, Malta Medal.
Main Theatres:	Malta, Europe, Middle East

In 1940, Ron Meadows was an Apprentice Engineer as well as a mean goalkeeper. On turning 19, he decided to join the RAF, enlisting at Padgate, Warrington in November 1940. Since he had an engineering background, he was considered a good candidate for aircrew and after basic training, he was sent to the Initial Training Wing at Stratford-upon-Avon. From here, he was sent onto the 39th Elementary Flying Training School at Swift Current, Canada. Many aircrews were at this time trained overseas in Canada or the U.S. He gained his wings in a Harvard in March 1942.

Many of his contemporaries opted to stay as trainers in Canada but Ron returned to England keen to put his new skills into practice in single seat fighters. Now a sergeant he went to the 57th Operational Training Unit at Hawarden, near Hull, to learn to fly Spitfires. He remained there until October 1942 where he moved Perranporth to join 130 Squadron. In early 1943 he joined 249 squadron at Malta. He arrived in a transport aircraft right in the middle of an air raid. Disembarking they had to race straight to the air raid shelters. The Germans and Italians had been bombing Malta heavily but by this time less was seen of the Luftwaffe as it concentrated its efforts on the Eastern Front. Most of Ron's 168 sorties were over Malta or flying fighter cover for the invasion of Sicily. Due to lack of enemy aircraft, his role was often to act as a dive-bomber as well as a fighter, the Spitfire having a small bomb under each wing. As well as bombing specified targets such as bridges and railway, they were also allowed to go on 'rhubarbs'. These were freewheeling flights over enemy-held Sicily, attacking targets of opportunity. It was around this time, that his CO shot down the 1000th aircraft claimed by the Malta squadrons, although it was an enemy training aircraft over Sicily. With the subsequent invasion of Italy, there was less need for aircrew based at Malta and Ron was thus transferred back to England to join 130th Squadron.

On D-Day, he took off at 0420 to cover the landings. On D-Day +2, he was shot down when flying at 800 feet, by a combination of German **and** Royal Naval anti-aircraft fire. He managed to ditch near the shore and taken to the beach-head by a Canadian Tank before being returned to England by Landing Craft.

He subsequently flew sorties in Europe, including flying cover for gliders at the Arnhem landings and later for the Americans at the Battle of the Bulge. Ron mentions that Spitfires at the time were preferred to US fighters as they were lighter and thus were more suitable for the softer winter airfields; but he also mentions that one of the peculiarities of the Spitfire was its poor frontal visibility when taxiing in. Ron described how he had to weave from side to side on the runway to see ahead.

It was during a transit stop at Brussels that Ron had the unpleasant experience of an air attack. He sheltered behind a handy marble pillar only later to discover, to his chagrin, that the marble was in fact papered wood and would have been no protection.

With Fist and Heels
249 Squadron _was formed as Seaplane squadron in 1918 at Dundee, and disbanded in 1919. It was reformed in May 1940, at Church Fenton with Spitfires, but replaced with Hurricanes. It took part in Battle of Britain, and it was then transferred to Malta in May 1941, taken by carrier. It was converted back to Spitfires. It moved to Italy in October 1943, and then converted to Mosquitoes. It was disbanded in Italy in August 1945._

130 squadron _was formed in 1918, but it did not become operational before being disbanded in 1919. Reformed on 20th June 1941 at Portreath, it undertook local air defence, convoy support until 1943. After being moved to Northern Ireland, Scotland, and northern England it was disbanded in Februarys 1994. On the 5th April 186 Squadron was renumbered 130 at Lympne, and it was this squadron that Ron joined in 1943. During this period it flew Spitfire XIV's._

From March to May 1945, Ron received training to become an instructor first at Hawarden and then at Central Gunnery School, Catfoss. In January 1945 he received his commission. He finished the war with 216 (Ferry and Transport) Group Cairo. He flew with the 3rd Ferry Unit operating from Blida, Algiers. His job here was to fly Spitfires out to either Cairo or Bordeaux, to avoid the possibility of them falling into the hands of the local Algerian insurgents. After the war, he remained in Cairo with 78 Squadron, flying Dakotas. During his service, Ron flew: Magister, Harvard, Master, Spitfires I, II, V, IX, XIV, Auster, Hurricane, Mustang I and III, Henley, Dakota III and IV. He took his discharge in January 1946 turning down the possibility of an RAF career. He returned to playing football professionally for Burnley. Later he decided to move back to Lancaster where he was Production Manager at Storeys until his retirement.

TEN of MY RULES for AIR FIGHTING

1. Wait until you see the whites of his eyes,
   fire short bursts of 1 to 2 seconds and only when your
   sights are definitely 'ON'.

2. Whilst shooting think of nothing else, brace the whole of the
   body, have both hands on the stick, concentrate on your
   ring sight.

3. Always keep a sharp lookout. "Keep your finger out"!

4. Height gives You the initiative.

5. Always turn and face the attack.

6. Make your decisions promptly. It is better to act quickly
   even though your tactics are not the best.

7. Never fly straight and level for more than 30 seconds in
   the combat area.

8. When diving to attack always leave a proportion of your
   formation above to act as top guard.

9. INITIATIVE, AGGRESSION, AIR DISCIPLINE, and
   TEAM WORK are words that MEAN something in
   Air Fighting.

10. Go in quickly – Punch hard – Get out!

Ron supplied us from a postcard of Ten Rules of Air fighting

'Greetings from Italy'

Fred Pickup

Corporal – Maintenance
No. 1434814

Born: 31st May 1920, Rossendale
Service Dates: 1941–December 1945
Place of Enlistment: Cardington
Units   RAF
Awards: Africa Star Italy Star 39–45 Medal.
Main Theatres: Egypt, Malta, Italy

Fred was 19 when he joined the RAF in 1941. He did his initial training at Scarborough. Here he had the most frightening experience of his whole war. He was in his room when suddenly a Bofors gun, just outside, opened fire on approaching enemy aircraft; 'Hearing something like that for the first time, made you jump right out of your skin.'

On completion of his training, he was transferred to Egypt as a carpenter in RAF maintenance unit based on the shore of the Red Sea. One of his first jobs was to collect the petrol drums. The problem was that Dhows dropped them just off shore in eight feet of water. You could not wade out to them you had to swim to get them and Fred's problem was he could not swim, but he learnt very quickly.

In 1942, he was transferred to Malta where his main task was cannibalising damaged aircraft and sending the parts to North Africa. While there, Malta was subject to repeated bombing. Casualties were lower than they might have been expected as the bomb shelters were dug deep into a soft and thus shock absorbing rock. While at Malta, Fred claims he had the distinction of packing up the 1000th plane shot down over Malta, a Messerschmitt, which was then sent onto England. His unit joined the allied invasion of Sicily and Italy. He remembers he was in Naples when Mount Vesuvius erupted. He commented that some of the streets of Naples were buried up to four feet in volcanic ash and dust.

His final assignment was back in England at Ringway (now Manchester Airport). During the war, this was the principal parachute-training centre. His job was to maintain the ground equipment including the swinging harness of the static parachute jump that was basically a rope slide. As part of his work there, he helped at the nearby 'spy school', where special agents were trained for night parachute drops. At the time of the interview Fred was an active member of the RAF association.

Keeping Them in the Air

Bill Ray (in Morecambe)

Flight Mechanic (Engineers)
RAF Ground Crew
No 1235045

Born:	16th December 1921, Newcastle-upon-Tyne
Service Dates:	29th April 1941–25th June 1946
Place of Enlistment:	Coventry
Units	Land Defence Volunteers (LDV) 1939, Squadrons: 110, India 4th, 60th and 211th.
Theatres:	Northwest Frontier, Burma
Awards:	39/45 Star, Burma Star, Defence Medal, 39/45 War Medal

Blenheim Mark IV

Bill was born in Newcastle upon Tyne but later moved to Manchester for seven years until his father was killed in a road accident. He then moved to Warwick, so it was at Coventry at 19 that he volunteered his services. It was1941 and he was told, 'We don't want any soldiers or sailors' – so he joined the RAF.

He was first sent to Cardington Camp in Bedfordshire for his induction and then to Morecambe for his training as an engine mechanic. The training was carried out in garage workshops. Bill kept a detailed 'Workshop and Laboratory Record', which contains beautifully hand drawn coloured plans of the Rolls Royce Merlin engines that he worked on. Fitters also had access to a Whitley Bomber that was parked on White Lund estate in Morecambe.

On completing his training, he was posted to 110 Squadron of Bomber command at Wattisham, Suffolk. Here Bill became very familiar with the Blenheim air-cooled radial engines.

Bill had volunteered for overseas service; in order, he said 'to see the world.' Therefore, Christmas 1941 found him sailing from Greenwich on the *SS Strathmore*, bound for Singapore. On route, they heard that Singapore had fallen so they were re–directed to Bombay. From here, he was posted to Kohat in the Tribal Territory on the North-West frontier, to join the new No.4 Squadron of the Indian Air Force.

I neither Fear nor despise

110 Squadron *was originally formed in 1917, as light bomber squadron, with first BE2.s then DH9's. It was reformed in 1927 at Waddington, first with Hinds then with Blenheim bombers. 107 Squadron carried out the first bombing raids of the war on coastal convoys. In 1942 it moved to India and for rest of war, was known as the 'Hyderabad' Squadron.*

*Maan Par Jaan –
Honour unto Death*

No 4 Squadron *was formed at Peshawar, February 1942, under command of Squadron Leader HU 'Bulbul' Khan and equipped with the Westland Lysanders. The Squadron was immediately moved to Miranshah, where its first flight remained. The squadron command and second flight were based at Kohat, where Bill Ray was sent. The squadron undertook reconnaissance and bombing role on the tribes of NW frontier.*

I strive through difficulties to the sky

60th Squadron *was formed in 1916 at Gosport. It was one of foremost fighter squadrons on the Western Front with aces such as Albert Ball and Billy Bishop. It was reformed in 1922 from the old 97 squadron at Lahore flying DH10's. It was equipped with Blenheims in 1939 and when Japan entered the war the squadron was based at Singapore. Re-equipped with Blenheim IV's in India May 1943, it operated against the Japanese until August '43 where it was the withdrawn to South India*

The pilots were Indian Sikhs that had been trained at RAF Cranwell. They flew Lysanders in an army co-operation role, dropping messages and occasionally bombs. The army also carried out punitive expeditions but they allowed villages to be evacuated before they were destroyed. Bill took part in a number of flights and they were often shot at by small arms fire from the ground. He and his friends were told in no uncertain terms do not allow yourself to be captured. The locals would simply hand them over to their women who would cut open their stomachs and fill them with hot stones. Fortunately, he never found out whether or not this was true. However, the locals regularly shot at their airfield, especially when there was a film on, (shown on an open-air screen.)

One day, Bill's mates found him flat out on his charpoy unable to rouse himself. They whisked him immediately to a military hospital where, diagnosed with sand fly fever, he was hospitalised for ten days with a bottle of Guinness a night. Bill remembers that there was a very competent matron to keep law and order and explains, 'I got out of bed for a 'jimmy riddle' and hadn't gone a yard or two, when I heard 'Airman get back into bed and don't move without permission.' You did not disobey!

In 1943, Bill joined No 60 Squadron of the Indian Air force in Assam where he was re-united with Blenheims. These were being used to support the 14th Army in Burma. It was a busy time with operations every day losses as they were being bombed many times. As the campaign progressed, Bill moved forward to Chiringa and then onto Dohazari.

The best pilot in the squadron, Bill commented, was Flying Officer Muller-Rowland and Bill followed him to 211 squadron, when the 60 Squadron was moved to South India to be re-equipped with Hurricanes. 211 squadron consisted of Beaufighters. As they worked on fitting the Beaufighters out for their next missions, they were increasing experiencing bombing raids from

Blenheim 60th Squadron, Chringa

—

direct hit no one hurt

Direct hit on Beaufighter Bill was working on

Japanese planes in groups of 9, 18 or 27 aircraft. He felt perfectly safe in his slit trench although they did lose people in these raids.

For example, he remembers two 'RAF blokes' saying that they would not take cover as 'the Japanese did not bomb the camp.' As a result, they had their 'heads blown off' when the Japanese did. On another occasion, Bill remembers running up the engines of a Beaufighter, the noise of which prevented him from hearing the approaching enemy bombers. Fortunately, a sergeant did and told him to take cover. He was so glad he did, as the Beaufighter he was about to work on, took a direct hit.

Eventually they found their own early warning system of imminent air attack, in the form of a dog called 'Gunner' which came from the artillery. When 'Gunner' made himself scarce, they knew it was time to take cover.

Bill had another lucky escape while back on a 'rest and recuperation' in India. He had just replaced a propeller on a Blenheim, when the pilot, a South African, invited him to join him on a test flight. Bill was unable to do so, which was lucky as the aircraft crashed later while flying to Bangalore. All that was found of the South African pilot were his arms still gripping the joystick.

During this period, Bill saw many famous commanders. For example, he was chosen to fly with an escort of two Beaus to cover General Wavell on his tour of the forward positions in Burma. On the first day, they landed at a strip called Kumbhirgram, a depot for the 110 'Hyderabad' Squadron. As was usual, the aircrew were whisked away to the mess, leaving Bill and the other ground crew to check the aircraft. Afterwards, they walked to the guardroom to find accommodation and a bite to eat. As they set off, a Vengeance dive-bomber of 110 squadron, returning from an operation came into land with its 500lb bomb still attached in its bomb bay, it having failed to release. As Bill stated, 'We certainly moved up that runway double quick.'

Lord Louis Montbatten's visit to 211 Squadron Dohazari 1944

After 211 Squadron had done its tour of scheduled operations, it was sent back to Ranchi to be equipped with 60lb Rockets and to receive training with them. Ranchi was also the HQ of the Chinese Army. One evening, while Bill was on duty crew; in flew a B17 (Flying Fortress) carrying no other than Chinese commander and nationalist leader, General Chiang Kai-shek and his wife.

211 Squadron, *originally formed as RNAS squadron in 1917, was later reformed at Mildenhall, in 1937 equipped with Audaxes, and then Hinds. In 1939, it moved to the Middle East. It was re-equipped with Blenheims and was sent to Greece in 1941. In 1942, it was sent to Java only to be disbanded in the field. It was reformed in 1943 in India, with Beaufighter X's, as a long-range strike fighter unit carrying out rocket and cannon attacks against river craft and other lines of communications. These operations continued until May 1945, when the squadron was withdrawn to India. Here it was re-equipped with Mosquito IV.*

After Ranchi, they were sent back to Dohazari, where they did a successful tour of operations mainly against Japanese supply boats. The Beaufighters now had the added firepower of eight rockets. They did take a number of losses though as the Beaufighters' operational height at the time was, 90 feet! While here Bill met another celebrity, Lord Mountbatten, (who had just replaced General Wavell as SEAC Commander-in-Chief) and was on a morale boosting tour.

In 1944 the Beaufighter was to be replaced with Mosquitoes and Bill was no longer needed, He was sent back to Karachi to work with a maintenance unit working mainly on Halifaxes. This he did not enjoy. Then, during a fortnight 'jankers' for being found in town without a visible means of identification, he received orders for his return to England. It was not a ship though. He travelled by train to Poona where on arrival a message came through that there was a seat left on a Dakota leaving almost immediately. On hearing this, Bill did not hesitate and went straight to the guardroom. He joined 23 Squaddies on a Dakota flying to England via Palestine and Sardinia. It took them a week to do the journey, but they saw the Pyramids from the air!

Bill finished the war at Lichfield, being finally discharged in 1946. At time of the interview he was chairperson of both Royal Air force Association and the Burma Star Association.

Burma Salvage

Harry Winder

Flight Mechanic
Royal Air force
No. 145321

Born:	25th June 1922 Dalton in Furness
Service Dates:	September 1941–July 1946
Place of Enlistment:	Lancaster
Units	132nd Rescue and Salvage Unit (RSU)
Awards:	39/45 Star, Burma Star. Defence Medal 39–45, Victoria Medal
Main Theatres:	India and Burma

Harry was born in Dalton in Furness before moving to Quernmore, just outside Lancaster as an infant. In September 1941, he volunteered for the RAF rather than wait for his call up. His basic training was at Bournemouth and, like so many other RAF personnel, he was quartered with civilians. From Bournemouth, he was transferred to Halton, Bucks, for a flight mechanics' and

Work of 132nd Repair and Salvage Unit –Imphal

fitters' course. On completion, he began work at Shawbury, Shropshire on pilot training aircraft, mainly Avro Ansons. There he broke his ankle landing badly from a vaulting horse and on his recovery he was greeted with the news that he was off to the Far East. It was September 1943 where he joined a convoy at Stranraer bound for Bombay, a one month trip. This was the first convoy to pass through the Suez Canal since the hostilities in the Mediterranean had closed it.

From Bombay, he entrained to Calcutta, followed by seven days on a narrow gauge railway and then followed by another 7 days drive to Imphal. Imphal was a major supply depot and on Harry's arrival the Japanese Army was surrounding it. This was early 1944 and Japanese 15th Army, had advanced in anticipation of a coming British offensive to seize this major supply depot on the Imphal plain.

Harry joined the 132nd Repair and Salvage Unit (RTU) where he worked mainly on Hurricanes involved in ground attack roles. He also worked on

Surrender at Singapore

Spitfires utilised for top cover. He was here for the next 12 months occasionally strafed by Japanese Zeros. By June, the siege of Imphal was broken, representing the greatest defeat sustained by the Japanese Army. The British 14th Army then began to push the enemy south. Harry's unit followed close behind the front line and on some occasions were so close that they came under Japanese artillery fire.

Finally, they arrived at Mingladang near Rangoon. With the war ending Harry was sent to Kallang airport, Singapore, where he had the disconcerting experience to find it was still manned by the Japanese, who however turned out to be friendly and accommodating. The end of war was clearly marked for Harry, as he was part of the full parade, formed up into a hollow square, to witness the formal surrender of the Japanese forces at Singapore. Harry now boarded a Victory ship which took him back to England again via Suez. His war was finally over when he was discharged at Kirkham, July 1946.

SECTION 3: AIRFORCE

Wizard Prangs

Norman Woodford

Born: 30th March 1921, Bradford
Service Dates: March 1941–September 1946
Place of Enlistment: Padgate
Units   53rd OTU, 56th OTU
Awards: Defence Medal 39–45
Main Theatres: England

Norman was born in Bradford but brought up in Morecambe from the age of three. At 20, he joined the RAF, signing up at Padgate near Warrington. Basic training was at Bridlington, followed by a 6-month course at Melksham, Wiltshire. Here he was trained to become an instrument repairer known as instrument 'bashers' because of their habit of tapping instruments to check for the zero. He had wanted to work on radios but his colour blindness ruled that out.

In 1942, he joined the 53rd Operational Training Unit based at Llandow in South Wales. The 53rd OTU had originally been based at Heston Middlesex but was moved to Llandow in July 1941. Here, pilots, who after passing basic

WAAF Ground Crew on Wing of a Spitfire of 53 OUT, 1942

training on such aircraft as Tiger Moths and Miles Master I and IIs, were upgraded to Spitfires. Norman was part of the RAF and WAAF crew (men and women) maintaining the aircraft. They were Mark 1 Spits which were now outdated for operational squadrons. Some of them were still in Battle of Britain colours and carried the sign of their victories – swastikas below the canopy.

Norman pointed out that Spitfires were not easy aircraft to land having a narrow undercarriage, leading to many 'wizard prangs' as they were called after the Merlin Engine. After 240 flying hours, the aircraft would be completely stripped down and virtually rebuilt.

After a year, the unit was moved to Kirton-in-Lindsey in Lincolnshire, This station, originally an RFC base in the Great War had reopened in 1940 as a fighter station for the Battle of Britain. It ceased to be a fighter base in 1943 and became the new base for the 53rd OTU on the 9th May 1943.

The station was packed with officers and to avoid the constant saluting required Norman always took the precaution of carrying a toolbox in each hand. At Kirton, Norman used his pre-war experience to run the camp cinemas.

On Christmas Eve 1944, Norman relates how he heard a rumbling sound coming in from the sea – 'like a couple of old motorbikes' He realized they were V1 rockets and prayed the engines would not cut out overhead, the signal for their rapid descent. He later found that they had been air launched from Heinkel IIIs and were aimed at Manchester. Most missed their target coming down across a wide arc of Northern England from Shropshire to York, even as far north as Scotland. One did hit a row of terraced houses in Oldham killing 37 people. This was the only V1 attack on the north and three weeks later, after a final V1 attack on London, Germany abandoned the air launch use of this weapon.

Norman remembers a time when he was arraigned before the CO on a charge of signing for an aircraft as being airworthy, when its altimeter was not visible. Instruments at the time were a luminous green and glowed in the dark. To check them, you illuminated them with ultra violet light, but with his colour blindness, Norman could not see that it did not. So for this reason, he was let off the charge.

On New Year's Day 1945 Norman was sent to 56th OTU in Northumberland (Brunton and Milfield) to work on the new Typhoons and Tempests. Typhoons he commented proved out to be poor fighters but an outstanding ground attack aircraft. The exhaust was so close to the cockpit that the pilot had to wear an oxygen mask even when on the ground.

Norman said he enjoyed his time in the RAF, but was not sorry to leave in September in 1946. At the time of his interview he was living his wife in Morecambe, in the house that Eric Morecambe was born in 1926.

Norman and a Spitfire Mk1 of 53rd OTU. Hendon, 1999

'By Air to Battle'

Leslie Arthur Kemp

Date of Birth: 15th March 1922, London
Service Dates: 1942–5
Units: RAF 1942–44, Glider Regiment 1944–5
Theatres: Germany

This account is a précis of three small booklets that Leslie wrote of his wartime experiences.

Joining the RAF 1942

Leslie was born in 1922 in North London but soon after his family moved to Dartford, where he grew up, attending Dartford Grammar School. After leaving school, he joined the civil service, working for the Admiralty. When the war broke out Leslie was working in Plymouth Dockyard and since he was working for the Admiralty, he was in a reserved occupation, thus unable to be in armed services. However, in 1942, he heard that the RAF was short of pilots and that they were prepared to take people from reserved occupations; Leslie immediately saw his chance and joined up.

In early 1943, Leslie was standing on a parade in Heaton Park, Manchester, with 200 other cadets in the pouring rain. They had all passed their initial ground school exams and 12 hours flying Tiger Moths at Grading School; they were now waiting nervously for the results of their assessments. Would they be Pilots, Navigators or Bomb Aimers? Leslie commented that he never met anyone who wanted to be a Bomb Aimer. As the water oozed into his socks, he recalled the Shakespearean lines 'There is a tide in the affairs of men, which taken at the flood, leads onto fortune' – surely, he thought, this must be such a time.

The large Lance Corporal who had marched them there returned with a small Squadron Leader, who was carrying a sturdy box and documents, protected by a transparent cover. He placed the box down and mounted it and began to announce the results. Beginning with 'Abbot S M 237 – Pilot' he proceeded down the list, alphabetically revealing their fate. Leslie said the Squadron Leader could not have had a more attentive audience. It felt like a long time, particularly through all the Jones's before 'Kemp L A 348 – Pilot' was called out. Leslie commented, 'I expelled a silent breath and I felt my body relax and a feeling of warmth flowed over me. I heard no more names.'

Training in America – Florida 1943–4

A few days later Leslie found himself at Liverpool Docks, bound for the US for training. The ship that was to take them was none other than the Queen Mary. Berthed with eight others in a cabin with three tiers of bunks, he soon got down to sleep as the Queen Mary departed. He woke up the next morning to find to his surprise that they were not at sea, but sailing up the Clyde. By midday the Queen Mary was anchored opposite Greenock, where she took on a VIP passenger, Winston Churchill, on his way to meet President Roosevelt. They then got underway, with an escort of a cruiser and two destroyers. They all felt they were in for a safe journey with Churchill on board. On the voyage across, Leslie remembers Sir William Beveridge giving them a lecture on his plans for a future Welfare State. Beveridge also mentioned the large number of cockroaches in his cabin.

One morning their escort left them, but by nightfall they were met by US Liberator bombers circling around them and then finally a US Naval escort of two destroyers. The following morning they entered the Hudson River and sailed up to New York. In the berth next to theirs, Leslie noticed a large

Admin Building, Riddle Airfield

burnt-out liner. This was the French liner Normandie, described as the most beautiful ship in the world. She had been in New York when the war broke out and the French Government had asked the US to harbour the ship until after the war. When the US entered the war, the Government decided to convert her into a troop ship. In the saloon, they had stored 14,000 life preservers, notorious for being highly inflammable. Thus, when a spark from an oxy-acetylene torch landed on them, the inevitable happened. With no fire extinguisher or trained firefighter, the fire soon spread to the whole ship, which then capsized, a burnt-out wreck.

Disembarking, they moved on to the holding base, which was the US Base, Camp Miles Standish, Massachusetts. After RAF camps it was a luxury! It had clean white sheets, cutlery with napkins and trays with compartments for different foods. Moreover, such food! – fruit juices, chops, varieties of vegetables, ice cream, apple pie, pumpkin pies, fresh fruit and delicious coffee. It had also three cinemas and three theatres – and it was just a 'Boot Camp!'

A few weeks later they were informed of which Training School they were to be sent to; the most coveted post was Number 5 British Training School, Clewiston, Florida. To his delight, Leslie was picked for this school. So began the long journey south, a train journey of several days. The seats of the coach converted into beds at night. They were allowed a number of stops on the way, including a six-hour stop in New York where they took the opportunity to see the sites. In New Jersey, the train slowed right down as it passed through a town. A crowd of girls spotted the fifty 20 year olds in unusual uniforms and started waving, so they wrote RAF on the windows and the girls became even more excited, blowing them kisses. Leslie wondered what would have happened if they could have opened the door. As they passed into the Carolinas, Leslie noticed that stations had 'Whites only' and 'Colored' on the seats. The temperature and humidity increased and they had to get an axe to try and prize open window. It broke the window, but the cool breeze was worth it.

After several long days, they came to Florida and after passing through Orange groves, they arrived at the small town of Orlando. Here they stopped for a while and a box of oranges was brought and put in their coach – a present from the orange growers of Orlando. The next stop was Clewiston, where they were picked up and taken the final ten miles to Riddle Airfield. This airfield was later to be where the 9/11 bombers trained to fly. After a journey of 4000 miles, three and a half weeks, pilot training at last was about to begin For the next six months they were to earn their wings, on Steermans and Harvards.

By January 1944, Leslie was nearing the end of his flying training and in a few weeks was expecting to get his wings. They were now on advanced exercises, such as aerobatics, formation flying, instrument flying under a hood and night cross-country flying. On the latter, Leslie had done one as the navigator, with fellow student Curly Gilliam as the pilot; they now had to do a second flight with their roles reversed. Leslie commented that he liked flying at night; the air was cooler and steadier, without the disturbance of the rising heat of the day. Before the flight, they of course got their briefing, including the weather forecast. It was down to a typical Florida night; no wind, clear sky and perfect visibility. Soon after they took off Leslie noticed wisps of patchy fog below and increasing. Ahead remained clear, but behind them the ground was now completely covered. Leslie decided as Captain of the aircraft that they should turn back. The ground was now thickly covered, but noticing a depression in the cloud Leslie steered the aircraft to it to find a hole and below, the lights of a town. Descending in a tight spiral, they discovered it was a town they knew just 15 miles from Riddle. This allowed Gilliam to gain a bearing and at 200 feet, they headed for the direction of Riddle. Five minutes later, they were relieved to see two lines of flares to guide them in and landed. The situation was very dangerous; two of the instructors had gone 10 miles to the landing strip to rig lights up there, to guide in other crews on night flights. One, sadly, did not

Harvards on Riddle Airfield

make it back and the bodies of fellow students John Parry and Tony Oakley were found later in their crashed plane. Leslie wrote up this whole story in article, entitled 'Death by Forecast'.

Finally, after 200 hours flying, Leslie was ready for his wings. It was now February 1944 and at the passing out parade Leslie was presented with his wings and commemorative document by John Riddle himself, the owner of the airfield. Now began what was to be a 2-month journey back to Britain. As the train travelled north, the warm temperatures gave way to cooler and cooler climates. In Newhaven, he remembers seeing powerful steam locomotives, whose every puff of steam came down again as minute ice pellets, like snow. By the time they reached Moncton, New Brunswick, Canada, the coach windows were all frosted up. Moncton proved not the nicest place to stay; it was much colder and with more basic facilities than they had been use too and there was little to do. They had to stay for weeks, until to passage back to Britain could be arranged. Frequently they were called to assemble in a large hangar to hear the names of those lucky few who had been allocated a place on a ship to Britain. This brought about much frustration and chants of 'Why are we waiting?' and 'We want to go home.' On one occasion, the hangar door had been left open and much snow had accumulated inside. One frustrated pilot scooped up a handful of snow and threw it at the Squadron leader announcing the names. Soon the squadron leader was deluged with snowballs and had to give up and leave.

On Palm Beach – Comrades Jimmy Morgan, Bert Edwards and on right Leslie Kemp
With little to do – idle pilots March – October 1944

Finally, after a tedious time at Moncton, Leslie got the news he was to embark for Britain. A week after Leslie's 22nd birthday (March) he finally go to board the liner *Andes* bound for England He assumed they must have taken a southerly route, as the air soon warmed up and they were soon able to lounge comfortably on the decks. There were also 200 nurses on board, but their quarters were out of bounds, so it was a quiet trip. One pilot though set himself up as a disc jockey, regularly playing in the morning over the loudspeaker the song 'Take it easy' – and they did.

They arrived at Glasgow and immediately got leave. After a week leave, Leslie was sent to Harrogate and installed with others in the Majestic Hotel. Their time ahead was to prove an anti-climax after all their training. When the training scheme had been set up back in 1942, there was a shortage of pilots; now there was a surplus awaiting a role in the war. For a while, all they could do was regularly parade in the grounds of the hotel; on one parade, they heard the familiar noise of a Tiger Moth, which came low over the parade ground and threw out a toilet roll, which unfurled to its full length across the parade. They all roared with laughter and it gave them a much need lift to their spirits.

This was their life ahead for the next few months. If you were lucky, they sent you on a course; Leslie was sent to a Naval School to learn ship recognition that consisted mainly of learning mnemonics. The only one Leslie could remember years later was 'Bandstand of the Maryland,' which was the side view of the USS Maryland, whose superstructure looked like rows of seaside circular bandstands. Leslie wondered how one could pick up such points in low cloud and poor visibility.

After the course, it was back to doing nothing; just waiting for some posting and being shuffled from one place to another. One day a notice appeared on the notice board, requesting RAF crew to volunteer to be railway engine firemen, as it explained there was a shortage of railway engine crew to take troops and supplies to the south coast. It was a strange request, but with nothing else to do, many put their names down, including Leslie. As the weeks went by nothing more was heard of it. At a 'not very useful' boring course in June at Whitley Bay, Leslie heard of the D-Day landings for the first time. Shortly afterwards he and his fellow pilots were told they were being sent to Doncaster.

RAF Doncaster was an active base, which seemed promising, but it was not the airfield they were being taken to but the railway yards! They were to become Railway fireman. On their arrival, they found that the railway yard staff knew nothing about it and they were taken totally aback. 'Was this a joke?' they asked; 'They had no use for RAF pilots as railway crew and had certainly made no such request.' Not sure what to do with them, the foreman of the yard sent the pilots over to the fitter's workshop, thinking they could be assistants there. Here they found some men in dirty oily overalls, who just ignored them and some women in clean overalls talking. When they explained they had come to help the fitters, the woman laughed. 'We are the fitters' mates,' they cried, 'and all we do is make tea.' The foreman then turned up and suggested the pilots just went to the canteen for tea and buns, while he tried to sort out what he was to do with them. At the canteen, they tried to explain to the other workmen why they were there, but no one believed them. They were convinced they were on secret work studying how to destroy railway yards on the continent. Therefore, as Leslie notes, 'we left it at that.' Finally the foreman came back to tell them they would turn up at the yards each morning, sign the book and then do whatever they wanted for the rest of the day. Over the years, Leslie tried to make sense of this episode. He concluded that the original notice, posted on accessible notice boards was part of a disinformation campaign to fool enemy agents about the date of the D-Day landings, but that no one had informed the RAF to ignore it. Hence, a few weeks after D-Day, Doncaster railway yards, to their utter amazement, found itself with a whole group of RAF pilots sent to work as railway engine crew!

After a few weeks at Doncaster, they were sent to Harrogate with nothing to do but enjoy the rest of the summer. Finally, at the end of summer Leslie got a posting to No 7 Elementary Flying Training Squadron (E.F.T.S.) at Desford Leicester. At last he could put in some flying, although only in Tiger Moths. Leslie noted that if you got lost while flying in the Midlands you just flew around taking in deep breaths until you smelt beer and then you knew you were over Burton on Trent.

On 23rd October, after seven months, Leslie finally got his posting to train for operational service. Would it be bombers or fighters? No, it was Bridgenorth for Glider pilot training. The previous month had seen the disastrous Arnhem action and so many army glider pilots had been lost that the only way to replace them was to transfer hundreds of RAF aircrew not on operational duties to the army. As Leslie said, he never wanted to be in the army and now he was. The training began in November 1944 and lasted to mid-January 1945. They were in groups of 330 and they stayed together until they joined their operational station. They had trained to use firearms in the RAF, but they now needed to train as infantry, which required the use of Sten guns, PIATs, Bren machine guns, trench mortars and practice in the use of hand grenades and bayonets. In addition, they had to attend courses on unarmed combat, how to kill sentries quietly, plenty of PT and route marches with rifle and pack.

After training, Leslie was sent to Brize Norton to fly Horsas. Its 88-foot wingspan made it the largest aircraft he had flown. It was three tons and carried 30 equipped soldiers, a jeep with a trailer and eight men, or a 75mm howitzer and gun crew. Its basic structure was wooden with a metal floor and Leslie remembers the wooden walls were green with mould. Training included loading and lashing the equipment to fittings at one-foot intervals on the floor. Correct loading was essential, for if it was too nose or tail heavy it would be disastrous. Equipment must not break free in a heavy or crash landing. The pilot's job was to get as close to the planned landing point as possible without injury to the occupants. The condition of the glider was not important, except to ensure the load could be removed okay. This would be either from the opening of the tail in a Mk 1 Horsa, or by the nose door in the Mk 11. The Horsa took two pilots; a 1st and 2nd Pilot. The first Pilot was always either an officer or NCO who had volunteered. Leslie's first pilot was Sgt Chas Haynes – described in his logbook as an 'outstanding pilot.'

Leslie describes what it was like to fly a glider:

> The initial movement forward as the tug pulled on the towrope was normally very gentle. As the tug accelerated down the runway the glider lifted off on its own, but immediately one had to hold it down a few feet above the runway in order that

it did not pull up the tail of the tug. When the tug was airborne with its gear up, the glider was kept in position above the aircraft as it increased height and speed. The gliders were flown by following every movement of the tug aircraft. It was seen through the glider's windscreen as the straight horizontal line of the wings and the glider's height was adjusted as the line moved up or down. Whenever the line left the horizontal, the glide banked to follow it. Thus, one needed to concentrate and the controls were quite heavy, so most glide pilots took turns every 15 minutes. To make a landing the glider pilot pulled a lever to release the towrope and dropped into the appropriate area. With an unloaded glider, the rate of descent was quite slow with flaps up. The airspeed of the tow was 130mph. This soon slowed down to 100mph. The next thing (apart from keeping clear of other gliders) was positioning on to a good final approach and then lowering the flaps at the appropriate point. The flaps were enormous, usually described 'like barn doors' and they had the effect of slowing the aircraft down to 80mph and putting it into a steep angle of descent. One could push the control column fully forward and the speed would stay at 80mph, which meant in action one could make a very steep descent without building up speed and then level off for a short landing run.

The whole process of landing, Leslie added, was very rough for the passengers. From January 1945 to March they were kept on practice manoeuvres, which included landing in daylight and at night, four mass airlift practices and one large cross country run with large numbers of aircraft involved. On the 10th March, Chas was called to the adjutant's office and was informed he was now a pilot officer. In fact, he had been for some time, but the paperwork had been mislaid. As was the custom in the RAF if you became an officer you were immediately transferred and so Chas had to leave. He was not happy, but at least he had a lot of back pay owing. Leslie's new number one was Ron and this was just ten days before the Operation was to begin. Although they did not know it at the time, their first flight together would be on the Operation itself.

Operation Varsity March 24th 1945

On 20th March, the squadron was assembled in the Camp Cinema to be informed by Chief Glider Pilot Brigadier Chatterton that they were now on standby. They were to take part in the crossing of the Rhine – Operation Varsity. It would take place on 24th March Leslie's glider was to take an Intelligence Major, eight men of the Devonshire Regiment and a Jeep and trailer. On the 23rd they were sent to Stores to collect their personal equipment, consisting of a camouflage jacket, steel helmet, rifle or Sten gun with 100 rounds, 24 hour ration parcel, a small cooking stove with solid fuel tablets, entrenching tool, clasp knife, first aid kit, toilet paper, Billy can, matches and a rucksack.

On the morning of the 24th, they assembled at their gliders. Lorry loads of troops arrived and the Stirling bombers (the tugs) began warming up. At 0730, the first aircraft got underway. At 3000 feet over East Anglia the squadron assembled and were joined by others to form an armada, (6th Air Landing Brigade) heading for the Rhine. It was a beautiful day, with a blue sky and good visibility. As they crossed the channel, Leslie saw a Horsa break free from its tug and descend into the sea in a huge white splash. In minutes, launches were heading for it. As they approached France, Leslie finished his stint as pilot, with two hours to go. He felt it was a good time for a break. Picking up a large flask of tea, Leslie went into the fuselage to offer the troops a drink. With no cups, they had to drink tea from the bowl-shaped covers from the row of lights in the ceiling. By 10.00am they were over Waterloo and now they were joined by another mass armada; Dakotas, pulling the American glider contingent (17th US Airborne Division) – the air was now a mass of aircraft. It must have been an awe-inspiring sight from the ground.

Soon the Rhine was visible and the tug signalled Point Alpha, which meant 10 minutes to target area. On the signal Point Bravo (five minutes to release) they crossed the Rhine and were met by heavy anti-aircraft fire. 'We could not hear them and they just floated in the still air as we passed by' Leslie noted. He added the gunners had got the altitude right and Leslie saw one Dakota close by descend in flames. Leslie, with the aid of supplied photographs, was navigating, but it was not going to be easy as the target area was now covered in smoke. With the signal Point Charlie (release point), the Horsas began their descent.

There was no wind, so they could land in any direction, but also with no wind, it would be harder to slow their airspeed. The descent was fast and they spotted what looked like a group of saplings, when Leslie realised these were big trees 'There're too big, go left' Leslie shouted and Ron turned at the last moment to the left and missed them. They came down on bare soft earth. There was a harsh grinding sound as the floor beneath their feet scraped along the ground; the nose wheel had broken off. They came to a stop in a very short distance. Although orders were to leave the aircraft as soon as possible on landing, they all sat there for a few minutes, to let their insides settle. Leslie released his harness and stood up on bare earth; the floor of the cockpit was gone. He and Ron joined the soldiers under the left wing – they were now all soldiers and battle was about to begin.

Leslie looked around, but he could not tell where they were or which direction the enemy could be found. All around were other gliders and suddenly a rushing sound was heard overhead as a glider came right over and landed 50 yards away. Leslie knew that his first task was to get the tail off so they could unload the jeep and trailer. In the meantime, the Major had found out where they were, just 200 yards short of their target. It had been a good landing, no one was hurt and marching alongside the jeep they all set off. At the end of the field, they could see a field with a dozen bodies in it – Germans. They took the track along the field and could soon hear automatic and rifle fire. Leslie asked the Group's sergeant:

> 'I haven't a clue what to do, Should I get down, take cover or what?'
> *'Is this your first time in action?' the Sergeant replied.*
> 'Yes.'
> 'Well, just keep your eyes on me and do what I do.'

They soon reached a farmhouse, where Leslie met some friends from his squadron, who were loitering around waiting for instructions. Ron went in and came out with instructions that 40 to 50 yards from the farmhouse was a low thin hedge (100 yards from the road) and beyond that was a large ploughed field. They were to dig in there, in some partially completed trenches made by the local German Home guard. Leslie and another member of his flight began digging out a trench for two. The entrenching tools were too small – so it was hard work. When they finished they cooked a meal and while eating, someone from the farmhouse came out to tell them their 'Bedtime Story,' a Panzer regiment was expected to retreat past them during the night. Leslie hoped it would be a case of 'You leave us alone, we will leave you alone.' As it had been a long, hard day the men soon fell asleep, only to be woken in the small hours by a very noisy artillery bombardment – it was the 3000 guns of Montgomery's 2nd Army artillery firing across the Rhine. Later they were woken again by the sound of aircraft, with sharp hissing sounds all around them. One of the pilots thought he recognised one of the aircraft as a Ju88 flying low, but they were not sure what the hissing sounds were; they did not sound all that threatening. When the morning came it was foggy and the danger from Panzers had proved a false alarm. As the sun came out, they 'loafed about' waiting for something to happen, the 'happening' was a brief mortar attack on their field. No one was hurt and it was so brief it was over before they got back into their trenches. Then activity increased; they could hear machine gun fire and then the sound of aircraft engines. Suddenly nine American Liberators with bomb doors open flew over at 100 feet. They dropped large canisters and, as they pulled off, a German Jet fighter at what seemed incredible speed shot past in the opposite direction. They were told to leave the canisters alone, as they contained medical supplies. One of Leslie's comrades could not resist looking anyway – it contained pyjamas.

In the afternoon tanks with pennants flying and allied markings on their side arrived. They were of the 51st Highland Division. Their arrival meant that the situation had changed; they were no longer in the front line. That night, Leslie saw a bright light slowly rising into the sky to their southeast. It then tilted to the west and at incredible speed disappeared. Leslie has no doubt it was a V2 rocket on its way to London.

Next morning they decided to explore the area. In the field next to them was a line of 25 pounders, firing by map and spotter aircraft. After they stopped, Leslie set off to see if he could locate their glider. They found it among many others, several burnt out. On the way back they picked up some parachutes; one white and one camouflaged. They cut them up and shared the pieces. Leslie's mother made shirts and underclothes from his share of the white chute and for a long time Leslie wore a 'camouflaged' scarf.

On the fourth day, Leslie and Ron decided to visit the local town of Hamminkeln. On the way, they met a long column of German prisoners with very few guards. He suspected the Germans were not a problem; they just looked totally dejected and miserable. While they waited for the column to pass, they explored a local farmhouse. It was deserted, but the walls were covered in religious pictures and texts. It did not fit the picture of Hitler's 'Godless Germany.' Later on the road, they met a corporal with two women on bicycles in tow. He explained that they were Dutch and the only word he could understand from them was 'Hollander.' The corporal looked embarrassed and hoped someone would take them off him. Leslie and Ron moved on to the town of Hamminkeln. They found the town had escaped significant damage and was very quiet, just various people like themselves wandering around and a few army vehicles. They were told that the local population had been rounded up; the men were in the school, the women and children in the church. They were directed to a house where a canteen had been set up but they found no one there, so they went out to explore further. They were on a path near the church when suddenly a machine gun fire opened up. Ron and Leslie crouched down against a wall, not knowing where it came from or where it was striking. There

From Cadets Handbook – Riddle Aeronautical Institute 1941

was a pause, then it started again and then quiet and after a few minutes, they decided there was no danger and they continued on their way. They learnt later that a woman had either escaped from the church or had been missed in the round up and had got hold of a gun left in an upstairs room. She had fired it out of a window, but had not hit anybody.

Next day back at the farmhouse they got news that they were moving out, walking six miles back to the Rhine, where Lorries would be waiting for them. They packed their backpacks, now heavier with the parachute material, but their spirits were high; they were on their way home. It proved a very pleasant walk, across flat sandy soil country with areas of forest and farmland. As they passed through one forest area, they reached a clearing with an awful smell; they had found the body of a dead German soldier. Later on, being hot and sweaty, they stopped at a farmhouse for a rest and a drink from their bottles. A number of men and women working in a nearby field waved and laughed at them. They were not sure whether they were Germans jeering or forced labourers happy to see their liberators.

Eventually they reached the Rhine. Here they got into the back of a lorry and were taken across on a pontoon bridge. Leslie said that the motion of the lorry on the pontoon bridge was boat-like. Across the Rhine, they turned and passed through a town, possibly Xanten. Leslie's sight of bombed towns in England had not prepared him for the devastation of the bombed towns of Germany. As they passed through, nothing above one storey was left standing. Finally, they reached a camp and settled into huts for the night, with hot showers and a change of underwear. Next day there was a parade, where a senior officer thanked them for 'a grand job' one, which had been a great success, although casualties among the glider pilots had been heavy, 30%, killed, wounded or missing. They spent the rest of the day exploring the local area, including being chased from a barn by an angry German housewife when they went looking for eggs. The evening was spent thoroughly enjoying an ENSA show.

The next day they continued by lorry into Holland, passing through Eindhoven and on to Helmond. Here they had a dinner waited on by local Dutch girls, full of smiles but no English. Afterwards they explored the town. There were few people about, except some boys who followed them around saying 'gum' and 'chocolate.' They gave them some of their rations. On the following day, they were taken back to Eindhoven and flown to England by Dakota. They arrived at Down Ampney Wiltshire at 9.00pm, hungry. Unfortunately, their arrival had taken the Orderly Officer by surprise; the airfield was still open, but the messes were shut! Eventually, after much heated discussion, some corned beef sandwiches and cocoa were supplied – thus ended Operation Varsity for Leslie. In that Operation of 440 British Gliders 10 were shot down, 284 damaged by anti-aircraft fire and only 88 came through undamaged. Fire destroyed a further 327 on landing. It brought in 3300 troops, 271 jeeps, 275

Brize Norton Glider Pilot Training Unit – Leslie on the right of first row

Brize Norton Glider Pilot Training Unit

trailers and 66 guns, plus other equipment such as trucks and bulldozers. Of the 880 glider pilots, 77 were wounded and 175 were killed or missing.

After the war, Leslie emigrated to Canada, where he joined the RCAF as Air Traffic Controller. He later returned to England to become a Civil Air Traffic Controller. He died in 2004, but two years before, on his 80th birthday, he had the opportunity to fly gliders again. Leslie asked the instructor how he was doing, 'I cannot comment' he replied, 'I have only flown light gliders, nothing compared to what you have flown.' Leslie recorded his glider flight in his flight log, a book he kept by his bed all his life.

Photograph of the landing area used by Leslie

Reconnaissance photo supplied showing landing area
marked As target, and actual place Leslie's glider landed

Nothing Daunted

Robert (Bob) Nuttall OBE

Group Captain

Born:	Sheffield 7th May 1919
Service Dates:	30th January 1940–16th January 1947
Unit:	RAF Manby, Hulhavington, Creden Hill, Kirkham, Jurby, 83rd & 85th Groups 2nd Tactical Air force (TAF) and 42nd AFAP
Theatres:	France, Germany
Awards;	1939–45 Star, France and Germany Star, Defence Medal and 1939–45 Medal

In 1939, Bob and his friend Verdin Barron, (a year older than Bob), were discussing whether as Christians they should support the war effort. They were part of a group of young people aged 19 to 20 years old who together with their Minster, Reverend Capewell, met to discuss the rights and wrongs of war. They found no definite answer and the advice given was for them to make up their own minds using the facts they had assimilated. Bob was at this time in a reserved occupation. This meant he would be unlikely to ever be called. He decided though that if he ever were he would go. His friend, Verdin decided otherwise and became a conscientious objector subsequently working in a market garden near Blackpool.

In January 1940, Bob did receive his call-up papers and was told to report to RAF Upwood by end of the month. The RAF was in great need at the end of 1940 and those in reserved occupations were being called up (see previous account)

On the day of his departure, the 30th, heavy snow had fallen and there was some doubt about whether the trains would be running. However, with tickets in hand, he set off for RAF Upwood somewhere in the South East of England. It proved to be one long and awful journey but finally wet, cold, exhausted and hungry he made it to the reception camp at Upwood.

The hut to which he was allocated was to accommodate 24 to 28 similar bewildered, wet and cold soon-to-be airmen. Three large coke-burning stoves provided the heat – usually red hot. Latrines were at one end and the corporals in charge had the two side rooms. There was quite a walk to the cookhouse or NAAFI. It really was a new experience to go up to the counter in the cookhouse, collect a tray and then to be given the food in a 'slap-dash' manner. His favourite was 'liver and bacon'. In the NAAFI, you also got a mug of tea and a rock bun, the latter was known as a 'WAD' while the tea was reputed to be laced with Bromide to keep them sexually quiet.

They were given basic training which included square bashing, how to salute and how to look after their uniforms. Then followed educational and aptitude tests at which Bob did not do well due to being completely frozen.

> I was called a dimwit or words to that effect and told I would be trained as an armourer. Of course, I hadn't the faintest idea what that meant but I soon found out when I was posted to RAF Manby in Lincolnshire.

It April 1940 he reported to the gates of RAF Manby and ordered to proceed to the guardroom. This time all his kit was in a kitbag – no civilian suitcase this time, all that was left at home. He was shown to his billet, a complete change to the wooded huts of RAF Upwood. These were warm brick buildings, (the 'artwork' of the regular Air Force, built around 1934). Apart from periods of 'square bashing and kit inspection' life was reasonably pleasant learning how to be an armourer. There were also visits to Louth (the nearest town) and meeting 'local folk 'at the church. He remembers doing quite well and after approximately three months of hard study, he passed out as an aircraftsman first class (AC1).

His first posting was to RAF Hulhavington in Wiltshire servicing second line aircraft, mainly biplanes like the Hawker Hind. It also included some night flying aircraft and Bob gained his first experience of flying in a fighter-bomber. He was enjoying the new work, but it was soon to end when the Armament Officer (a Flight Lieutenant) recommended him for a Fitters Armourer course. Two weeks later he was at RAF Creden Hill near Hereford for the course.

RAF Creden Hill was another hutted camp like RAF Upwood but in addition had large workshops. Here at his nominated bench he soon learnt how to turn a piece of 3ft long round mild steel bar into a hexagon shape. Then he would take a rough 6ft by 3ft block of cast iron and shape it with hammer, chisel and file to make it into a clean piece ready to remove its centre. This was done by drilling and filing until his mild steel hexagon piece could fit perfectly into the centre with all six sides having only two 'thou' tolerance. The officer in charge was a Flight Lieutenant, a smallish well-built and pleasant gentleman. He thought Bob was getting along too quickly so he took away his one-pound hammer and gave him a two-pound club hammer to slow him down. Bob's final piece was considered so good that it went on display in the special cabinet at RAF Cosford – the Fitters Alma Mata.

Later in the course, he was to make, a teapot, a sugar bowl and milk jug in aluminium as well as items for Browning Machine guns. This included the art of tinsmithing and welding. In addition, he did courses in Maths, English and Engineering Drawing. He did well and was promoted to a Leading Aircraftman (LAC) and made a Corporal Instructor. Given seven days leave before the start of the next course, Bob said, 'It was good to be home even for a short time.'

As a Corporal Instructor at Creden, he had his own small room at the end of the hut with the 20–24 trainees occupying the main area of the hut, just like at Upwood. It was not long before he became the owner of a bicycle and a radio. Never one to miss an opportunity Bob found a market for the hire of bicycles and radios and started a business. He did very well at it but it was short lived as six months later he was promoted to sergeant on the Trade Test Board, he found himself at RAF Kirkham.

Bob believes that this must have been late 1941 or early 1942. It was from Kirkham where he rode his bicycle to Great Harwood to meet his fiancé Lena whom he married on 4th April 1942. The honeymoon was at the residence of his favourite uncle and aunt, Harry and Gladys in Rhos-on-Sea, North Wales. This seven-day leave sadly passed all too quickly.

On his return, he was posted once again to RAF Manby to do a specialist armament instruction course. As the first non-regular airman on the course, the 'Old Sweats' Sergeants and Flight Sergeants treated him very well. He got to renew his flying experience and trained as an Air Gunner/Bomb Aimer on a number of aircraft such as Wellingtons, Hampdens, Blenheims and Stirlings. He did so well on the course that they retained him as an instructor. His time here passed very quickly and enjoyably. As the senior 'Bod' in charge of Air Gunnery and Bomb Aiming, he got to use the most modern equipment available. Bob comments that he also gained more freedom to do other things and became involved in station sports, ecumenical activities and outside visits. The latter included a local farm he knew on the way to the bombing range. The farmer's wife made the most wonderful pork pies. They got on so well that they gave him a 'ham' to take home – 'worth a real fortune in wartime'. Home was at Great Harwood where his wife was staying with her parents.

It was now the start of thousand bomber raids on Germany and Air Chief Marshal 'Bomber' Harris needed aircraft from the Training Establishments such as Kirkham, to bolster those available to him from the Front Line squadrons. It was thus decided to release two Wellington bomber aircraft complete with crews and a maintenance team. Bob together with three instructors were chosen to be 'Air Gunners', while two others were to be 'Bomb Aimers', each aircraft having two gunners and one aimer. Bob's main role was to be the tail gunner but if the need arose he would cover the mid upper turret position. They joined the Bomber Command at RAF Waddington and immediately after settling in, they were off on their first mission. The target was to be Cologne. As Bob commented,

> Little did I realise what was to happen. I sat in the rear turret on the first sortie and we passed over the channel in bright moonlight. Aircraft were all around us and above. At the command from the skipper, I tested the guns and it was quite eerie to watch the tracer shell sweep out over the rear of the aircraft, which together, with the firing from the aircraft, was like a firework display. We could see the Lancasters a few thousand feet above us. It was a majestic spectacle.

The initial journey to Cologne was uneventful but as they approached the target, searchlights picked them out. Their skipper, a Squadron Leader Pilot with a DFC, had seen it all before and was adept at evading the searchlights but still made Bob's stomach turn as the pilot weaved and bucked the aircraft in evasive action. The run up to the target was quite 'hairy' with tracer and shells from the Ack-ack batteries below piercing the night sky around them. The skipper held the aircraft steady until the bomb aimer shouted 'bombs gone'. The aircraft turned left over the target and the navigator plotted the route back to Waddington. As the aircraft turned steeply away, Bob had an excellent view of the burning city below. On the return journey, Bob had little to do except watch out for enemy fighters. 'We were fortunate but some of the other Lancasters were not', Bob commented, 'and I saw a few of them twist round and round on fire as they fell to earth. It was a sickening moment never to be forgotten.'

They returned to base to a warm meal, a debriefing and bed. There were to be four such sorties to Cologne and Dusseldorf over the next few weeks. Some of these were intercepted and they had to fight off enemy fighters – a real hairy experience. Fortunately, Bob commented, there was not much damage to our aircraft, although on the other hand there was no record of a 'hit' by him or the other gunners. As more aircraft and aircrew did become available, their roles as bomber crew were not as necessary. It was felt they were more valuable training others.

Then quite unexpected Bob got the opportunity to apply for a commission. The Flight Lieutenant in charge of the instructors and a real gentleman, thought him to be a very suitable candidate. He was to be one of six or seven local NCOs who were to attend the Board of Officers for an interview. As Bob noted 'It was with a certain amount of trepidation that at the age of 22 years and being quite a service 'rookie' that I might just be accepted'. There were all the usual questions on education, experience, reasons for the application for a commission and sporting activities. He had expertise at cricket and football, but it was his experience as a Cumberland Style Wrestler though that caused much interest and a request was made for a demonstration. Bob asked the warrant officer in charge of the applications to send for a special rubber mat used in training. As Bob said, 'they found me ready to demonstrate.' The youngest member of the panel was chosen as Bob's opponent. 'I don't think he was too happy being placed in various holds and then thrown on to the mat in a demonstration of different falls,' Bob commented. Bob supposed the demonstration took fifteen to twenty minutes a longish time for an interview. However, by the end of all the interviews later that day he was informed that of all the candidates he was the only one accepted and that he would be going to RAF Cosford for a commissioning course.

Soon he was on his way, his old badges of rank removed and wearing a white cap band to denote that he was an Officer Cadet. The course was of twelve weeks with only one 48-hour pass. He was fortunate in having two friends, a Warrant Officer 'Paddy' McGrath and a Flight Sergeant 'Ginger' Nichols, both of whom were regular airmen. Bob felt they taught him a lot and kept him out of trouble. That did not prevent him though gaining a minor rebuke from the Squadron Leader of Waddington who was in charge of the course. They had been taught not to salute when on a bicycle but Bob did so when he passed the Squadron Leader.

> I saluted, but in so doing my arm happened to get entwined in his, with the result that we collapsed on the ground. Paddy and Ginger came to the rescue and valiantly extricated the Squadron leader and myself from the bicycle. Fortunately, it did not affect my passing out as a pilot officer.

His first posting was to RAF Jurby on the Isle of Man, where once again he was involved in the training of air gunners. A lot of the flying took place from modified Ansons fitted with 'scarfe rings' mounted with Lewis guns. During his short stay at RAF Jurby Bob was telephoned by his brother to inform him that his wife had given birth to a daughter. His trainee aircrew gave him much advice as to the name. After much discussion, they all opted for 'Susan Lesley', which Bob duly relayed to his wife for approval.

His short tour at Jurby ended with a return to Manby to undergo a Specialist Armament Officer's course. This allowed more flying from Hampdens and Blenheims. As a result, of his experience as an instructor he was occasionally asked to be in charge of the other students, some of them were actual ex aircrew. One gunnery exercise nearly proved fatal. They were using a Blenheim modified with an under body blister, shaped somewhat like a bath, connected front and rear with quick release catches painted red. This modification was to permit two or three students with the instructor to carry out the gunnery or bombing exercises. On take-off one of the students, an ex-Veteran pilot, sat in this 'blister' and when told not to tamper with the red painted catches he tersely replied, 'I'm an old hand at this and know all the rules.' He may have known the rules but unfortunately he could not keep his hands to himself and he uncoupled the catches. The result was that just as the aircraft commenced take off on the reinforced grass runway, he and blister departed the aircraft and went careening down the runway doing about 80 to 90 knots. He ended up luckily only with one sore backside and a much-bruised body. The Group Captain commanding was not pleased and Bob as the instructor was responsible. It was an awkward thirty minutes explaining to the Group Captain how it had all happened. It did not though effect Bob's standing overall and he finished the course with an 'Excellent.'

Officers were needed for bomb disposal and inspection of explosives for a possible invasion of France through Germany, so Bob was now trained how to a) control of the safety of explosives used by the Air Force and b) disposal of booby traps and mines located in the forward movement after the invasion.

After the training, Bob was sent to 85 Group Headquarters, a secret tented area in the south of England and part of 2nd Tactical Air Force. It was here Bob got his promotion to Flight Lieutenant. His job was to inspect the storage of explosives and the quality of various items at the squadrons based along the southern part of England. At this time, in addition to 'strikes' on the Continent, the squadron aircraft were used to destroy the Doodlebugs (V1s) now being used against London. He went to visit a Typhoon Squadron, under the command of Wing Commander (Wg Cdr) Beaumont whose armament officer was a Flt. Lt. 'Tubby' Cottingham DFC. The Typhoons were armed with 30mm cannon and the irate Wing Commander collared Bob and complained about the poor quality of the ammunition, which apparently caused stoppages during an attack on the Doodlebugs. He wanted the ammunition taken away and a new lot supplied immediately. 'Tubby' Cottingham was most concerned and hastened to obtain some three-ton Bedford trucks, some armourers and a 'belting machine'. Bob knew it was impossible to obtain new supplies, therefore with a faint heart; he found a wooded area some miles from the camp and took the ammunition, belting machine and the armourers there. During the night, they re-belted and oiled the 30mm cannon, ensured they were properly aligned and then returned them early the next morning in time for the first sorties of the day. He also supervised the loading in the aircraft gun bays and checked the connections to the 30mm cannon. He stayed for a further 24 hours and was pleased when a number of 'Doodlebugs' kills were recorded and received a 'thank you' from the Wing Commander and 'Tubby' Cottingham. Bob returned to HQ. His life continued like that with the odd 48-hour passes home until D-Day was announced and now they were all on full alert.

> We are all agog, the invasion had started and our party of three 3-ton Bedford trucks, to act as laboratories, myself with three drivers and five NCOs were to embark on a landing craft tank (LCT) on the morning of 24th June.

Eighteen days after D-Day, Bob was on his way to France to rendezvous at a staging post just outside Bayeux, Normandy. The day dawned in the pale sunshine about 6 am, as Bob and his party boarded the Landing Craft Tank (LCT) that was to take them to France. The Landing Craft was also loaded with Sherman tanks. The channel crossing was relatively smooth with their Bedford trucks cramped by the side of the LCT walls. Halfway across the channel Bob had a meeting with the Lt Col. in charge, to discuss his party's disembarkation on the Arromanches Beach Head. As Bob commented, 'Imagine my dismay to learn as the next 'senior' officer I was in control of disembarking the tanks before my party was allowed to leave – a 24-year-old Flight Lieutenant in charge of tanks!' They gave him the briefing papers for the procedures for disembarkation of the tanks and Bob hurriedly read them. When the LCT Captain beached the craft and the ramp was lowered, Bob was ready to lead the way. The sea was not too cold and Bob was only wet up to his knees, the depth being six to eight inches. Then he supervised the tanks coming off, before finally he could disembark his own vehicles and men. The Lt. Col. thanked him and wished him good luck. He now needed it to find his way as dusk was falling. Of course, there were no signposts, but by the aid of his map he set off into the night, with his still salt stained and wet trousers making him cold and uncomfortable as night drew in. By good fortune more than good management he 'navigated' his party to a base reception area a few miles outside Bayeux. Having ensured that the vehicles and men were properly accommodated he was escorted to his sleeping quarters, a tent in the middle of an orchard, sharing with a Group Captain. Their stay amongst the apple trees and wasps was only a short one and in a couple of days, they were on their way to Caen. At that time, there was still fighting in Caen and captured and destroyed German tanks with their dead crew littered the route. They bypassed the town and found a base inland.

Their work now began in earnest with the building up of 424 Aviation Fuel and Ammunition Depot. From then on their progress was east with a mixture of destroying mines on German airfields, demolishing unexploded bombs and clearing booby traps. The latter from the buildings required for accommodation by those following on. By this time his party had increased to a larger unit with more bomb disposal trained airmen and administration. As they proceeded through Normandy, the army had penetrated past the Seine taking the northern route towards Belgium. Their party was set up near Evreux awaiting orders to move to Brussels when they heard that the Americans were ready to take Paris. A group of four officers, two squadron leaders and two flight lieutenants including Bob, decided to divert to Paris in their four by four vehicles. They set off, leaving the main party to head into Beauvais and

Amiens and headed for Paris. On their way, they ran into General Patton's tank force blocking the roads. Fortunately, 'Freddie' a French speaking Flt. Lt. who knew the area well, he had been wine rep in the past, directed them down small French by-ways to the outskirts of Paris. There he took them to a farm that he frequented before the war. He knocked on the door. The farmhouse was dark, uninviting with little or no light showing. They wondered if anyone was there. Then the door slowly opened and whilst still slightly ajar an elderly female screamed 'Freddie.' With that they were welcomed with open arms and given food and drink i.e. beefsteaks and local red wine. They slept well, sneaked into Paris in one of the 4x4s the following morning and parked near the Eiffel Tower. They took the lift to the top. From there they watched General Patton lead his task force into the centre of Paris. It was quite a thrill to see the capitulation of that great city. The following morning they set off back to join the main party at Amiens. The route was quiet, but near the small town of Creil, they saw two shaven heads of what they subsequently found to be naked ladies buried up to their necks. They dug them out, but whilst doing so some Frenchmen on a nearby hillside shot at them. As Bob was the official marksman, he flopped down with his Enfield .303 and winged a couple of them after which they ran off. They cleaned the girls, wrapped them up with blankets and took them with them until they could find a Red Cross tent. They did not find one, so took them all the way to the base camp at Amiens. The two women were very grateful to be with the nurses who agreed to fix them up with clothing and accommodation.

The stay in Amiens was short, as Bob's small party had to reach Ghent, not far from Brussels. Here, they were to set up a co-ordinating centre at a large school. When the coastal towns of Ostende, Blankenberg and Knokke-sur-Mer were liberated, the bomb disposal team was sent in to remove the booby traps from hotels and boarding houses to provide accommodation for the troops. This was a tricky operation, as toilet seats, flushing handles and doorknobs were all fixed with an assortment of explosive devices to go off when used. Even the odd ball point pens lying on desks were similarly booby-trapped. It was fortunate that they suffered only minor injuries in learning the deviousness of the enemy and it made the team all that more careful and experienced.

One day in Ghent Bob with Squadron Leader Bill Adams were looking out of their office window, when from nowhere, the building was attacked by a number of Messerschmitts. They ducked as the windows were smashed and bullets burst against the opposite walls and cupboards. Then the next day a V1 flying bomb landed in the forecourt outside the offices, but failed to explode. It was left to Bob to make it safe. This turned out to be a problem at first, as he had no experience with these German weapons, 'I suppose I was just fortunate that time.' he explained.

A fuel and ammunition dump was set up in a Belgium Army explosives storage area in Eckloo between Ghent and Bruges and Bob was dispatched to take charge. He could not drive, so a staff car was supplied for the journey and on arrival, he was billeted in a house with a batman. The next morning he arose, had breakfast and wondered how he was to get to the storage areas some four kilometres outside Eckloo with no transport. Then his batman informed him his vehicle was outside the door ready for him – a 15cwt Bedford truck but with no driver. Bob set out and with much double de-clutching and with a lot of clanging and banging, he finally managed to drive to the nearby storage area. Eventually a driver had to be found to instruct him on how to drive.

Bob soon found his way about and introduced himself to the NCOs and airmen, some of whom he already knew. They all lived in a big house, which also accommodated three NCOs and fifteen airmen. He subsequently found out that the German Army were still in occupation across the river on the Belgium/Holland border. 'We often heard the big guns firing.'

Bob found the Belgian captain a nice enough chap but he thought his safety arrangements, explosives inspection and servicing techniques were poor. His fears were founded when one of his explosive servicing buildings was blown up, killing the three servicemen within. The Belgian captain then came to Bob for help. Bob with one of his NCOs, inspected the damage, collected what was left of the three servicemen and made the area safe. 'I don't know what happened to the captain, I never saw him again,' Bob commented.

By this time, it was well into 1945 and they were hearing the news of the advance into Germany. Part of their main depot at Louvain (Leuven) had moved further north to supply airfields in Belgium and Holland. Eckloo was too close and the ammunition moved to Leuven where Bob was to be based for the next few months. The depot was about ten kilometres on the road between Leuven and Liege.

Just after Bob's arrival, there the Germans began their counter attack in the Ardennes. They came within twenty kilometres of the explosives storage depot. All the local army back up units and civilians in the vicinity were evacuated, leaving Bob, an equipment officer, a Flight Lieutenant plus the NCOs and airmen remaining. There was plenty of air activity, mostly Typhoons on tank busting sorties and Bob's team remained to supply them. Then a signal came for them to insert seventy-two hour delay fuses in one of the bombs on each bomb stack around the perimeter of the storage area. Bob commented, 'Then we knew that things were not good'. The locals were worried and some were distinctly hostile towards Bob and his men as they travelled back and forth from their billets to the town.

Then six hours before the fused bombs were due to go off, came the news of the German retreat. Orders then came to remove the fuses. This was no easy task and Bob and his six NCOs had to work all night. They took out the last fuse out with just ten minutes to spare. Then the bomb detonators had to be removed, checked to see if they still functioning (all were), before being packed away in special containers. All would be replaced at some future date. The equipment officer had missed all this drama, as he been on compassionate leave to see his sick wife. He returned to find the NCOs and Bob a little inebriated and very tired.

> He came bustling into my bedroom and trying to make me wake up it was six in the morning but I had not slept for the past twenty-four hours and was not well pleased.

With the German threat gone, they soon got back into the routine of removing explosive items such as ammunition and bombs from crashed aircraft in the surrounding area. The ammunition had to be destroyed in the explosive storage area specially prepared for that purpose. The bombs were taken to a demolition area about fifteen kilometres on the other side of Leuven. There was one incident at that site that Bob would never forget. He had to demolish a damaged four thousand pound bomb. The crater at the demolition site had by this time, become about twelve or fifteen feet deep so that they had to use a ladder to get to the bottom. They lowered the bombs very gingerly into the crater and then went down. They fixed the two-pound guncotton slabs plus detonators all wired up to a manually operated exploder situated at the appropriate distance from the crater. The safety hut was further back from that point and the airmen with their NCO were safely accommodated there. Bob went to operate the exploder to blow up the bomb and of course, it went off but not as expected. The blast blew him off his feet and into a tree twenty feet behind him not far from the safety hut. His NCO ran out to help him and found him slightly concussed, with his trousers, jacket and hat ruined and one shoe missing.

His back was damaged and subsequently, in hospital, he was encased in a plaster cast from hip to neck. An investigation revealed that the army had not cleared all the explosive debris on leaving the site after they had last used it and the combination of the four thousand pounds of explosive and an unspecified amount left by the army had resulted in the increase of explosive power. He

The crater site for demolition

also found out that it had blown out a few windows of the Leuven cathedral. The RAF supplied the money to replace them.

> I think I had forty-eight hours respite before being passed well enough for duty, notwithstanding the plaster cast. The doctor made a point that I should stay off alcohol, which proved very dispiriting; even more so some months later when I returned for a check-up and to have my plaster cast removed. He asked if I would like a strong drink and when I reminded him of his previous advice to abstain he replied, 'But I meant only in working hours!'

Bob and his men celebrated VE Day with a special issue of beer and spirits obtained from the main depot in Brussels. He revisited Eckloo to have a small celebration with Belgian friends and took with him a small party of an NCO and six airmen. Unknown to Bob one of the airmen had taken a Vary pistol and that night in the square, fired a few cartridges into the air. A local then grabbed the loaded pistol and fired a cartridge that went into the clock tower and set fire to its wooden facing. Bob and his men were amused the next day to read in the local paper a report of the incident, as 'that an irresponsible airmen had set fire to our ancient clock face but its fate was prevented by one of our intrepid citizens who climbed up and put the fire out by pissing on it'.

Back at base there was still much to do in support of the RAF as the Germans retreated into Germany. Usually the local population were very friendly and were eager to help, particularly the local shopkeepers and hotels, but they did have some trouble with a cadre of German sympathisers based in the rear of a café and one of Bob's NCOs was attacked in the café and had his fingers badly damaged. Bob had the café closed and the individuals put in prison.

The war in Germany now ended, but the war in Burma was continuing and there was a need for additional supplies. An order came to move all explosive stores, fuel and equipment from Germany. Bob was part of an advance party that moved to a Luftwaffe ammunition depot at a place they called 'Hesedorf', not far from Hamburg. On the way, they came across the headquarters of Admiral Raeder and stayed the night there. One of Bob's senior NCOs found a Chippendale dining table and six chairs and suggested that they would be an excellent addition to Bob's 'office'. Sadly, he had only room for the table, which he had until his return to the UK. On arriving at the gates of the German ammunition depot, they found the Black Watch in possession. The Colonel commanding was adamant that his troops would stay in the wonderful accommodation, the first decent accommodation since they had landed on Normandy D-Day beaches a year before. He could not be persuaded that all Luftwaffe bases were the responsibility of the RAF and he had to leave. Even Bob's warning of the danger of unstable explosives in the depot did not move him. A few controlled explosions during the night though did and the Black Watch moved out next morning – taking with them a number of baths. Bob's party had slept in their vehicles that night and were delighted o find the depot empty of troops the next morning. They had much preparation to do not least of which was to retrieve the baths. This involved a twenty-kilometre road journey to No 21 Army Group Headquarters and then a few hours negotiation with the Major Quartermaster in charge of equip-ment. The encounter with him had proved a real headache but not as bad as the road journey itself, driving around so many potholes. Relative calm now followed as they settled in and explored the facilities and take stock of all the explosive stores, i.e. bombs, fuses and ammunition together with their serviceability.

Food and domestic equipment was no problem but the NAAFI HQ in Hamburg refused to set up a shop although they would allow bulk purchases by cash. Beer was also difficult to obtain. A civilian German engineer, employed by the RAF at the depot, told them of a defunct local brewery

Flight Lieutenant Bob Nuttall at Leuven, 1945

nearby. If Bob could locate some hops, they could brew German beer for a small fee. Thus, Bob order his trucks back to the UK to obtain hops from a 'friendly' supplier in Kent. Soon a full working partnership was set up to provide what was needed to satisfy the thirsty airmen and NCOs. Cash was a bit of a problem but this was overcome through the black market in Hamburg. They now got the supply train into motion to send the refurbished and serviceable explosive stores to Burma, many of which remained in use in the Far East long after the war, as well as their own supply train of hops from Kent to the German Brewery, which was now making a nice profit, which helped supply their NAAFI

Control Commission Officers arrived to oversee the gradual hand over of the depot back to the Germans. A snag arose when the headquarters auditors wished to know where the money had come from to purchase the items from the brewery and their locally operated NAAFI. They explained to the auditors that the money came from contributions from the officers, NCOs and airmen themselves, not mentioning the real source, the profits from the brewery, and this seemed to satisfy them. However auditors did request a list of all who contributed, a bit of a headache, but then the auditors insisted in reimbursing them all for their contributions, a nice bonus.

Bob's unit was also involved in the reparation and accommodation programme for a number of the German personnel including fifty German prisoners of war under a Luftwaffe captain. One 'little calamity' was averted here. The Luftwaffe captain explained that his men were complaining that all the bedding were riddled with lice. On Bob's orders, the bedding was removed and burnt, the huts fumigated. However, it was three days before a new supply of bedding was forthcoming and Luftwaffe captain was furious that his men had to sleep on the bedsprings without mattresses or bedding. Bob merely informed him that it was his fault and if his men were not 'clean' that his fault as well. They had no further trouble.'

It was now nearing the end of 1946 and Bob was due home. An interview with the Air Commander, Air Marshal Sir Sholto Douglas at his headquarters resulted in a recommendation for a permanent commission, which he received on his return to the UK. Bob was glad to be home with his wife and daughter.

'Forewarned and Forearmed'

Pat Fernihough (née Harper)

Woman Observer Officer

Born:	24th October 1925, Leek, North Staffs.
Service Dates:	1943–1945, recalled 1947–1981
Place of Enlistment:	Lancaster
Units	Royal Observer Corp (ROC) – 29 Group HQ, 21 Group HQ (ROC) UKWMO
Awards:	British Empire Medal, ROC medal and clasp, Coronation Medal (Elizabeth II)
Main Theatres:	NW England

Pat was born in Leek, North Staffordshire and at the outbreak of the war was living with her parents in Morecambe. Her mother supplied billets for RAF and WAAF personnel in the area. Pat's mother was shocked by catching a WAAF in a compromising position on their porch, so when Pat came to join up in 1943 her mother told her that she had to join the Royal Observer Corps not the WAAF.

Site of Heysham Master Post

Pat was part of B Crew in 29 Group HQ, based in Lancaster, operating from both the Castle and the basement of a bank in Church Street. The HQ controlled groups of four observations posts five to ten miles apart. They sent in their reports of air activity aided by their Micklethwaite height finders to the HQ. Any report was entered onto a thin strip called a plaque. This gave it a track number (I.D), the type of aircraft (F=fighter B= Bomber) and the number of aircraft. If was believed to be hostile, it was coloured red and if friendly white. If the track took it out of the sector, they passed it onto the next appropriate sector, which could be Manchester if heading south, Leeds if heading east, or Carlisle if heading north.

As part of ROC, Pat came under the RAF and she mentioned how once she got a reprimand for walking on Morecambe promenade without a hat.

As well as plotting movement, the ROC could also contact damaged aircraft and talk them down to a safe landing. It was also their responsibility to set off the air raid sirens when necessary. Air raid wardens situated in the 'Ops room' did this. During the D-Day landings, ROC was also posted onto allied ships to minimize the friendly fire on allied aircraft. Pat was not so posted but she was on duty the eve of D-Day and remembers the mass of air traffic they had to monitor that night.

Rubble that was Heysham Master Post

Opening Day 21 Group Preston – Pat is left with the headphones on

At the end of the war, the ROC stood down, but with the advent of the Cold War, it was re-instated in 1947. Towards the end of the fifties, its role had changed from aircraft warning to Fallout Warning. As Pat commented, 'We were in the front line of the battle for survival' It became the heart of the UK Warning and Monitoring Organization (UKWMO). This meant moving from aircraft spotting to being underground in mainly new 4-person, two level and radiation and bomb-blast proof bunkers. Between 1956 and 1962, over 1500 such posts were built. Pat was at Heysham Master Post, reporting to the Group HQ Ops room.

Pat informed us, that in the event of a nuclear war, surviving posts would broadcast the word TOXIN. They could then plot where the explosion took place and measure the magnitude and local level of radiation on various instruments. This information would be used to predict the movement of a radioactive plume, so that the services could assess the relative safety of different areas. These bunkers were all closed in 1992 with end of the Cold War.

Heysham post was situated just 20 yards east off Money Close Lane, with some irony next to the present day Heysham Nuclear Power stations. In 2000, it was dug up and destroyed and all that remains is a pile of rubble by a fairway of the local golf course.

While still involved in the ROC, Pat in 1948 started work with air traffic control at Barton Hall, near Preston. She made officer and from the early 1960s was involved in training personnel from numerous countries who were setting up their own air traffic control systems.

She married in the 1976, her husband joining her in the ROC. She left in 1981 when he was becoming too infirm to get in and out of the underground bunkers. In addition in 1969, she was awarded the British Empire Medal (BEM).

From Brigands to Vulcan – an RAF Fitter

Flight Sergeant Lawrence J Braithwaite

Airframe Fitter/Aircraft fitter
Service Number K1922397

Born:	1st July 1934, Sawry
Service Dates:	27th September 1949–1989
Place of Enlistment:	RAF Locking, Weston-super-mare
Units:	2nd Allied Tactical Air force Germany. RAF Coningsby, RAF Goose Bay, RAF Wattisham, RAF Cranwell, RAF Marham, RAF Waddington and Offutt AFB USA
Awards:	British Empire Medal. LSGCM plus clasp
Main Theatres:	England, Germany, Canada, USA, Ascension Island

Lawrence produced his own account of his life as an RAF fitter, over 300 pages, as an E-book. He kindly allowed us to précis this account for this book. We have tried to remain true to the overall account by selecting the stories, which not only reflect his experiences, but also his feelings of being a fitter in the RAF.

Childhood 1934–49

Lawrence was born on the 1st July 1934, on a very hot summer day. His mother's landlady, Mrs Heelis (Beatrix Potter), was not amused, telling Lawrence's mother 'Don't be a silly woman; it can't be coming, as the district nurse is on holiday.' Well Lawrence did come, although Mrs Heelis revealed her dislike of children, for she let it be clearly known that if she had been aware that Lawrence's mum was pregnant she would not have rented them the cottage.

Lawrence grew up in the Lakes during the war and had a great childhood. His father was an Air Raid Warden and his grandfather a Special Constable. He remembers on the far side of Windermere the building of a factory, for the construction of Sunderland flying boats. He remembers distinctly the first one they constructed, brought down the slipway, into the water and then flown. He and his mates used to swim out to the Sunderlands and use their float to dive off, until the patrols chased them off with dire threats ringing in their ears.

As Lawrence approached 15 and the time to leave school approached, he decided to become either an apprentice or a Boy entrant for the RAF. He decided on the latter and was sent for his Boy Entrant exam and medical to RAF Hornchurch. The journey south was an adventure in itself: the train from Windermere was full of serviceman and an old local sailor (a Royal Navy deep-sea diver) took the young Lawrence under his wing for the journey. When he finally arrived at Hornchurch, he was given a meal of fried eggs, bacon, fried bread and beans – but cold!

The next day he went down to the selection hangar. He noted that there were some interesting things to see: some shot down Messerschmitts, a Doodlebug (V1 – flying bomb) and some Japanese Baka bombs. Lawrence elected that he wanted either to be an Electrician or to work in Armaments or in Engines. He was selected for Airframes. After a second medical, he returned home, getting back to Lancaster late, so having to hitchhike back to Windermere.

Soon after, he heard he had made it into the RAF as a Boy Entrant Airframe Mechanic.

Boy Entrant 1949–51

He was ordered to RAF Locking, near Weston-super-mare for the 25th September. The journey down was such a miserable one that, seeing on his arrival a sign on the platform opposite indicating 'Lakes Express,' he was tempted to take it back.

On getting to RAF Locking, he found he was to be in the 'No 8 Boy Entrants,' numbering 34 boys. His mistake was to be the first to arrive; he was shown a wooden hut with 16 beds and told to learn to make them RAF style all 16 of them – a chance to get thorough practice. The tannoy system played records, but only two; 'Put another nickel in the Nickelodeon' and Ghost riders in the Sky.' The sound of these, Lawrence says still makes him shudder today.

Life at RAF Locking had its strange rituals. No more so than the F.F.Is (Forced Foreskin Inspection). The boys were lined up with just their trousers on and as the Medical Officer passed down the line the lad would drop his trousers and the MO would use his cane to lift the boys' 'bits', then turn him around and bend him over so he could inspect the rear. The object was to inspect for crabs or Venereal disease, but as Lawrence says; 'What a way to do it!'

Two afternoons were reserved for basic training: Wednesday was for sport (mandatory), Sunday for Church (mandatory) and the rest to trade training. Saturday and Sunday afternoons were the only free time. Pay was five shillings in hand and five shillings put into a savings account by the service. It was paid to you on your leave, minus any damages. Since the 8th Entrants were the junior entrants, they also had to do the chores for the senior entrants (the 4th).

While at RAF Locking, Lawrence got a surprise visit from his father. He worked as a driver for Jack Pooley of Hawkshead. Since he was down in the area delivering furniture he decided to drop in. He gave Lawrence ten shillings, which he remembers was like the crown jewels in those days and probably more than his dad could afford. After the visit, Lawrence felt really homesick and ill for several days, but time is a great healer and after a while, he got back into the swing of things.

On one occasion, Lawrence met a young lady in Weston and took her to the cinema. She did not tell him that she had a 'steady boyfriend.' He found out the next Sunday afternoon, when the boyfriend and his mates from the Engine Mechanic Training Wing grabbed him, took him to the bathhouse and beat him up. When he staggered back to his hut his mates insisted on him telling them what had happened. Some of the 'hard men' in his unit organized a retaliation squad and justice was meted out on his behalf. One stood by one's mates.

RAF Locking, they were informed, was to be their base for the length of their training. However half way through the course and for no apparent reason, the whole boy entrant wing was moved to RAF Cosford, near Wolverhampton. They travelled by train. Lawrence recalls that stops for food were at sidings in the middle of nowhere and they were closely watched, in case anyone tried to escape – some did try. At Cosford, they were accommodated in wooden huts; however, they were all mixed up so it was a case of getting to know your room-mates all over again.

Ahead of them lay months of work on Hydraulics, Pneumatics, Wheels and Tyres, Bostics and Plastics, Workshop Practice, Airframe Structures, Metal Repairs, Riveting, Welding, Fabric Repairs and Doping – a hectic 18 months! Lawrence passed his final exams, as an LAC (Leading Aircraftman) with the recommendation he be promoted to SAC (Senior Aircraftman) after six months. There was a slight problem as he was only just 17 and could not hold that rank until he was 18!

RAF Leeming – Boy Entrant to Senior Aircraftman 1951–2

Lawrence's first posting was RAF Leeming, although Cosford did not inform him where it was and he had to work it out from his Railway Warrant. He arrived on 1st July 1951, completing the last part of his journey by bus. As it approached the camp, he was met by a mass of ambulances and fire engines: one of the Mosquitoes had run off the runway across the grass, through a hedge and hit a lorry and trailer carrying cheeses. Lawrence says there were no fatalities as he remembers, but they did have a lot of cheese pie over the next few weeks!

On his arrival, there were immediate problems: as Lawrence was under 18 he was not allowed to be in the adult male accommodation, so where was he to stay? RAF Leeming's barracks were made up of H block buildings, at the centre of which were a shower/washing room, with a drying room downstairs. The drying room was to be Lawrence's home for the next six months. The other problem with being under 18 was that he could not sign for anything and was thus unable to do any work. They sent him over to a Brigand squadron to see if there was anything he could do. An old flight sergeant, called Goody Bennet took pity on him and took him on, as long as he kept out of the way. Work was soon found for Lawrence. The first job he got was riding the brakes of the Brigands as they were taken out in the morning and brought back in the evening. He soon found himself helping other lads in repair and rectification work, as long as they signed the F700 forms for him. The worst job he got he recalls was to renew the plywood skinning at the rear of the toilet on the station's old runabout, an Airspeed Oxford. He hoped that the gunners and bomb aimers had better aim with their guns and bombs than when they used the loo.

Aircraft accidents, Lawrence added, were a way of life at RAF Leeming. Lawrence remembers that many a time after night flying had taken place he would get up in the morning to find crashed aircraft somewhere on the airfield. One morning, he recalls, he found two Mosquitoes in a nose-to-nose embrace and further on was a Brigand with its undercarriage collapsed.

A Bristol Brigand T4 at RAF Leeming

Accidents even took place in the hangar. He remembers working with SAC Sammy Service, an engine mechanic, refuelling an aircraft on a dark night, with no moon or stars. Sammy was on the wing and having passed down the refuelling hose, he closed up the fuel caps and began to whistle his way back to the fuselage. Then the whistle stopped, followed by a yell. He had turned the wrong way and, to his surprise, dropped off the end of the wing instead. Luckily he was not hurt, except for his pride. More seriously, Lawrence recalls the time when he was returning from lunch and a call came out for everyone to report to the ASF Hanger. As they made their way to the Hanger, an Austin flatbed truck passed with fire extinguishers. Everyone grabbed one and on entering, the hangar saw a Wellington on fire in the corner, defeating all current efforts to extinguish it. In the hangar were also two Mosquitoes, an Anson, a Martinet under repair and a Brigand on the stocks – all had to be urgently removed. They kept the hangar door closed, to stifle the fire, briefly opening to let each aircraft out before shutting it again. The last to leave was the Anson and in their exuberance to close the door, the lads nearly cut its tail off. Meanwhile the fight to save the Wellington was lost, it was left a burnt out wreck.

The cause of the fire turned out to be a corporal who had pulled out a trolley plug without switching the power off, thus creating a spark. The aircraft had just been cleaned and in those days, they used 100 Octane gasoline for cleaning with a lot of discarded rags. The corporal was cleared of blame at his court martial, but the use of high-octane gasoline to clean aircraft soon ceased at RAF Leeming.

On his 18th Birthday Lawrence was promoted to LAC then SAC. He was now allowed into the barrack block with everyone else and he could sign for his own work.

From SAC to Corporal – Becoming a Fitter 1952–3

After his promotion Lawrence was lucky enough to be recommended to do the fitter's course at RAF St Athan, however the downside to this was that first he had to do General Service Training at RAF Credenen Hill, Hereford. Four weeks of purgatory followed of drill, kit inspections and unarmed combat – a time best forgotten.

Finally back at RAF Leeming, Lawrence remembered he had a vivid night-mare. It was so bad that he woke up in a sweat, with the lads having turned on the light to see what was the matter. He had dreamt he was flying in a Buckmaster with one of the pilots of the squadron; he was letting Lawrence have a go, showing him the controls, when he suddenly collapsed and sent the aircraft into a nosedive. Lawrence grabbed the column and pulled it back so the aircraft was climbing, allowing the pilot to slump back into his seat. Lawrence fastened his harness to stop him slumping forward again and then he contacted Leeming tower. A Brigand was sent out to escort him in and to tell him to what to do. Following the Brigand, he obeyed their instructions, but as he landed, he pulled on the brake too hard and over it went onto its nose – as bits of propeller flew off in all directions, he awoke. A week after this dream, while having a mug of tea in the crew room, a pilot popped in and asked if anyone wanted to go on a cross-country flight in the Buckmaster. Any other time Lawrence would have jumped at the chance, but this time he declined. As he looked at the pilot, he recognized him from the dream... the aircraft did not return from that flight.

On the 6th April, Lawrence began his Fitters course at St Athan, which would set him up for years to come. It covered the same material he had learnt as a Boy entrant, but in far greater depth. It was an enjoyable 6 months with weekend afternoons off, during which time Lawrence took every opportunity to go to Barry Island or Cardiff to chat up Welsh girls, or the local WRAF. On completion, he returned to his Brigand Squadron (No 2. OCU), now at RAF Colerne. Hangers at Colerne were smaller than at RAF Leeming and as a Brigand's wingspan was greater than the width of the hanger doors they had to manoeuvre them in at 45 degrees; a tedious job, particularly if all had to be got out or in and in the pouring rain.

In the morning, after the planes were out of the hangar, it was a downhill journey to the flight lines. Thus they had to put an experienced man to ride the brakes, while they gave the Brigand a good push and let it roll. The only problem was that a road to the Communications Squadron crossed the taxiway and of course, on one occasion the inevitable happened, when the Brigand and a car from the AOC reached the crossing point at the same time. Fortunately, the car was there first and the man in the Brigand was able to slam on the brakes, causing the nose to hit the ground avoiding the accident. After that they stationed a man on the cross roads as a lookout.

On 15th July 1953, Lawrence was promoted to Corporal and was formally introduced to the Corporal's club by an Engine Corporal called Jock Kirk. Lawrence recalls many amusing incidents at Colerne, such as one of the riggers, standing on the edges of a forty-gallon oil drum. Suddenly someone at the front of their aircraft tapped their ankles together, causing the rigger to respond by coming smartly to attention, only to disappear into the drum. He had to go to Sick Quarters in order to be cleaned up. No one found out who it was that tapped their ankles in the first place. Another time while on Duty Crew, Lawrence was called to assist a visiting pair of Group Captains who had come over for a function. They were now planning to return in their Anson. Lawrence got up onto the wing with a starting handle, waiting for the signal to start the engines. No signal came and on looking to see why he found the two Group Captains arguing on who should fly the aircraft, an argument resolved immediately when they saw Lawrence watching them. Lawrence started up the right engine, but got no response from the left. On inspection he found they had not switched the 'mags' on. When he turned it this time, the throttle must have been half on, as it blew him nearly off the wing. Getting down, he had only gone two steps when the aircraft shot off and Lawrence had to dive onto the grass as the tail plane passed over the top of him. He watched it weave its way into the air and disappear. He assumes they got back all right, as no more was heard.

2nd Allied Tactical Air force – Germany 1953–6

The 10th December saw Lawrence with all his kit at RAF Buckeburg, Germany, which was the distribution centre for all manpower posted to Europe. He had joined the 2nd Allied Tactical Air force and he was soon sent to RAF Celle. The RAF takes the name of their bases from the nearest town and RAF Celle was an ex-Luftwaffe base and showcase base.

On his arrival, the flight sergeant (FS) met him. He asked him for his name and trade and on being discovered to be a rigger, he was immediately ordered to go down to the stores, get his kit and overalls and begin work on a Vampire, (Jet fighter) in the corner. Lawrence explained he needed first to finish arrival procedures and get accommodation. The FS called for someone to get Lawrence to Squadron accommodation, but to be back 'double quick'. On arriving back, he found his overalls, toolkit and the Vampire all waiting for him. First, however he had to get hold of volumes one to six of the instruction manual to find out what made a Vampire tick. He did his research in an office and while doing so, he decided to cover his back by ringing General office in SHQ to explain why he had not completed his arrivals procedure. After a few days, the FS called him in and told him to stop what he was doing and go and finish his arrival procedures.

Lawrence was working with the 16th Squadron (Vampire Mk5s and 9s), commanded by Squadron Leader De Burg. It had two officers, two Flt Lieutenants as Flight commanders with the rest of the Squadron being all SNCO aircrew, plus the 'techies,' of which the FS was the boss. The morale of the squadron was high,

By the summer of 1954, Venom FB1s were replacing Vampires. These aircraft looked the same, but were in fact quite different: the 'Ghost' engine of the Venom was more powerful and a tighter fit in the airframe, making the engine change much harder. It had a cartridge starter system which didn't always perform as designed and with some unfortunate results. The starter exhaust pipe spewed out gasses across the wing and this meant that after a couple of starts the wing was black and its lift properties seriously affected – more like a brick than a modern aerofoil, was Lawrence's observation. This meant hours of cleaning work until a Sergeant Tom, invented an ingenious modification to the starter exhaust pipe. It was a simple piece of curved metal, not unlike an orange peel, which fitted to the outer end of the exhaust pipe and deflected the gasses upwards about 30 degrees away from the wings. The technicians also had another use for the starter cartridges. During the winter, they found the quickest way to light their Nissan Hut coke stove was by placing a great chunk of the internals of a starter cartridge at the bottom of the stove, under the coke and lighting it. Everyone would then retire from the hut for five minutes until the resulting blast of smoke cleared.

May 22nd saw the Squadron moving to the Island of Sylt in Northern Germany. This was the air firing practice camp for all squadrons based on mainland Europe. As all the aircraft were behaving themselves, airframe wise, the riggers were gainfully employed helping the armourers to belt up the ammo, running the belts through the alignment jig and finally painting the nose of the rounds with coloured paint. (The latter was to allow the shell to mark the target banner when it struck) One day, Lawrence recalls, as they were helping the armourers on the flight line, the air was suddenly filled with a burst of cannon fire. One of the lads in the cockpit had accidentally pressed the button. No one was hurt, however the lad in question remembering that the punishment for this was a day's jankers for each round fired, leapt out, started picking up rounds and stuffing them into his overalls. His ruse meant he received just two days jankers, but he got some nasty burns around the waist as he only had on a pair of shorts under his overall.

In June 1955, the Squadron was transferred to Florennes, Belgium operating from an air force base, near Dinant. After a spell there, they were returned to Celle. A week after their return they were paraded before the station commander. He gave them a 'right old rollicking', because the British Embassy in Belgium had sent a whole list of objects that had gone missing while the squadron was in Florennes. It was regarded with such diplomatic seriousness that an aircraft had been sent to collect these items. However some of the items were missed off that list, so they kept for example their two 'new' bar stools in their mess.

After this excitement, it was back to work, the worst part of which was working on the flight line. Here aircraft were coming and going, some still armed with live rockets and guns whilst around them were refuelling trucks dispensing their flammable cargoes and armourers walking around with 20mm cannon belts draped over their shoulders. It was, as Lawrence put it, 'a scary place to work.'

Arrival of the Vulcans – RAF Coningsby 1956–64

By 1956 Lawrence was back home, based at RAF Coningsby. On his arrival he found the base on 'Care and Maintenance,' with contractors everywhere. RAF Coningsby, it transpired, had been picked for the still top secret TSR2 supersonic fighter jet, In the meantime, it was being used as a Bomber Command Holding Unit for some Canberra B2s, although what the purpose these Canberras were Lawrence never did discover. He had now become a permanent member of the Modification unit and second in command. RAF Coningsby would be his base for the next ten years.

He was working now with some National Service men, including a former worker for Lockheed Hydraulics, a Machine tool designer and an ex-undertaker. Another, a steel erector called Pete, used to give the old FS (Flight Sergeant) a fright, as he walked from one side of the hangar to the other along the steel girders in the roof. A fellow Boy entrant, Digger Holden, joined Lawrence at Coningsby and they then heard that the RAF was being equipped with C130 transport planes and was short of aircrew. They saw their chance to take up a flying career and so they put in their General Applications. They soon went up to Hornchurch, but Lawrence was turned down as 'medically unfit' due to dryness of the skin on his elbows and knees! (It was suggested he would not look good in shorts in the mess.) Diggers got in and it got to Lawrence that but for 'dry skin on knees and elbows' he could have followed Digger into the more lucrative and prestigious career of flight engineer.

Vulcans were now due to arrive at Coningsby and construction of the new buildings got underway. The water table at Coningsby is only 4 feet down and Lawrence remembers a construction crew laying a concrete floor for a new filter plant, only to come back after a weekend of heavy rain to discover that the floor had risen several inches. It had to be dug-out and redone. Finally, the first Vulcan Mk 1, arrived and was kept in a hangar under Police guard.

Lawrence was now seconded to RAF Bedford, to work on the new Fairy Delta 2 operating there. His job was to be the liaison between civilians and the RAF. It was an interesting six weeks with the trials for the TSR2 going on, but in the end, the British abandoned the TSR2 programme. Their co-partners, the French did not and went on to produce the successful Dassault family of aircraft from the design.

Now back at Coningsby, Lawrence discovered the base had received a lot of new Vulcan ground equipment and some of his mates had been sent on the Vulcan course. In addition Vulcan Aircraft Servicing Chiefs (ASC) had arrived and started to settle in. Then suddenly Coningsby ceased to be in No 1 Group and was instead placed in No 3 Group. This meant it was now to be equipped with Victors, not Vulcans. So the new ground equipment was dismantled and sent on, the ASCs departed and they all now waited for the Victors to arrive. In the meantime, there was still the Canberras. Lawrence was asked to make some modifications that consisted of putting in a new canopy with fiberglass, reinforcing the strip where the plastic joined the metalwork of the aircraft. It took all week to do the job even with two lads to help. Just before the last plane was due to arrive to be fitted Lawrence requested leave; on the basis he would 'mentally lose it' if he did not have a break. (This he was entitled to as laid down by the administrators). Five days later he returned to find the last aircraft was still waiting to be done! His replacement could not do it and a fitter from the factory had been sent for, all the way from Shorts, Belfast. Lawrence was furious – all it needed was more metal to be cut away. Lawrence had it all done before the fitter from Shorts arrived.

The new Victor ground equipment had barely arrived along with the Victor Service chiefs, when Coningsby was reassigned back to Group one, which meant Vulcans, not Victors. Thus, the Victor ground equipment was dismantled and the Victor Aircraft Servicing chiefs departed. It was all a farce. Although in the short time they were a Victor airbase, one Victor did land there , in clouds of dust as it careered into the undershoot at the end of the runway. It then taxied to a hangar, where someone got out (possibly with a set of golf clubs,) before the plane then taxied back to the runway and took off. That was it. Soon new Vulcan ground equipment arrived and the Vulcan ASCs returned and with that the Canberras finally left and the holding unit was disbanded. It was now at last a Vulcan base, although now with Mks 2s.

With the newly arrived 'Tatty' Vulcan Mk2s a great deal of overtime was needed to get them up to date with many modifications required by 'us learners,' as Lawrence put it. In fact, those planes were still not up to date with the new modifications before the newer 'Mk 2 Phase 2 XM Series' Vulcans started to arrive at the base. At this time, Lawrence was put in charge of the Tyre bay, with the task of getting it up and running before the flying began. Again much overtime was needed and more alarmingly they had only eight spare wheels for two squadrons of aircraft! (each aircraft had eight wheels.) One day a lad from the supply Squadron rang up to ask if they could store some supply boxes in the bay storeroom. Lawrence could not believe what he saw when they arrived; they contained the Mark 2 wheel hubs, which he had long sought and been endlessly, reassured were not available yet.

Later, during an inspection of the bay, the AOC (Air Officer Commanding) was impressed with Lawrence's work and assured him, he would get on well in the service. Lawrence replied he did not think so, which stopped the AOC in his tracks. On being asked why not, Lawrence explained he was unable to stay on for further service as there were no vacancies in his rank and trade. The AOC asked Lawrence's boss if this was true and when it was confirmed he added, 'Oh, we will see.' Within two days, Lawrence was called to sign on the dotted line for another 22 years, with a promotion to sergeant. It was now 1964.

Flight Sergeant – Goose Bay, Canada 1964–5

He had been on Vulcan and Victor courses now, but while doing a Valiant course the aircraft structure gave up the ghost on the second day, causing the course to be cancelled. Thus, Lawrence found himself instead, with four

Vulcan XM645

others, posted to the RAF detachment at RCAF Goose Bay base in Labrador, Canada. On the 1st July 1964, he set off to RAF Innsworth, for the first leg of his journey to 'The Goose.'

They flew to Gander International, Halifax, only to discover that Trans Canadian airlines, (TCA) with whom they were travelling, had no connecting flights to Goose Bay. They would have to fly on to Montreal, which ironically would have been the next destination of the original flight, now just departed. So instead TCA found them tickets with a provincial airline flying DC4s which could take them to Goose Bay, however it meant staying overnight at the expense of the British Embassy in Ottawa. Eventually they set off in a well-worn DC4 along with Indians, Eskimos and their livestock. As they approached the 'Goose' airbase, they saw a huge pall of smoke rising up to greet them. The officer's mess on the USAF side of the base was on fire. Once landed, they sent a message back to Britain about the mix up at Gander International over transfers to ensure it did not happen again, (and of course, one week later it did.)

Goose Bay was originally part of RAF Transport Command. It had an officer, a chief electrician and seven men, but was now rapidly expanding to accommodate the V bombers, who would use it as a base for training in low-level flying. The base was to expand by 70 new members and thus the original nine who had happily integrated themselves into the local population and gone native, suddenly found themselves back in the RAF world.

Lawrence was working on V bombers and for the first few months this was mainly on Mk 2 Vulcans. (Victors did not yet have the underwing tanks to fly into the westerly headwinds to make it across the Atlantic to Goose Bay.) Lawrence worked on the Canadian side of the base, in the hangar shared with

Trans Canadian Airways (TCA). Overhead on the corner of the hangar was the Air Traffic Control tower (ATC), so care had to be taken when closing the doors, otherwise the noise it produced, made the ATC 'feel as if the world was coming to an end.' Weather-wise July was good at Goose Bay, where it could be warm to hot, but the downside was the mosquitoes and more importantly the black fly, whose bites would often go septic. As autumn came the vast woods around them would burst into bright yellow light, as mountain ash and birch leaves changed colour against the dark contrast of the fir trees around them. Suddenly it would be winter. Dress code for summer was Khaki Dress (KD kit), but on a certain date they would go over to warm blue uniforms. The service set the date, but Mother Nature did not know it and one week before they were due to change it snowed. They all changed to their blue uniforms, only to be ordered back to KD kit, as they still had a week to go before the date set by the RAF for winter. Therefore, for a week they wore summer dress, covered over with fur parkas and boots – not an aesthetic sight and an ongoing joke to the 4000 US personnel stationed there.

The base may have been isolated, but it was not short of entertainment. Lawrence soon found himself playing Ice Hockey team before a capacity audience at the Winter Carnival. It began when Lawrence met a nice lady on an ice rink. She took him in hand and taught him to skate reasonably well. Then he got friendly with some Canadians with whom he shared accommodation mainly civilians who worked for the Royal Bank of Canada or the Mounted Police and one of which, Doug, , was a star ice hockey player. Lawrence recruited him to coach an RAF Ice Hockey team. His work was cut out, as only Lawrence and two others could skate well. Despite this, the team was whipped into shape to play a Canadian female team at the Winter Carnival. They began promisingly by taking a three nil lead, but then in the last three minutes, they scored three own goals to equalize the match. They got a standing ovation for being good sports. The referee, a RCAF officer, was dressed in a tutu, battle dress and wig. It was the stuff of comedies and he added that the 'ladies' did not exactly play to the rules either. Lawrence had a good time at Goose Bay, so much so that when he was 70 and he was told he had a major heart problems which could shorten his life, he immediately flew back to Canada and drove hundreds of miles to visit the old base, once more.

Becoming a Vulcan Aircraft Servicing Chief 1965–66

In the summer of 1965, Lawrence completed his exams to become a Chief Technician. He could now volunteer to be an ASC (Aircraft Servicing Chief) for V bombers. Thus the RAF in its infinite wisdom, posted him back the UK to RAF Wattisham with English Electric Lightnings (56th Squadron), aircraft he had never worked on. They told him he would just have to go on a course to learn. Lawrence had had enough: he had been on a course on V bombers for nine months, why did he want to go on another. He wanted to volunteer to do ASC duties on the Vulcan force. The response was that he was 'silly' and that the application would not leave the station, but Lawrence persisted and persisted, until after six weeks a letter arrived giving him a date to join a Vulcan ASC course; the first volunteer for such a course for some time. While waiting he got to work on the Lightnings, an aircraft that although of the same era as the Vulcans, had been constructed in a very different way. It was thus a sharp learning curve. Before he left for the ASC course Lawrence had become a team leader, having worked on four Mk 6s Lightnings, a T3, plus one of the brand new T5 Lightnings. The latter only had ten hours on the clock. It also had a leak on the 'standby pilot head' in the cockpit, which required the removal of the canopy, ejection seats, RH instrument panel, cockpit floor and many numerous bits and pieces. It took a whole week to do the job. Lawrence hoped he would get a chance to be involved in the Air test, but missed out – thus missing his chance of a Supersonic flight. Lawrence also resolved an ongoing fuel leak problem with the four Mk 6s. This leak was between the flap tank fuel transfer pipe and the fuselage and the fitters were constantly changing the seal. What Lawrence discovered was that none of the grease guns fitted the grease nipples servicing the flaps. Thus the hinges were not being lubricated. Lawrence designed, with the help of the station workshops, a modified grease gun, which remedied this issue once and for all. At this point, a new Junior Engineer Officer arrived at the station and to give him something to do the Engineer Boss got him to do the paperwork for this modification to be sanctioned and authorized. Lawrence thought no more of the matter, but some months later when he was on the ASC course a letter of commendation arrived from the AOC in C Fighter Command, plus a £5 financial award for his modification.

Lawrence also commented that in the short time he was with 56th Squadron he never got used to coming through the hangar doors each morning and seeing it full of aircraft being serviced, all of them dripping fuel from someplace into a pile of sawdust on the floor and LOX fumes drifting across the room like an early morning mist. There would be Engine fitters filling up the AVPIN tanks, ('a fiendish liquid if there ever was one'.) One of the power sets would inevitably be running and plugged into an aircraft, increasing the noise and fumes and then to finish it off someone would bring a tractor into the hangar in readiness to tow an aircraft out, spewing out clouds of black smoke. To Lawrence's mind, it was like 'the devil's kitchen, or a place, waiting for an accident to happen. He was not sorry to leave.

In 1966, Lawrence began his training to be an Aircraft Service Chief (ASC) for Vulcan Bombers. To be an ASC meant 12-hour shifts, weeks away from home and a lot of responsibility and loads of hassle. Many of the early ASCs developed ulcers and other ailments due to the diabolical workload and the divorce rate was a little bit higher than for the rest of the Airframe and Propulsion trades. Thus to be an ASC was not 'top of the pops,' which is why people were nominated rather than volunteered, with the exception of Lawrence. The only way off the course was to leave the service, die, or as happened to one of his fellow course mates – get a commission.

The course was six weeks training at RAF St Athan on Jet Propulsion, then onto Electrics at RAF Newton. Towards the end of the latter course, they were told they were going to learn and be examined on the Main Generating System not of Vulcans, but of Victors! When Lawrence queried why since they were destined to be Vulcan ASCs, he was informed that the circuit diagrams for Vulcans were unavailable. Lawrence retorted, 'What did they think the Vulcan school at Finningley was using... and also what every Vulcan unit was using to service their aircraft?' It was remedied. From Electrics they were moved onto Instruments and finally to RAF Finningley for the practical side of the course. On completing the course, Lawrence was posted to RAF Waddington; 28th December 1966 as an ASC for three squadrons of Vulcans: 44th, 50th and 101st. There was only one slight problem, they were all Mk1s and Lawrence had been trained for Mk2s. The upside was that the Vulcans would on occasion fly 'Rangers,' meaning they went overseas and ASCs would be selected to fly with them in order to do any required maintenance. It was Lawrence's chance to be airborne. First, he had to do a Pressure Breathing course at RAF North Luffenham, however on completion he got his first chance to take off as the on-board ASC, destination Goose Bay – a chance to meet old friends.

RAF Waddington – A Ranger the chance to be Airborne 1966–72

The first Vulcan that Lawrence signed for was XA910 and as he says, it was the first time he had ever signed for a single item worth one million pounds! The Vulcan had five crew, with the potential for two more seats, although 'seats' was a loose description; in fact these were just the platforms where the Navigator stood to take his astronomical readings with his sextant. For take-off and landing, the ASC sat on one of these platforms and if you were over five and a half feet tall you had to have your knees jammed into your chin

Vulcan XA910

with little chance of strapping in. The second 'seat' was a bonus, as it allowed a new boy ASC to go up with an old hand on his first 'ranger.' Thus on the 17th April 1967, Lawrence found himself airborne on XA910, in the 7th seat, with C/T Johnny Walker in the 6th seat. The pilot was Flight Lieutenant Brian Petit. The flight would be four hours and 50 minutes to Goose Bay. It was a momentous occasion for Lawrence, although he was a little alarmed at the sight of smoke pouring through all the conditioning outlets, so thick you could not see across the cabin. However it was not smoke just moisture, condensation. The XA910 would do 20 landings and 70 hours in low and high level flying without a problem – a good mission. On its return to RAF Waddington XA910 it was sent on to Malta. Lawrence was to fly in XA910 only one more time and it was to be XA910's last flight before it was scrapped, (17th November 1967.)

Life as an ASC was hard, they operated a three-shift system; two main shifts from 0800–1700 and 1700–0200 hours and a small 'graveyard' shift 0200–0800. In this shift, the first two aircraft had to prepared and ready for launch by 0800. Lawrence hated this shift; it was hard motivating people at four in the morning, on a bleak and desolate airfield and in winter when de-icing often had to be performed. Thankfully, this shift came round only once a year. By the end of his time at Waddington it was not uncommon for one ASC to be looking after four Vulcans out on B or C dispersals, furthest away Line HQ. You would head out at 0800 an could be stuck there until your relief came at 1700. The tradesman would then take the bus back, but the ASC still had to brief the next ASC and sign over responsibility – not a five-minute job! If you were in middle of launching one of the aircraft, then you would also have to stay there until finished, even if it took you finish well over your shift time. The demands of the job Lawrence emphasized just increased as time went on.

There were a number of chances to get away and to fly. Lawrence remembers in 1969 when an XM650 was fitted with a new pair of Drum tanks. These were fitted into the bomb bay, leaving room for just one bomb, though of course a bomb of significance. This added fuel allowed the XM650 to take part in the second of the new OILBURNER low level flying sorties from Offutt, near Omaha, Nebraska, USA. Lawrence was to be its ASC. They flew out to Goose Bay and then took off for the Great Lakes where they dropped to 250 feet. It was smooth over the frozen lake, but rough over the landmass. Lawrence describes it as being like driving an E type Jaguar flat out, with flat tyres, on cobbles! – 'Exciting yes, forgettable No!' With low-level flying over, they returned to the relative peace and quiet of high-level flying; but the state of the suits of the crew testified to the workload and stress!

Over the next six years Lawrence was able to fly to other parts of the world including Singapore, Guam, Australia, Maldives, the Mediterranean, as well as the US and Canada. In 1969, he was selected to part of the team for the 16th Strategic Air Command Combat Competitions, always held in the US.

Strategic Air Command Combat Competition 1969–70

The 16th Strategic Air Command Combat Competition was to take place from the 7th–13th October 1969 at Fairchild AFB in Washington State, USA. Three crews and aircraft would represent the RAF at the event. Code named 'Giant Voice' the RAF had picked four sets of aircraft, aircrew, ASCs and ground crew, the fourth to act as a reserve. Lawrence was assigned to the Vulcan XM599 to be the fourth on the list, with Flight Lieutenant Dennis as the pilot. However, they moved to second place out of the four to their immense delight. On September 18th, they set out for Offutt US Air Force Base via Goose Bay and on their arrival did a fly by for the press before landing and settling in. As only three aircraft were to take part, the competition was high to be selected. XM599 had to work hard to maintain its second place. After a week of practice flights, it moved up to being tied for the first place slot, then came the bad news. The USAF insisted that the three to take part were to be the three at the head of the original list and thus the XM599 was to be grounded. RAF argued that the order of the planes on their list was a purely administrative one, but the USAF would not give ground. (Maybe because they had seen how well the XM599 was doing.) Thus, Lawrence became part of the static show.

One consolation was that he was invited to see the new Lockheed SR1 (Spy plane) in its secure hangar. This was quite a privilege, as the security around this aircraft was very tight – one US airman had been arrested on the day it arrived for taking pictures. It was a great moment for Lawrence who felt compelled to touch this 2000mph projectile of an aircraft and he was interested to see the suits the crew needed to wear, similar to astronaut units, not to mention the looks that he got for being a British person allowed around the hangar.

The following year Lawrence was picked to be one of ASCs for the 17th Strategic Air Command Combat Competition, this time at McCoy AFB in Florida – the results were good. He felt that the good results helped the careers of the Air and Ground crew in the USAF, but sadly he felt this did not seem to be the case for the RAF personnel involved.

Chief Technician – Offutt Air Force Base, USA 1972–75

After six years as an ASC at Waddington, Lawrence landed a plum tour as the Chief Technician to an RAF detachment at Offutt AFB (November 1972–May 1975.) Lawrence took the family with him. On his arrival he made good friends with the Ground Equipment Chief who was in need of an ally as the detachment had gained a bad reputation. This was why a C/Tech (ex-Victor ASC) and Lawrence (an ex Vulcan ASC) were sent out. Lawrence saw the problem when he met the CO of the detachment – 'a man who thought he was God.' For example, everyone had to do the job of being his 'Duty Driver;' that is picking him up in the morning from his rented home in the local town, then driving him back home when he felt necessary. It was also known for him to ask the driver to take the scenic route to his home. The driver could therefore be quite late back and he would still be expected to return to his work on the aircraft.

When it came to Lawrence's turn, he was determined to be no lackey. It was raining, so on his arrival at the CO's house he sounded his horn and waited. Procedure dictated that he was supposed to get out of the car, go to the door, ring the bell and then return to the car and wait. Lawrence was not having this, it was pouring with rain. What with the rain and need to get an aircraft ready to fly, he waited for only 15 minutes before deciding to leave. As he was about to go the CO came charging down the drive. 'Was he mad?' the CO wanted to know, 'What was he playing at?' Lawrence's reply was that he was a 'misemployed Chief Technician Aircraft Fitter,' who had been posted to this detachment to service aircraft, as required by Strike Command HQ. The journey was very quiet and later Lawrence got a dressing down in the Flight Sergeant's Office. However, it was the end of the 'Duty Driver.' Lawrence was to have more disagreements with this CO, whom he felt may have been sent to Offutt to be 'got rid of.' By the time the CO was replaced, Lawrence was a bit of a celebrity at the base.

Lawrence commented on how helpful the USAF was in any way they could be. He felt their help kept the RAF detachment going. One nice idea the USAF provided, was to give Lawrence and his family tickets for Disneyland when he went on leave.

The RAF at Offutt hosted not just the usual Vulcans and occasional Victors, but also other RAF visitors. For example an early Jaguar arrived, on its cold weather trials, accompanied by two Victor tankers. A regular visitor was a Short Belfast with a cargo, which shall remain nameless as Lawrence put it, except to say it had to have heaters kept running during the winter nights. RAF C130 transport aircraft also flew in, with all sorts of cargo and visitors.

RAF College Cranwell 1975–82

In 1975, Lawrence was posted back to England, to RAF College Cranwell, where he was to stay until 1982. Lawrence was to be the NCO in charge of a HS-125 Dominie Flight. There were six 'Dominie' training aircraft belonging to the Department of Air Warfare. The job was to service these aircraft. They were used to train Navigation Officers to evaluate their equipment, however it did cause some problems as the Decca Navigation equipment had seen better days and the Navigators were evaluating it against its original specifications. The aircraft were all close to their 'sell by dates' and they were being operated on a two-shift system, which was 0600 to 1700 and 1700 to finish and these latter night shifts could be quite long. Lawrence remembers one aircraft had a port wing that would drop violently as it came in to land. The only thing Lawrence could think of was that the port wing must have a rough surface to its leading edge slats, possibly because of the way it had been painted. So, with an element of tongue in cheek, he ordered the whole edge of the wing to get a good rub down and then called the boss, who sceptically took the plane up, only to have it come in to land perfectly. He then did it six times more to make sure. It proved to everyone the importance of Laminar Flow and that one needs to be very fussy about painting the surface to ensure a good finish. After that, all the painters and finishers were dispatched to clean up the rest of the aircraft of the flight.

Lawrence was also to have a problem with the Flight Commander. One morning he came in to see the Flight Commander who was sitting in an easy chair, jacket undone, boots on the table, and drinking Lawrence's work team's milk. Lawrence chose to ignore him and went back out. The officer followed him, began to chastise him for ignoring an officer. Lawrence replied, 'If I had seen my Flight Commander I would have most certainly have said good morning, but as I hadn't, how could I?' The Flight commander replied 'But you just saw me in the crew room,' to which Lawrence replied, 'all I saw in there was an improperly dressed person stealing my men's rations.' The Flight Commander swore and left, but Lawrence's Warrant Officer (WO) told him later he had made an enemy. Despite Lawrence's intentions of not crossing him again, he was to have another bust up with the officer. The problem, as Lawrence's WO pointed out to him, was that at the end of the year his assessments from people like this may not be helpful for Lawrence's future promotion prospects. Just after the New Year, Lawrence got a letter from the College Commandant, offering his congratulations on being awarded the British Empire Medal. Lawrence was to discover later that after this was made known on the base, his end of year assessments were quickly recovered and rewritten. It appeared the Award and what they had originally written about him, just did not go together.

Lawrence moved on from the Dominies to Jet Provosts. Here one had Flight Line Mechanics (FLMs) – Flems. In Lawrence's opinion the worst thing the RAF ever did was to devise this trade. Flems were young lads with A levels or GCSEs taken on to be trained to work on just **one** aircraft for anything up to ten years. In addition, all prospects of promotion stopped at SAC. They soon became a demoralized bunch of lads. Lawrence championed the cause of Flems and his Flems responded. On one occasion, a Group Captain paid a visit. Lawrence's bosses told him he was to stay in his office as they knew his feelings on the issue and did not want them passed onto the Group Captain. So Lawrence stood in his doorway and naturally when the Group Captain saw him, he went over to chat to Lawrence. Lawrence tactfully and diplomatically let his feelings be known on Flems. The Group Captain talked to the Flems as well and it was not long after that visit that the rules for Flems were changed, until eventually the trade was effectively done away with.

Later, Lawrence was to move sideways to the Engineering Wing HQ. On his last day his Senior FLM and all the lads on his line presented him with a Silver Goblet engraved 'To Vince from the Line.' (Vince was his old nickname.) The Senior FLM made a short speech on how they felt, Lawrence had been the only one to stand up for them and make them feel worth anything and how sorry they were to see him go, Lawrence was moved.

In his new role at the Engineering Wing HQ Lawrence had to deal with female staff for the first time, but found it no problem. He also used his day releases to learn the art of silverwork, which he was to pursue in his retirement. It was also at this time that the OC Engineer (the boss) wandered into his office and asked him if he would like to stay in the RAF until he was 55. Lawrence rapidly signed on.

During the Falklands War in 1982, Lawrence was miffed that, as an experienced Vulcan man, he had to remain at RAF Marham with the Victors. It was not a good time for Lawrence; he was frustrated with some of the politics thrown up in the RAF, though he did manage to get away in August to Ascension Island, to look after the Victors operating there until a new airport/base was built at Port Stanley.

The Final Tour 1986

1986 saw Lawrence undertake his final tour of duty, back at RAF Waddington. He was to be the Flight Sergeant (FS) at the newly established Nimrod AEW 3 Major Servicing Section. It was a shambles and a major servicing would have been a nightmare. The aircraft were suffering from chronic corrosion problems due to their previous service life and the new electronics were diabolical. He remembers being pleased to hear later that the Nimrod AEW was cancelled, although his celebrations were tempered at the thought of the millions of taxpayers' money that had been wasted on them. In July 1989, Lawrence's long RAF career came to an end. Just before his departure, he had one final disagreement with the authorities above him. On 20th March there was an Officers Mess Ball and thus there were no officers to be found on the airfield. Lawrence found himself the highest ranked person on the airfield. Due in were a flight of C130s when a sudden change of wind by 180 degrees, threatened their landing. Prompt action was needed and along with the aid of the Air Operations Corporal, Lawrence put into motion the procedures required to redirect the C130s in their landing. All went well and Lawrence felt it was a job well done. However, the next morning there was an outcry over who had authorized the change of procedures and Lawrence's CO told him *'Engineers DO NOT make decisions in the air force, Only Ops and Aircrew Officers do that.'* Those words and the whole incident, for Lawrence, summed up a good deal of his experience of the RAF. On his retirement after 39 years' service he moved north to Morecambe, but his involvement with the RAF and Vulcans was not over.

First, he had to deal with a condition he had long recognized in himself that is of gender dysphoria, i.e. born the wrong sex. It is quite common for those born with this condition to enter the military, to attempt to deny the problem. It is though impossible to deny and so Lawrence became Lynne. He also set up his Silversmith business, (LJB Models) modelling aircraft in silver and 9ct gold. Then in 2005 at the age of 72, Lynne was once more to become directly involved with Vulcans. The Walton family, who owned Bruntingthorpe airfield, had purchased the Vulcan, XH558 from the RAF in 1993. They stored it along with other preserved aircraft. The aim was to eventually restore this Vulcan to its flying glory. To achieve this, the Walton family had purchased over 800 tons of spare parts. A business, Vulcan Operating Company purchased the aircraft from the Walton family to finish the restoration of the aircraft – a project that took 15 years and £7 million to achieve.

In 2005, Lynne was asked to be the consultant on the project and, in August 2005, Lynne found herself once more working with a Vulcan. 'A delight,' she

XH558

Lynne with some of the guys under wing of XH558

said, although it was nice now just to survey the plane for problems, rather than be the one to do the actually work of putting them right. She still had to put in a lot of travelling and long hours, for as she commented in her diary: '30th June 2007 – I am getting too old for travelling and long days at the hangar.' However she felt it was more than worth it and when on the 18th October, 2007 XH558 took to the air Lynne's comments were that this was "where she truly deserves to be; and didn't she look and sound wonderful." Early in 2008, following more test flights XH558 was finally certified to fly for air shows. She has a finite life of ten years before she must be retired to a museum. Interviewing Lynne, you could feel the pride she felt in being part of getting this last fully service-able Vulcan to fly. Sadly, on 12th August 2008, Lynne died, but as a tribute to her, Vulcan XH558 gave a fly past at her funeral; a tribute to this long serving aircraft fitter and maybe the only member in RAF ground crew history to get such an honour.

Lynne J. Braithwaite BEM LSGCM &Clasp – Consultant Aircraft Engineer 2007

Index by Theatre

Main Theatres	
Home Front (Wartime)	Toms (1938–42), Hool (1939–45), Grimes (1940), Dunn (1940), Leach (1940–1), Nuttall (1940–4), Wilson (1942–4), Woodford (1941–6), Kemp (1943–5), Fernihough (1943–5).
Home Front (Peacetime)	Phillips (1946), Fernihough (1947–81), Dix (1948–50),Braithwaite (1949–53, 1956–72, 1975–89) Potter (1955–7),, Rainford (1957, 1959), Hill (1957–8), Spooner (1988–91). Lodge (1989), Martindale (1954–77),
Naval Base	Dix (1948–50 – RNAS Nuthatch), Potter (1956–7–Portsmouth)
Ireland	Coggins, (1921) Spooner (1972–73)
France	Coggins (1917–8), Grimes (1940), Laidler (1940), Dowding (1940), Henson (1940 & 1944), Nuttall, (1944), Theobald (1944,) Meadows (1944)
Bef	Henson
Little Bef	Dowding, Grimes Laidler
D Day	Theobald, Meadows, Nuttall
Belgium	Nuttall (1944), Braithwaite (1955)
Holland	Kemp(1945)
Germany	Fitzsimmons(1945) ,Kemp (1945), Henson (1945–6), Wright (1945), Nuttall (1945), Wilson (1945), Hayton (1953), Braithwaite (1953–6), Parnham (1959)
Operation Varsity (1945)	Wright, Kemp
Norway	Grimes (1945), Laidler (1945)
Italy	Coggins (1918), Meadows (1943), Wetton (1943–5), Todd (1943–5) Fitzsimmons (1943–4), Dunn (1944–5), Hill C. (1954–6)
North Africa	Hays (1940–1) Dunn(1940–3), Grimes (1941–2), Laidler (1941–2), Wetton (1942–3)
Tobruk	Grimes, Laidler, Dunn,
Malta	Meadows (1943), Pickup (1942–4)
Palestine	Grimes (1941), Dunn (1943), Fitzsimmons (1944–5), Todd (1945–7), Phillips (1946), Holden (1949)
Sudan	Parker G & D (1950–2)

Libya	Warmsley (1956–7)
Egpyt	Pickup,(1941), Grimes (1942–3)
Canal Zone	Parker G & D (1952) Gill (1953–5)
Emergency	Warmsley (1955), White (1954–6), Fletcher (1953).
Suez Crisis (1956)	Hill C, White.
Cyprus	Hill W(1956), Fletcher (1971–2)
Aden	Rainford (1958), Theobold (1965)
Bahrain	Gill (1966–9)
South Africa	Hays (1940), Wetton (1942), Grimes (1941)
East Africa	Rainford (1958–9) Spooner (1989)
India	Ray (1941–3), Grimes (1942–3), Ladiler (1942–3) Adams (1943)
Burma Campaign	Knowles (1940–5) Hays (1941–5), Adams (1943–45), Leach (1943–5), Les Parker (1943–5), Ray (1943–6), Winder (1943–5), Grimes (1944), Laidler (1944), Lyons (1945–7)
Imphal and Kohima	Grimes, Laidler, Leach, Winder,
Singapore	Knowles (1941), Winder (1945)
Malaya	Parnham 1957–9) Hudson (1957–1959), Boyd (1958–60) Fletcher (1951–2)
Hong Kong	Hill W (1954–6)
Korea	Hayton (1951–3)
Christmas Island	Hill A (1958–60)
Canada	Braithwaite (Goose Bay – 1964–5) Spooner (1990)
USA	Kemp (1943–4), Braithwaite (1972–5)
Belize	Spooner, Lodge (1986)
Iceland (Cod Wars)	Stokes (1961–2)

Index by Units

National Servicemen	Wyatt (1947–9), Dix (1948–50), Hayton (1951–3) ,Warmsley (1955–7), Parker G & Parker D (1950–2), Gill (1953–5), White (1953–6), Hill W (1954–6), Hill C (1954–6) ,Martindale (1954–6), Potter (1955–7), Rainford (1957–59), Hill (1957–9), Parnham 1957–9), Hudson (1957–1959), Boyd (1957–60)
Infantry	Coggins (1914–34), Henson (1932–48), Dowding (1938–43), Grimes (1939–47), Laidler (1939–46) Anderson (1940–54), Hill (1954–60), Hayton (1951–53), Spooner (1972–3), Parker D & G (1950–52), Gill (1953–86), Hudson (1957–9), Reuben (1957–60), Phillips(1946), White (1953–57), Spooner (1986–91)
Artillery	Hays (1940–6)
Territorials	Grimes (1939–40), Wetton (RTR TA) (1939–45), Coggins (1940–5), Wyatt (1949–84), Martindale (1958–77)
Home Guard	Hudson (1953 – Kirkham)
Signal	Wilson (1942–47), Dowding (1943–5)
Airborne (Army)	Wright (1942–46), Kemp (1944–5 from RAF), Wyatt (1947–49)
Reconnaissance	Fitzsimmons (5th RR), Knowles (Loyals), Les Parker (1942–5 2nd RR)
Tanks	Wetton (1939–45 7th RTR)
Chindits	Anderson (1943–5)
Musicians	Henson (1932–48 Piper), Parker G (1950–52 Bugler), Martindale (1958–77 – Drummer)
Anti-Aircraft	Hool (1939–45), Dunn (1939–46)
Auxiliary Territorial Service	Hool (1939–45)
Engineers	Theobold (1938–74), Wright (1939–42)
Stores & Ordnance	Grimes (1940), Dix (1948–50 RN), Warmsley (1955–7), Rainford, (1957–59)
Catering	Hill C (1954–6), Armstrong (1940–6)
East Indies Fleet	Lyon (1945–6), Webster(1944–5), Lyons

Index by Topics